THE DISTRIBUTIONAL IMPACTS OF PUBLIC POLICIES

POLICY STUDIES ORGANIZATION SERIES

General Editor: Stuart S. Nagel, Professor of Political Science, University of Illinois at Urbana-Champaign

Sheldon H. Danziger and Kent E. Portney (*editors*)
THE DISTRIBUTIONAL IMPACTS OF PUBLIC POLICIES

Don F. Hadwiger and William P. Browne (*editors*)
PUBLIC POLICY AND AGRICULTURAL TECHNOLOGY

Richard C. Hula (*editor*)
MARKET-BASED PUBLIC POLICY

Rita Mae Kelly (*editor*)
PROMOTING PRODUCTIVITY IN THE PUBLIC SECTOR: Problems, Strategies and Prospects

Fred Lazin, Samuel Aroni and Yehuda Gradus (*editors*)
DEVELOPING AREAS AND PUBLIC POLICY

J. David Roessner (*editor*)
GOVERNMENT INNOVATION POLICY: Design, Implementation, Evaluation

The Distributional Impacts of Public Policies

Edited by

Sheldon H. Danziger

Professor of Social Work and Director,
Institute for Research on Poverty,
University of Wisconsin-Madison

and

Kent E. Portney

Associate Professor of Political Science and
Director, Citizen Survey Program,
Lincoln Filene Center, Tufts University

M
MACMILLAN
PRESS

in association with the
POLICY STUDIES ORGANIZATION

First published 1988

Published by
THE MACMILLAN PRESS LTD
Houndmills, Basingstoke, Hampshire RG21 2XS
and London
Companies and representatives
throughout the world

Printed in Hong Kong

British Library Cataloguing in Publication Data
The Distributional impacts of public policies.
— (Policy Studies Organization series)
1. Public welfare—United States
2. Poor—Government policy—United
States 3. Economic assistance, Domestic
—United States
I. Danziger, Sheldon H. II. Portney, Kent E.
III. Series
362.5'80973 HV95
ISBN 0–333–42192–2

To our parents
Sarah and Calman Danziger
Helen Portney

Contents

List of Figures

List of Tables

Notes on the Contributors

Sandra R. Baum is Assistant Professor of Economics at Wellesley College, Massachusetts. Her research has focused on the distributional effects of public policy, particularly in the area of financial aid to college students. She is the author of a forthcoming Macmillan Press book on the history of economic theories of income distribution.

David M. Betson is Assistant Professor of Economics at the University of Notre Dame, Indiana. Prior to this appointment he was a Research Associate at the Institute for Research on Poverty, University of Wisconsin-Madison. Between 1975 and 1979, he worked in the Office of Income Security Policy of the Assistant Secretary for Planning and Evaluation in the Department of Health, Education and Welfare where he was involved in the design and planning of the Carter Administration's reform of the welfare system. His published work has been mainly in the area of the efficiency and distributional effects of the tax-transfer system.

Robert X. Browning is Assistant Professor of Political Science at Purdue University, Indiana. He received his PhD from the University of Wisconsin in 1981. His publications include *Politics and Social Welfare Policy in the United States* (University of Tennessee Press, 1986), from which his contribution here is adapted.

William H. H. Cranmer lives and writes in Hudson, Wisconsin. He attended Stanford University and the University of Wisconsin at Madison, obtaining his PhD in 1982. He has taught comparative politics and international relations at the University of South Dakota, DePauw University, and the University of Minnesota.

Sheldon H. Danziger is Professor of Social Work, Romnes Faculty Fellow, and Director of the Institute for Research on Poverty at the University of Wisconsin-Madison. He received his bachelor's degree in economics at Columbia University in 1970, and his doctorate in economics from the Massachusetts Institute of Technology in 1976. His research is concerned with the effects of government social welfare programs on poverty, work effort, and the family. He is the co-editor of *Fighting Poverty: What Works and What Doesn't* (Harvard University Press) and the author of numerous scholarly articles. Recent papers have appeared in the *American Economic Review*, *Journal of Economic Literature*, *Quarterly Journal of Economics*, *Review of Economics and Statistics*, *Social Service Review*, and *Journal of Social Policy*.

Irwin Garfinkel is Professor of Social Work at the University of Wisconsin-Madison, where he has been Director of the Institute for Research on Poverty and Director of the School of Social Work. His research centers on poverty and income maintenance programs, the evaluation of social programs, and child support. He has published numerous articles, books, book reviews, and newspaper columns. His articles have appeared in The *American Economic Review*, *Quarterly Journal of Economics*, *Journal of Public Economics*, and *Journal of Human Resources*. His most recent book is *Single Mothers and Their Children: A New American Dilemma*, co-authored with Sara S. McLanahan (Urban Institute, 1986).

Richard A. Kasten is a Principal Analyst in the Tax Analysis Division of the Congressional Budget Office. Prior to joining the Congressional Budget Office, he was employed in the Office of the Assistant Secretary for Planning and Evaluation in the Department of Health and Human Services. He has worked on income security issues for over ten years. His work includes analyses of numerous Welfare and Social Security reform proposals. He is co-author of a number of microsimulation models including the KGB model (a model used to simulate Carter Administration welfare reform proposals), the ASPE Benefit and Tax Simulation model (a model used to analyze alternative Social Security reform proposals including taxation of benefits and earnings sharing) and the CBO Individual Income Tax Simulation model.

Donald T. Oellerich is Assistant Professor of Social Work at Boston University. He received his doctorate in Social Welfare from the University of Wisconsin-Madison in 1984 for a dissertation titled, 'The Potential of Child Support to Reduce Welfare Costs and Caseloads, and Improve the Economic Well-Being of AFDC Families: A Wisconsin Example'.

Kent E. Portney is Associate Professor of Political Science and the Director of the Citizen Survey Program at the Lincoln Filene Center for Citizenship and Public Affairs, Tufts University, Massachusetts.

Andrew Reschovsky is Associate Professor of Economics at Tufts University, Massachusetts. He is the author of *State Tax Policy: Evaluating the Issues* and numerous articles in professional journals. He is currently conducting research on the impact of federal tax reform on state and local governments and on the poor, and is participating with several French economists in a study on fiscal decentralization.

Frank J. Sammartino is a Principal Analyst in the Tax Analysis Division of the Congressional Budget Office. Prior to joining the Congressional Budget Office he was employed in the Office of the Assistant Secretary for Planning and Evaluation in the Department of Health and Human Services. He has worked on issues relating to retirement security and the income of the aged for over seven years. His work includes analyses of numerous Social Security reform proposals. He is co-author of a number of microsimulation models including the ASPE Benefit and Tax Simulation model (a model used to analyze alternative Social Security reform proposals including taxation of benefits and earnings sharing) and the CBO Individual Income Tax Simulation model.

Jane Sjogren is Assistant Professor of Economics at Simmons College, Boston, Massachusetts. Her main research interest is in financial conditions of the elderly.

Timothy M. Smeeding is Professor of Economics and Director of Social Science Research at the University of Utah. He also directs the Luxembourg Income Study. Smeeding has published widely on the economics of poverty, especially the effects of in-kind transfers and the relative economic status of the elderly.

Jennifer L. Warlick, PhD (University of Wisconsin, 1979), is Assistant Professor of Economics at the University of Notre Dame, Indiana (1982 to present). During 1976–79 she served as an economist in the Office of Income Security Policy, US Department of Health, Education, and Welfare, where she was responsible for the formulation and evaluation of policy regarding social insurance and income maintenance for the aged and disabled. During 1979–82 she was Assistant Professor of Economics and Research Associate at the Institute for Research on Poverty, University of Wisconsin. She has published in both national and international journals including the *Review of Income and Wealth*, *Journal of Human Resources*, *Journal* *of Gerontology*, and *Consommation*: *Revue de Socio-Economie*, and in numerous books regarding income maintenance policy for the aged. Her current research focuses on the adequacy of the Social Security Disability program and the economic status of older women and SSI recipients.

John F. Witte is Associate Professor in the Department of Political Science and Associate Director of the Robert LaFollette Institute of Public Affairs at the University of Wisconsin-Madison. He received his PhD from Yale University. Hc is the author of *Democracy, Authority and Alienation in Work: Workers' Participation in an American Corporation* and *The Politics and Development of the Federal Income Tax*.

Preface

The chapters in this volume were selected by the editors, with the assistance of numerous anonymous referees, from over 40 manuscripts submitted in response to a call for papers on the distributional impacts of public policies that appeared in the *Policy Studies Journal*. An earlier version of Chapters 3, 5, 6, 9, and 10 appeared as part of a symposium in the September 1983 issue of that journal. All chapters were revised in early 1986.

We would like to thank Thomas Dye, who asked us to co-edit the September 1983 symposium; Stuart Nagel, general editor of the Policy Studies Organization Series; and Laura Friedrichs, who managed a large quantity of correspondence between the editors and the chapter authors.

SHELDON H. DANZIGER
KENT E. PORTNEY

1 Introduction: The Distributional Impacts of Public Policies

Sheldon H. Danziger and Kent E. Portney

Over the past 20 years economists, political scientists, sociologists, and other social scientists have put substantial effort into examining the different kinds of 'distributional impacts' of various public policies. The disciplines begin with different underlying theories and notions of what are the interesting and important questions. For example, economists often study the trade-offs between efficiency and the achievement of a particular distribution of benefits (Okun, 1975; Thurow, 1980), sociologists are more interested in a policy's implications for the perpetuation and modification of class differences in society (Parkin, 1971; Heller, 1972), and political scientists focus on theories of power and regime stability (Russett, 1964; Midlarksy and Tanter, 1967) and more recently on the nature of domestic policy-making processes (Lowi, 1964; Lowi, 1972; Ripley and Franklin, 1980).

Given such a broad range of researchable issues, we used a rather general definition of distributional impacts to select papers for this volume. In this introduction we offer a simple classification of how the benefits and costs of public policies can be distributed across numerous types of units, such as income classes, geographic areas, interest groups, races, genders, and so on. We then briefly summarize the papers selected for this volume and attempt to integrate their findings with those of other relevant works.

WHAT ARE DISTRIBUTIONAL IMPACTS?

Although the various disciplines have developed their own implicit or explicit definitions of 'impact', we suggest a fairly broad definition here. Distributional impact studies are those which investigate the distribution of actual benefits or burdens to various groups or persons in some specified population; or compare the 'actual' distribution of benefits or costs to the 'intended' distribution; or focus on alternative policy interventions or implementation schemes as a means for achieving some desired distribution of benefits or burdens. Distributional impact studies also identify conditions under which various distributional impacts might occur, and delineate the specific trade-offs necessary to achieve them. Or they compare the distribution of some characteristic of the population (such as income, health, or educational status, and so on) before the adoption/implementation of a policy, to the distribution of that characteristic after the policy has been in effect. Most distributional impact studies are *ex post facto* empirical evaluations of existing policies pursued by federal, state, or local governments. Others consist of *ex ante* simulations of the impacts of proposed policy alternatives.

In general, whenever a government pursues a course of action toward the achievement of a specific goal, some people are affected differently from others. Sometimes these differences are intended. For example, a federal income transfer policy designed to alleviate poverty is expected to benefit poorer people more than wealthier people. At other times, however, the pursuit of a nondistributive goal produces unintended distributional impacts. For example, the intended purpose of oil and natural gas deregulation is to stimulate exploration and expanded production. An unintended consequence is the redistribution of income from one sector of the economy or income class of people to another. Ideally, studies of distributional impacts examine both the intended and unintended consequences of governmental programs or policies.

Some policy studies distinguish between 'policy impacts' and 'policy outcomes' or 'outputs'. For example, Bryan Jones (1981) argues in the case of public service distributions that 'impacts' constitute the ultimate costs or benefits from service utilization or provision, while 'outcomes' and 'outputs' represent the results of antecedent steps in the service provision process. Jones cites an example of a drug treatment program, where the outputs consist of the client utilization rates, outcomes consist of changes in drug dependency attributable to the program, and impacts consist of changes in measures of drug-related health problems. In this sense, distributional impacts might differ from distributional outcomes. Thus, in Jones's example, the distribution of utilization rates could be quite different from the distribution of health problems, even for the same population.

In practice, however, it is difficult to know whether one is looking at the ultimate costs or benefits of a particular public policy. Public finance economists, for example, have successfully differentiated between who pays a tax and who bears the tax burden (Pechman and Okner, 1974). Consider the social security tax, one half of which is paid by the employer. Research suggests that the employers' payment reduces employee wages so that the employee actually bears the entire tax burden.

WHAT GETS DISTRIBUTED TO AND FROM WHOM?

Before examining distributional impacts, one must identify the relevant characteristics (costs or benefits) and units of analysis. The distributional characteristic refers to 'what is being distributed'; the units refer 'to whom and from whom that characteristic is distributed'. Given our rather broad definition of distributional impacts, a variety of distributed characteristics and units potentially could be examined in such studies. In this volume, for example, we have included papers which examine the distribution of government transfers to people below the poverty level, child support payments from absent fathers to their children, tax burdens resulting from the recent taxation of social security benefits, and others.

In Table 1.1 we list some policy areas cross-classified according to several different distributional characteristics and units. The four columns reflecting 'what is being distributed' are: (1) income/earnings/wealth; (2) occupational status or opportunity; (3) health and quality of life indicators; and (4) political access, participation, representation, or power. These outcomes might be distributed across the units listed in the rows of the table: income classes (as in tax incidence); racial groups (as in affirmative action programs); between the genders (as in anti-sex-discrimination policies); geographic areas (as in intergovernmental aid); between political parties, or special interest groups (as in campaign finance laws); among sectors of the economy (as in oil deregulation); or among nearly any other identifiable 'status' group.

Consider, for example, the upper left-hand cell. Income transfer policies (and others) distribute income differently across income classes. The cell immediately beneath suggests that the effects of these transfer policies (and others) differ among various racial groups. Obviously the distributional impacts in some of the cells have been investigated more rigorously than those in others.

This table does not represent the entire range of distributed

Table 1.1 What is being distributed to and from whom? A classification of research on the distributional impacts of public policies

To and from whom benefits or burdens are distributed	*What types of benefit or burden are distributed?* *Income/ earnings/ wealth* (1)	*Occupational status or opportunity* (2)	*Health and quality of life* (3)	*Political access/ participation/ representation* (4)
Income classes of people	Taxes Income transfers Health Environment Energy Transportation Manpower Employment Inflation School finance Deregulation	Manpower Employment Education Transportation	Health Income transfers Environment Manpower Employment Police and justice	Reapportionment Redistricting Transportation
Racial groups of people	Affirmative action Income transfers Manpower Employment Transportation Inflation Health Police and Justice	Affirmative action Income transfers Manpower Employment Education Transportation	Health Income transfers Manpower Employment Police and justice	Affirmative action Citizen participation Police and justice Reapportionment Redistricting Transportation

Sexes	Affirmative action Abortion/family planning Equal rights amendment	Affirmative action	Abortion/family planning Equal rights amendment	Affirmative action Equal rights amendment Intergovernmental transfers
Geographic areas or regions	Intergovernmental transfers	Education Intergovernmental transfers	Environment Energy Intergovernmental transfers	Reapportionment Redistricting
Political parties	–	–	–	Campaign contributions Reapportionment Redistricting Votes Citizen participation
Interest groups	Environment Energy Inflation Agriculture	Education Agriculture	–	Campaign contributions Intergovernmental transfers Education Environment Energy Agriculture Inflation Income transfers
Industrial or economic sectors	Taxes Energy Environment Deregulation Inflation	Taxes Labor and employment	–	–

continued on page 6

Table 1.1 *continued*

To and from whom benefits or burdens are distributed	*What types of benefit or burden are distributed?* *Income/earnings/wealth* (1)	*Occupational status or opportunity* (2)	*Health and quality of life* (3)	*Political access/participation/representation* (4)
OTHER 'STATUS' GROUPS				
Home-owners versus renters	Taxes Housing Inflation	Education	Energy Housing Taxes Inflation	–
Voters versus non-voters	–	–	–	Reapportionment Redistricting Referenda/initiatives Police and justice Transportation
Age groups (old versus young)	Taxes Income security Retirement Income transfers Health Housing Inflation	Education Housing	Income security Taxes Health	

characteristics or units. Moreover, as in Witte's paper on the distributional impacts of federal tax expenditures, one policy might involve the distribution of one or more characteristics between several different types of units.

Nevertheless, the table does provide a basic guide to existing and potential distributional impact research. Each of the cells of the table lists some policy areas where distributional impact research has appeared or where we believe prospective research is likely to be most fruitful.

THE PAPERS IN THIS VOLUME

With this framework in mind, we chose papers that fit into various cells of the table. Each paper develops its own methodology, and extends our understanding of the respective topic. We now turn to a brief summary of each paper's contribution.

Following in the genre of studies of Steiner (1971) and Storey (1983), Browning reviews the growth of US social welfare programs since the New Deal. He shows that much of this program growth occurred during the Nixon and Ford administrations, and in many cases had Republican support. Browning also shows that programs targeted for the largest cuts by the Reagan administration are, for the most part, those which grew most rapidly since 1968.

Flowing from their own previous works (Danziger and Plotnick, 1982; Smeeding, 1982), Danziger and Smeeding present papers which examine recent trends in poverty and the antipoverty impacts of public policies. Danziger finds that the impacts of income transfer policies reached a peak in the late 1970s and have declined during the Reagan administration. None the less, he shows that transfers continue to reduce poverty substantially, relative to what it would be in their absence.

Smeeding examines problems in official poverty estimates. He concludes that in-kind benefits reduce poverty more than official estimates indicate. He also finds that, due to Reagan administration policies, the more comprehensive poverty measure has increased more rapidly than the official one.

The next four papers analyze the distributional impacts of proposed policy changes in child support systems, the impact of cost-of-living adjustments to Social Security benefits on incomes of the elderly, the impact of three deficit reduction proposals aimed at

Social Security benefits, and the distributional impact of taxing unemployment benefits, respectively.

Oellerich and Garfinkel use the 1979 Current Population Survey – Child Support Supplement data to estimate the effects of existing and proposed programs designed to transfer income from an absent parent to a child. They focus on the antipoverty impact of such programs for children living in families headed by their mothers. They find that the present system, even if it were to operate at peak efficiency, can do little to reduce poverty. However, a new program they propose for 'taxing' absent fathers to support their children could significantly reduce poverty.

Baum and Sjogren use the Retirement History Survey data for 1970 through 1977 to study the distributional impact of seven alternative ways of indexing Social Security benefits. They conclude that the legislated indexing in 1973 of Social Security benefits to the Consumer Price Index has reduced poverty substantially compared to what it would have been without indexation. Attempts to alleviate social security difficulties by altering cost-of-living adjustments will very likely increase poverty among the elderly. However, minor modifications in the indexing scheme, such as the use of an alternative wage or price index, would not have a major impact.

Sammartino and Kasten simulate the distributional implications of three proposals to tax Social Security benefits. Each of the proposals would potentially achieve an equal reduction in total expenditures or increases in revenues. Using the Department of Health and Human Services' Benefit and Tax Simulation model, and data from the 1985 Current Population Survey, they show that the proposals produce very different distributional impacts.

Betson, Warlick, and Smeeding examine the effects of taxing Unemployment Insurance benefits as income. Using the Survey of Income and Education, they attempt to adjust revenue impact estimates according to induced labor supply responses. They find that because Unemployment Insurance recipients return to work sooner when their benefits are taxed, revenues raised through this tax would very likely be higher than previously estimated. And it produces this result without seriously affecting the distribution of personal income.

The two subsequent papers address tax-related issues. Witte examines the distributional impacts of federal tax expenditures (revenue losses due to special tax exclusions, credits, exemptions, or liability deferrals). He uses Treasury Department data to analyze the distribution of benefits from some 67 such provisions in the tax code.

He concludes that all income groups receive some benefits from tax expenditures, which may be judged to be either regressive or proportional depending on whether one distributes them across population groups, income classes, or by taxes paid.

Reschovsky develops a microsimulation model to assess the distributional impacts of changes in state taxes. He uses Massachusetts as an example and simulates how the tax burden would change if a single income tax rate on all income were adopted instead of the current dual rate on earned and unearned income. He looks at the effect of this proposal on burdens borne by elderly taxpayers, and compares it to simulated impacts from a tax deduction targeted for elderly persons, and broadening the state sales tax base. He finds that the single rate income tax would reduce over-all tax progressivity; the deduction for the elderly would have little impact; and the sales tax expansion would make the sales tax more regressive, but the income tax more progressive.

The final two papers focus on several political aspects of distributional impacts. Cranmer analyzes the temporal changes in benefits enjoyed by several different political interests. He develops a methodology for analyzing the benefits accruing to groups in developing nations, and applies it to Sri Lanka.

The final paper, by Portney, examines distributional impact studies within their policy-making process context. He suggests that distributional impact analysts face something of a dilemma because many policy-makers are not well prepared to receive their findings. He argues that policy-makers are not likely to appreciate distributional impact studies in particular until they develop a 'need to know'. Using concepts from policy-making process research, Portney suggests that the need to know is not likely to develop until economic and social conditions force policy-makers to confront the specific trade-offs involved with their policy decisions. Distributional impact analysts may, however, be able to structure their analyses in order to maximize the chances that policy-makers will utilize their research.

References

DANZIGER, S. H. and PLOTNICK, R. (1982) 'The War on Income Poverty: Achievements and Failures', in P. M. SOMMERS (ed.) (1982) *Welfare Reform in America*, p. 31–52 (Boston: Kluwer-Nijhoff).

HELLER, C. (ed.) (1972) *Structured Social Inequality: A Reader in Comparative Social Stratification* (New York: Macmillan).

JONES, B. D. (1981) 'Assessing the Products of Government: What Gets Distributed?' *Policy Studies Journal*, 9 (7): 963–70.
LOWI, T. (1964) 'American Business, Public Policy, Case Studies, and Political Theory', *World Affairs*, 16 (4): 677–715.
LOWI, T. (1972) 'Four Systems of Politics, Policy, and Choice', *Public Administration Review*, 32: 298–310.
MIDLARSKY, M. and TANTER, R. (1967) 'Toward a Theory of Political Instability in Latin America', *Journal of Peace Research*, 3: 209–27.
OKUN, A. M. (1975) *Equality and Efficiency: The Big Tradeoff* (Washington, D.C.: Brookings Institution).
PARKIN, F. (1971) *Class Inequality and Political Order: Social Stratification in Capitalist and Communist Societies* (London: MacGibbons & Kee).
PECHMAN, J. A. and OKNER, B. A. (1974) *Who Bears the Tax Burden?* (Washington, D.C.: Brookings Institution).
RIPLEY, R. B. and FRANKLIN, G. A. (1980) *Congress, the Bureaucracy, and Public Policy* (Homewood, Ill.: Dorsey).
RUSSETT, B. M. (1964) 'Inequality and Instability: The Relation of Land Tenure to Politics', *World Politics*, 16 (3): 442–54.
SMEEDING, T. M. (1982) 'The Antipoverty Effects of In-Kind Transfers', *Policy Studies Journal*, 10: 499–521.
STEINER, G. (1971) *The State of Welfare* (Washington, D.C.: Brookings Institution).
STOREY, J. (1983) *Older Americans in the Reagan Era: Impacts of Federal Policy Changes* (Washington, D.C.: Urban Institute).
THUROW, L. (1980) *The Zero Sum Society: Distribution and the Possibilities for Economic Change* (New York: Penguin).

Part I
Spending on Social Programs: Its Growth and Distributional Impacts

2 Priorities, Programs, and Presidents: Assessing Patterns of Growth in US Social Welfare Programs, 1950–1985

Robert X. Browning

Much has been written about the election of 1964 and the resulting enactment of the War on Poverty and Great Society social programs. Much more will be written, to be sure, on the effect of the 1980 election and the Reagan administration efforts to scale down or terminate much of the federal social welfare effort. The difficulty with these efforts is that they overlook the enactment of social programs and adjustments to programs which have occurred during every administration in the post-war period. The impetus for some of these changes has been presidential; for others, the initiative was congressional. A look back at patterns of growth in social expenditures across time and presidential administrations may yield surprises for some. Most importantly, it puts policies in perspective and provides a basis for assessing presidential efforts to expand or control social expenditures.

In this paper we explore the patterns of growth in federal social expenditures from 1950 to 1985. The analysis seeks to show the periods when we have seen new program enactment, and when we have seen adjustments to current programs. These adjustments include changes in benefit formulas, or modifications in eligibility conditions. Throughout this period there has been differential growth across administrations and within programs. Exploring these patterns of growth and, when possible, their underlying program roots, may help to dispel some myths about presidents and social welfare spending priorities which arise from an overemphasis on particular cases of program enactment. Furthermore, these patterns show how the growth of US social expenditures has resulted from political control of the government interacting with economic conditions. We conclude with some observations on the cuts in federal social expenditures initiated by the Reagan administration in 1981.

CLASSIFYING US SOCIAL WELFARE POLICY

We rely in these paper on the definition of social welfare expenditures long used by the Social Security Administration. These are cash and in-kind programs which 'are of direct benefit to individuals. Included are programs for income maintenance through social insurance and public aid, and those providing support of health, education, housing, and other welfare services' (McMillan and Bixby, 1980, p. 3). US social welfare policy includes over 70 programs paying $200 billion in benefits to 40 million households.[1] They range from the largest, Social Security retirement, to one of the smallest, the Indian Health Scholarship program.

The federal budget classifies the bulk of US social programs in four functional categories.[2] These are income security; education, training, employment, and social services; health; and veterans' benefits and services. Two direct loan programs to provide for rural housing and housing for the elderly and handicapped are classified in the commerce and housing credit category. A few programs are found in the community and regional development functional budget category.

Within the budget categories, programs can be further classified into categories based on type and condition of assistance. The types of assistance are cash versus in-kind, and the conditions are whether the program is means tested or non-means tested. Means-tested policies have an income test for benefit eligibility. These programs are generally targeted toward the poor. Non-means tested programs base eligibility on some other criteria. The most common of these is eligibility based on previous employment. Social Security, other public retirement programs, disability programs, and unemployment compensation are all based on previous employment. These programs are termed social insurance and pay benefits in some proportion to the duration and salary of the worker's employment. Each functional budget category contains a mix of cash and in-kind programs and means-tested and non-means-tested programs. For example, veterans' pensions are a means-tested benefit to veterans with low incomes. Veterans' compensation payments are not means tested;

rather, eligibility is based on a disability which may be service or non-service connected.

The classification by type and condition of assistance is a useful one because it indirectly relates to the target beneficiary groups and highlights the categorical nature of federal social policy. Non-means-tested cash programs are considered to be 'earned' benefits and are primarily directed toward the middle class. The poor certainly benefit from these programs, but that is not the expressed purpose of the programs.[3] Expenditures for means-tested cash programs are small relative to means-tested in-kind programs. A characteristic feature of US social programs has been a greater willingness to provide services to the poor rather than cash (Steiner, 1971; Patterson, 1981; Garfinkel and Haveman, 1982). Arguments for the effectiveness of the latter are met with concerns about work disincentives and a fear that the poor would frivolously squander welfare checks. Consequently, assistance to the poor is provided in many in-kind forms which intend to target the money for food, housing, health, and social services.

Many have lamented the categorical and fragmented nature of US social policy. This absence of a comprehensive approach to US social welfare policy was described in 1972 by a staff study for the Subcommittee on Fiscal Policy of the Congressional Joint Economic Committee (US Congress, 1972, p. 1):

> In general an incremental approach has been followed, but it is no longer possible – if, indeed, it ever was – to provide a convincing rationale for the programs as they exist in terms of who is covered and who is excluded, benefit amounts, and eligibility conditions. No coherent rationale binds them together as a system. Additionally, the programs are extraordinarily complex, and the eligibility conditions and entitlement provisions lack uniformity even among programs with similar objectives and structures. Public retirement programs, for example, differ widely in their generosity to covered workers. And, a number of the income-tested programs reach the same part of the population but have been developed separately without apparent consistency of objectives, operating features, and equity.

A similar observation was made in 1975 by David Stockman, the first Office of Management and Budget (OMB) director in the Reagan administration (Stockman, 1975, p. 11). He wrote:

> In a small percentage of instances, the current panoply of cash assistance and in-kind benefit programs provides a comfortable income equivalent of more than $8,000 annually for female-headed families in areas like New York City, as demonstrated by the Griffiths Subcommittee on Fiscal Policy. In most states and most instances, however, it is not this cumulative benefit package which is available, but instead a grab-bag of uncoordinated, gap-ridden programs that simultaneously provide both inadequate income maintenance and marginal tax rates which we shrink from levying even on millionaires.

The approach of this paper is to show when and how the expenditures for this 'grab-bag' of programs have grown. Then we might be better able to understand the noncomprehensive nature of US social programs and appreciate the priorities which have been placed on particular programs during post-war presidential administrations.

SOCIAL WELFARE PROGRAM GROWTH

Most federal programs have their origin in the New Deal. Before that time social welfare was a mix of state, local, and private efforts. While the role of the federal government has vastly changed and the size of the present federal programs dwarf the modest New Deal beginnings, the basic shape and character of present-day programs still reflect much of their New Deal origin.

The Social Security Act of 1935, signed by President Franklin D. Roosevelt, contained provisions for Old Age Insurance, unemployment compensation, assistance to the needy who were aged, blind, or had dependent children (Witte, 1963; Altmeyer, 1966; Derthick, 1979). It also provided for child welfare and maternal and child health services. Since that time, health and disability insurance have been added. Benefit coverage has been expanded to widows, spouses, children, and students. Today benefits paid under the provisions of the Social Security Act constitute 59 per cent of all US federal social welfare expenditures and 31 per cent of all US federal expenditures (McMillan and Bixby, 1980, p. 12). Beyond the social insurance programs, federal program expansion has been seen in in-kind expenditures. These include expenditures for food, housing, health, education, and manpower training programs. Few new cash programs have been enacted since the New Deal. The new program

Table 2.1 Share of cash and in-kind expenditures, 1950–80 (millions of dollars and percentage)

Fiscal year	*In-kind*	*Cash*	*Total*	*In-kind percentage*
1950	2 393.9	5 114.1	7 508.0	31.9
1955	965.7	10 100.5	11 066.2	8.7
1960	1 578.8	19 999.2	21 578.0	7.3
1965	5 378.9	27 555.2	32 934.1	16.3
1970	23 869.1	46 061.4	69 930.5	34.1
1975	57 353.8	94 640.5	151 994.3	37.7
1980	121 663.3	181 681.6	303 344.9	40.1

Source: Calculations by author from Social Security Administration data. Excludes all administrative, construction, and research expenditures except for 1980. All figures in nominal dollars.

enactments since 1940 have been in-kind rather than cash programs. In-kind expenditures as a percentage of total expenditures steadily declined from 35 per cent in 1949 to 7 per cent in the late 1950s as veterans benefit programs declined in participation (see Table 2.1).[4] This percentage rose again rapidly in the early to mid 1960s, however, as Democratic Congresses enacted new social service and Great Society programs. By 1980 in-kind expenditures constituted 40 per cent of total federal social welfare spending, reflecting ever increasing expenditures for health and food programs.

Expenditures for social welfare have been increasing steadily since 1950. The annual percentage increases range from a low of 0.6 per cent in fiscal year 1949 to a high of 20.1 per cent in 1975.[5] These percentage change figures do mask the increases in the size of federal expenditures seen in Table 2.1 as well as the relative size of the categories (Table 2.2). Percentage change figures are useful, however, in showing the increases from year to year in standardized units.

From the summary shown in Table 2.3, some differences across presidential administrations can be observed.[6] The figures show that the percentage changes for social welfare have generally been larger in Republican administrations than Democratic administrations. The major exceptions are the large increase in the Johnson Administration and the very small increase during Reagan's first term.[7] When considering real expenditure changes, the percentage increases in

Table 2.2 Federal social welfare expenditures by category, 1950–80 (in millions of dollars)

	1950	*1960*	*1970*	*1980*
Social insurance	2 103.0	14 307.2	45 245.6	191 106.9
Public assistance	1 103.2	2 116.9	9 648.6	49 252.2
Veterans	6 386.2	5 367.3	8 951.5	21 253.6
Education	156.7	867.9	5 875.8	12 990.2
Health and medical	603.5	1 737.1	4 775.2	13 348.0
Housing	14.6	143.5	581.6	6 608.1
Other	174.0	416.7	2 258.9	8 785.9
Total	10 541.2	24 956.6	77 337.2	303 344.9
Total in 1972 dollars	18 924.9	35 100.7	85 361.1	169 277.3

Federal social welfare expenditures by category (as percentage of total)

	1950	*1960*	*1970*	*1980*
Social insurance	20.0	57.3	58.5	63.0
Public assistance	10.5	8.5	12.5	16.2
Veterans	60.6	21.5	11.6	7.0
Education	1.5	3.5	7.6	4.3
Health and medical	5.7	7.0	6.2	4.4
Housing	0.1	0.6	0.7	2.2
Other	1.6	1.7	2.9	2.9
Total	100.0	100.0	100.0	100.0

Note: All figures are in nominal dollars except as noted, and include all administrative, construction, and research expenditures. Categories are those used by the Social Security Administration.
Source: A. K. Bixby (1983) 'Social Welfare Expenditures, Fiscal Year 1980', *Social Security Bulletin*, 46:9–17.

federal social welfare spending during the Eisenhower (9.7 and 11.3%), Nixon (11.3%), and Nixon-Ford (8.2%) presidencies exceed that of the Truman (1.6%), Kennedy-Johnson (3.9%), and Carter (3.7%) presidencies. Republican presidents have been more successful in controlling total and nonsocial welfare expenditures than social welfare expenditures.

Looking beyond these totals the different priorities in social programs begin to emerge in the budget category percentage change figures. Table 2.3 shows these differences for the four major budget

Table 2.3 Real annual percentage change in budget outlays by presidential administration, 1950–85

		All expenditures			*Social welfare*			
		Total	*Non-social welfare*	*Social welfare*	*Income security*	*Education, Manpower and social services*	*Health*	*Veterans*
D	Truman	16.0	21.1	1.6	12.0	23.4	12.0	−7.8
R	Eisenhower I	−1.2	−3.6	9.7	15.1	7.6	8.9	1.0
R	Eisenhower II	4.4	2.0	11.3	14.5	14.1	15.5	1.5
D	Kennedy-Johnson	3.5	3.4	3.9	3.7	18.0	17.3	−1.2
D	Johnson	8.3	6.5	12.2	6.7	38.0	57.2	4.4
R	Nixon	3.1	−2.5	11.3	13.3	9.6	7.9	7.3
R	Nixon-Ford	4.6	1.0	8.2	8.6	5.4	11.5	2.7
D	Carter	4.0	4.5	3.7	4.0	2.1	6.5	−2.4
R	Reagan I	3.9	6.5	1.6	1.4	−7.0	6.5	−1.0

Note: Calculations from US Budget data. Social welfare expenditures include all expenditures in income security, education, manpower, and social services, health, and veterans' benefit functional categories. Trust funds are included.

Table 2.4 Average real percentage changes in payments to individuals by presidential administration for cash and in-kind benefits, 1950–85*

	All expenditures			*Low-income expenditures*			
	Cash	*In-kind*	*Total*	*Cash*	*In-kind*	*AFDC*	*Total*
Truman	12.8	6.9	12.6	6.9	5.9	6.9	7.0
Eisenhower I	15.3	9.5	15.1	2.5	13.1	2.5	3.4
Eisenhower II	14.9	14.5	14.9	6.5	19.0	6.5	7.9
Kennedy-Johnson	3.6	15.1	4.0	5.4	16.0	5.4	7.3
Johnson	6.6	84.6	12.4	3.8	71.0	3.8	35.3
Nixon	11.6	15.1	12.4	9.6	26.2	9.4	18.9
Nixon-Ford	8.5	11.9	9.4	11.9	12.5	−5.3	12.3
Carter	3.4	8.2	4.8	1.9	7.0	−1.0	5.2
Reagan I	1.6	4.8	2.6	−3.8	0.8	−8.7	−0.3

*Excludes veterans' benefits.
Source: US Budget data. Reagan administration changes based on four-year averages using estimated outlays for FY84 and FY85.

categories. The figures reveal that the Johnson and Kennedy administrations, which show the smallest percentage change increases for income security programs, have the largest percentage increases for the in-kind categories: health and social services. These Democratic administrations had a different program emphasis from the preceding and following Republican administrations. The Carter administration looks much more like the Republican administrations it follows than the previous Democratic administrations. The changes in the veterans category reflect, in part, the cyclical effects of war efforts.

To further understand the bases of these differences within budget categories, the distinction between cash and in-kind programs and in means-tested versus non-means-tested programs is potentially illuminating. Table 2.4 shows cash and in-kind percentage changes without veterans' dollars. The in-kind changes show the effect of the Johnson administration and the subsequent Republican administrations. Democratic administrations have been periods for increases in in-kind, rather than cash, programs.

The means-tested versus non-means-tested cash benefit comparison shows a reversal of Republican and Democratic positions. First, the figures in Table 2.4 indicate that cash benefits were increased the most in the Truman administration. This reflects the first efforts to adjust Social Security and the public assistance benefit programs (OAA, AB, ADC).[8] The former is non-means tested; the latter are means tested. After the Truman administration, the three Republican administrations lead the Kennedy and Johnson administrations in increases for non-means-tested cash benefit programs, the social insurance programs. The increases in low-income cash programs are much lower than are non-means cash benefit increases.

The Democratic social priorities are also seen if one examines all means-tested programs, regardless of whether they are cash or in-kind. The figures presented in Table 2.4 show that these programs increased the most in the Johnson and Truman presidencies. The Nixon and Ford presidencies are not far behind, however, reflecting the increases in means tested in-kind programs during this period. While the emphasis was on low income cash benefits in the Truman administration, it was on means tested in-kind programs in the Kennedy and Johnson years.

SOURCES OF PROGRAM GROWTH AND EXPANSION

In order to understand the causes of this differential program growth we must take a closer look at when and how programs have grown. Since the programs we are describing are payments to individuals, increases in expenditures most often result from adjustments in eligibility conditions or benefit amounts. The following six causes underlie most social welfare expenditure increases. First, new entitlement programs may be added or additional family members may be made eligible for an existing entitlement. Secondly, benefit payments may be increased. Thirdly, eligibility conditions may be modified in a way which affects program participation. Fourthly, expenditures are responsive to economic conditions, demographic changes, and changes in household composition. Fifthly, the federal share of program costs may be increased. Finally, total federal program appropriations may be increased. These last two reasons primarily apply to programs which require a state or local contribution or for programs in which funds are not appropriated or calculated on an individual basis. An example of the latter would be grants to states for social services.

Growth in cash programs

Since the enactment of the New Deal programs there have been very few new cash entitlement programs. Consequently, cash programs have grown because of benefit adjustments and expansion of eligibility. All presidents, regardless of party, have supported cost-of-living adjustments in Social Security at the onset of their terms of office (Browning, 1986). Beyond these recommendations, the impetus for benefit increases and the gains in real benefits have come from the Congress.

Increasing Social Security and public assistance benefits was a social welfare priority during the Truman administration. Benefits were increased an average of 77 per cent in 1950. Throughout the 1950s Congress enacted Social Security benefit increases on a two-year cycle just prior to elections. Benefit increases for the public assistance cash programs were usually added in floor amendments at the same time. Since veterans' pension benefits were reduced by the amount of Social Security increases, the veterans interests in and out of the Congress pressed for increases in this cash program following each Social Security benefit increase.

In the 1960s Social Security increases were less frequent than in the 1950s and AFDC payments, the most visible welfare program, were not increased with other public assistance cash benefit programs. However, inflation pressures in the early 1970s resulted in frequent Social Security benefit increases and in pressures on the House Ways and Means committee, the guardian of Social Security policy, to make Social Security increases automatic.[9] What soon followed was an extension of indexing to most cash and in-kind benefit programs. The most notable exception was AFDC, which remained unindexed (US Congress, 1981).

In addition to these benefit increases, cash entitlement programs have been marked by many modifications designed to expand eligibility. In the social insurance cash programs these changes have usually meant making family members eligible for some portion of the insured worker's benefit. Surviving spouses and children have been made eligible. The conditions under which the worker is eligible have been modified to provide benefits at earlier retirement ages or in cases of disability. This pattern was observed throughout the 1950s and has been attributed to a strategy of the program executives of the Social Security system (Derthick, 1979; Berkowitz and McQuaid, 1980).

These two phenomena underlie the patterns of expenditure increases observed earlier in cash programs. Benefit increases and expansion of eligibility in the 1950s and 1970s account for the observed increases during these periods. The presidential policy posture during these periods has been one of assent to bureaucratic and congressional interests. Elections and economic conditions determined the amount and timing of the increases.

Growth in in-kind programs

It is in the in-kind programs that the initiation of new programs is observed. While not technically entitlements, these programs became *de facto* entitlements since Congress authorized benefits to all eligible beneficiaries and appropriated additional funds when actual costs exceeded estimated costs. Most of these in-kind programs were enacted in the 1960s and 1970s, but the program design usually reflected previous programs or previous policy debates. In-kind programs were enacted as innovative responses to public problems, and as the result of the reluctance of policy-makers to provide cash benefits to needy individuals.

The War on Poverty signaled a major effort to provide the poor with the skills – political and educational – to better their conditions. Prior to these Great Society programs there had been few in-kind policy initiatives, either from Congress or the president. There was an emphasis on vocational rehabilitation services in the Eisenhower administration. The Kennedy initiatives were in social services for the poor, the first Manpower Development and Training Act, and the Area Redevelopment Act. Kennedy also initiated a pilot food stamp program which had been resisted by the Eisenhower administration in the previous years (Ripley, 1969).

With the War on Poverty came the in-kind programs such as Community Action Programs (CAP), legal services for the poor, adult education, neighborhood health centers, Job Corps, Neighborhood Youth Corps, Head Start, and Upward Bound. The Office of Economic Opportunity (OEO) programs were never large in terms of the money spent (Plotnick and Skidmore, 1975; Levitan and Taggart, 1976). The total appropriation for the first year budget was only $800 million. Their importance, and the reason they attracted so much opposition is that they challenged existing community power structures. Consequently, they were the target of congressional critics and a major priority for termination in the Nixon administration. The lasting importance of the War on Poverty was that it elevated the plight of the poor to a national concern and created a new test for public policy: 'What does it do for the poor?' (Lampman, 1974).

Far more important in terms of spending were the in-kind initiatives passed following the 1964 election. The passage of Medicare, Medicaid, and the Elementary and Secondary Education Act were the culmination of struggles which occurred in every Congress prior to the 89th. The election of 194 northern Democratic representatives in 1964 provided the necessary margins to pass these acts over the longstanding objections of conservative southern congressmen. The effects of these acts can be seen in increased levels of federal social welfare expenditures in the years following 1967.

Program growth in the post-Johnson administrations

Two other in-kind program initiatives during the Johnson years which would also later become major spending programs were manpower programs and the food and nutrition programs. Neither of these were ideas which originated with the Johnson administration. They had been on the congressional agenda since the late 1950s. Senate Democrats had been pushing for a Youth Conservation Corps patterned after the New Deal programs since 1958. The Manpower Development and Training Act (MDTA) of 1962 and the 1962 Public Welfare Amendments to the Social Security Act were designed to help the chronically unemployed. Manpower programs did constitute an important policy emphasis of the original OEO act comprising over 50 per cent of the requested appropriations. In subsequent extensions of this act numerous additional manpower training programs were initiated and were ultimately consolidated into the Comprehensive Employment and Training Act (CETA). Expenditures for the MDTA program were less than $500 million annually prior to the War on Poverty changes. By 1968 there were a dozen programs with annual expenditures totaling $2.2 billion annually. But with manpower programs as with food programs, the major expenditures occurred in the years following the Johnson presidency.

The post-Johnson years were marked by high unemployment, presidential interest in consolidating manpower programs in block grants, and presidential – congressional struggles over public works employment programs. Nixon vetoed two jobs bills which authorized public service employment programs. This struggle culminated in 1973 with the passage of CETA which contained provisions for $250 million annual authorization for public service employment in 1974 and 1975 and open-ended authorization for 1976–7. Continued high unemployment motivated the Congress to pass additional jobs programs such as Title VI to the CETA program authorizing $2.5 billion in emergency jobs programs. Only six months later the Congress passed an additional $2.3 billion emergency jobs bill which was vetoed by President Ford. As unemployment continued to increase, President Ford proposed a $2 billion program and Congress successfully enacted bills authorizing $3 billion for public service and summer youth jobs in 1975.

This struggle over jobs programs continued into 1976. As the election neared, Ford abandoned his resistance to the Title VI CETA extension which authorized $1.6 billion for emergency public sector employment. Also in 1976, the Democratic Congress enacted a public works employment bill over President Ford's veto. The first veto of the $6 billion program was sustained. The second veto of the pared down $4 billion program for state and local public works projects and countercyclical aid was overridden. Total federal spending for manpower and employment programs had reached almost $8 billion in 1977. An additional $4 billion was authorized for public works jobs during the Carter administration. CETA was reauthorized but with few changes and without the Title VI funding.

While the Democratic presidents, Kennedy and Johnson, supported efforts to make food stamps a national program to assist the poor, its transformation into one of the more costly and uniform national programs was furthered by the initiatives of a Republican president, Richard Nixon.[10] In 1969 Nixon recommended a doubling of food stamp appropriations from $340 million to $610 million for FY70 and an increase to one billion for FY71. Included was a proposal of free stamps for the poor. The 1970 changes provided for $1.75 billion appropriation for FY71 and open-ended appropriations after that. More importantly, the bill required national eligibility and benefit standards. In subsequent enactments, the Congress mandated participation by all counties. By 1980 the federal cost of food stamps was over $11 billion.

A similar post-Johnson increase is observed with the other federal nutrition programs which increased from $500 million to almost $3 billion during the period 1965–78. The increases in the school lunch programs, and the initiation of additional nutrition programs for breakfast, for children in child care, for summer programs, for the elderly, and supplemental food assistance for women, infants and children were enacted despite presidential resistance from Presidents Johnson to Ford. In 1967, for example, Johnson recommended cutting school milk funds for FY67 from $103 million to $21 million and a $20 million cut in school lunch appropriations. Congress ignored these recommendations. Similarly, in the early 1970s Congress continued to expand the nutrition programs providing free meals to children from families with incomes up to 175 per cent of the poverty line. Eligibility and appropriations for nutrition and the food stamp programs were automatically adjusted semiannually for increases in the Consumer Price Index (CPI) for food. Carter's positions on child nutrition programs were similar to previous presidents. He proposed restrictions on the growth to the Women, Infant and Children (WIC) nutrition program, an end to the special milk program, and targcting breakfast funds to the poor.

Assessing the effect of program lags is one of the more difficult issues in analyzing social program expenditures (Browning, 1986). Some of the increases observed from FY70 to FY77 result from decisions made during the Johnson years. The Elementary and Secondary Education Act resulted in increased education expenditures. Additional programs expanded aid for college education. Following the enactment of Medicare and Medicaid, expenditures for health were influenced by exogenous factors such as physician and hospital charges and the demand for medical care. With nutrition and manpower programs the post-War-on-Poverty increases observed in these programs result from presidential and congressional decisions during the Ford and Nixon years.

Few new programs were enacted during the Carter administration. While total expenditures continued toward new heights, the annual growth figures were much lower. This slowdown in growth and concern about program uncontrollability set the stage for the reductions enacted in the Reagan administration.

A NEW PRESIDENT AND NEW PRIORITIES: RONALD REAGAN

This analysis of previous spending decisions provides a perspective to understand the priorities of the Reagan administration which came into office committed to stemming the increases in federal social welfare spending. Approximately 75 per cent of the federal budget was termed 'relatively uncontrollable' indicating that spending would continue at that level unless Congress altered existing laws and previous commitments. Spending for social programs consumed over half of the $700 billion budget. To an administration philosophically opposed to many of these social programs, and with its own priorities to increase the defense budget and lower taxes, cuts in social programs were a major priority.

In a very early policy document David Stockman indicated that he knew where he would achieve the social welfare savings. Setting aside Social Security, which he wrote 'would be a political disaster to tinker with in the first round . . .' (Greider, 1981, p. 153), he zeroed in on the non-Social Security entitlements. In the December 1980 so-called Dunkirk paper he wrote (Greider, 1981, pp. 155–6):

> Current expenditures for food stamps, cash assistance, Medicaid, disability, heating assistance, WIC, school lunches, and unemployment compensation amount to $100 billion. A carefully tailored package to reduce eligibility, overlap, and abuse should be developed for these areas – with potential savings of $10–20 billion.

The 1981 Omnibus Budget Reconciliation Act did implement cuts in many of these programs. The importance of this bill was that it changed existing laws and altered statutory eligibility criteria for *de facto* entitlement programs. An FY82 budget savings of $35.2 billion was projected from the cuts made in 17 federal programs (Congressional Quarterly, 1982, pp. 102–3). These cuts primarily altered the liberalized eligibility requirements and benefit adjustments enacted in the 1970–76 period. For programs such as Pell grants for education, CETA job training, WIC, energy assistance, and Title XX services a cap was placed on total expenditures to reduce program costs. Federal program contributions to Medicaid and school nutrition programs were reduced. Eligibility was restricted for food stamps and school lunches while benefits for AFDC recipients were reduced. Two programs, CETA public works jobs (Title VI) and the Social Security minimum benefit, were eliminated.

Throughout this debate the administration emphasized its support for the 'safety net' – those programs targeted to those who 'rely on government for their very existence' (Congressional Quarterly, 1982, p. 99). These programs were identified as Social Security; Medicare; veterans' pensions and compensation; Supplemental Security Income (SSI); Head Start; summer jobs for disadvantaged youths; and free school lunches and breakfasts. What this emphasis reinforced was the concept of a federal welfare commitment to the elderly, the veterans, and the destitute. Those who were barely above the poverty line, or who were only above the poverty line by virtue of the federal in-kind benefits they received, would bear the brunt of the cuts in non-Social Security entitlements. While ostensibly seeking to end benefits to those who could pay, the Reagan cuts hit the hardest at the working poor.

Most important from the standpoint of this paper is to understand that the Reagan administration priorities were not targeted primarily at War on Poverty programs, but at the expansion of the welfare state realized in the post-Johnson years. Most of these eligibility changes and new programs were enacted during the Nixon and Ford presidencies. Nixon had already done battle with the War on Poverty and the original OEO programs had been modified and placed under new auspices. The increases in program benefits of the 'safety net' programs were also enacted in the post-Johnson years. Although the poor, and especially the elderly poor, have benefited from these increases, the bulk of the 'safety-net' programs (Social Security, Medicare, and veterans' benefits) are not specifically targeted to the poor (Plotnick, 1979).

PRIORITIES, PROGRAMS, AND PRESIDENTS: A SUMMARY

In summary, we see throughout this analysis that the largest per cent increases have been observed in Republican rather than Democratic administrations. Removing inflation increases alters the ranking of the Republican administrations, but does not change the relative position of Democratic and Republican administrations. Within program categories and across administrations, one does see differences in social welfare program priorities. The enactment of new in-kind programs is observed in Democratic administrations. The Republican administrations have been periods of adjustments in cash benefits which are not income tested, and expansion of programs enacted in previous years. Many of these enactments originated in the Democratic Congress over the resistance, or with the acquiescence, of Republican presidents. More than any other Republican president, Nixon furthered the expansion of the welfare expenditures by his support for welfare reform, food stamp expansion, and Social Security increases. Congressional actions during the Carter presidency signaled a rising concern about the cost of social benefit programs.

Throughout this period economic conditions have influenced the amount and timing of benefit and expenditure increases. In the 1950s elections determined the timing of Social Security benefits coupled with first term presidential recommendations for inflation adjustments. In the late 1960s and early 1970s persistent inflation created pressures for benefit increases and led Congress to index over 60 programs to various consumer price indices. A similar effect resulted from the increased unemployment realized from 1970 to 1976. This led to the enactment of public works and emergency jobs programs as well as to semi-automatic increases in entitlement and open-ended appropriations programs.

CONCLUSION

The legacy of US federal social welfare policy-making is one of incremental adjustments to the basic New Deal social programs. Eligibility has been expanded and benefits increased in the cash non-means-tested, social insurance programs. These adjustments have by and large been greater during Republican administrations than during Democratic administrations. Beyond these cash expenditures for social insurance, the major growth and program proliferation has been in in-kind programs.

Decisions made in previous administrations certainly affect the options available to the current president. This is seen in several ways. First, policy-making is incremental. US social welfare policy making is the culmination of continuous program adjustments through the addition of new beneficiaries or benefits to entitled recipients. Secondly, there are few really new programs.[11] Instead, old ideas are resurrected, redirected, or reissued. Thirdly, the nature of entitlements, actual or *de facto*, limits the policy discretion of the current president. Hence, some part of the spending observed during the Nixon and Ford administrations was the direct result of the priorities and programs of the previous administration. The same is true of all other administrations.

To understand the Reagan social priorities, we must understand the priorities of previous presidents. Furthermore, we must examine the nature and kind of benefit programs which comprise the US welfare state. Finally, we must explore the process of policy decisions. This involves decomposing the automatic economic effects from the political decisions to authorize those effects, disentangling the lagged effects of previous policy decisions, and separating presidential priorities from congressional priorities. Only then will we be able to fully understand how politics influences who benefits from US social welfare policy.

Notes

1. Exhaustive lists of federal social programs, their benefits and conditions are not easily obtained. A good starting point for current programs is a US Congressional Research Service publication (1981), *Indexation of Federal Programs* (see also, the annual *Catalog of Federal Domestic Assistance*). The social welfare expenditure figures are from the Social Security Administration figures. The household recipient estimates are from Current Population Survey data.
2. The federal budget categories are often changed to reflect program changes and administration emphases. The categories referred to here were in use at the beginning of the Reagan administration.
3. Indeed, it can be argued that the progress against poverty has been realized through increases in non-means-tested programs whose benefits are also received by the poor. Social Security is such a program (see, for example, Burkhauser and Smeeding, 1981. See also, Plotnick and Skidmore, 1975; Plotnick, 1979; Danziger and Plotnick, 1982).
4. The expenditure data are taken from the social welfare expenditure series published in the *Social Security Bulletin*. Programmatic details are found in the publication: US Department of Health, Education and Welfare (1968) *Social Welfare Expenditures Under Public Programs in the United States, 1929–66* and for subsequent years from unpublished data made available by the Office of Research and Statistics, Social Security Administration (SSA). Generally, all expenditure data follow the classification of Robert Plotnick in Plotnick and Skidmore (1975). The SSA series provides consistent definitions across time and permits the separation of program expenditures from administrative expenditures. Before 1980 we include only programs which are of direct benefit to individuals. Model Cities and Community Action Program funds are the only social programs included in which individuals are not the direct program recipients. All research, construction, and administrative expenditures are excluded. The only departure from Plotnick's series is the exclusion of administrative and construction expenditures and payments to farmers. Plotnick (1979) excludes payments to farmers in his subsequent analysis. Some program expenditures are taken from the US budget and annual reports of the Veterans Administration.
5. The expenditure data for the federal government is on a fiscal year basis – 1 July to 30 June – and members of Congress and the president serve terms of office based on the calendar year. For example, the fiscal year, 1 July 1969 to 30 June 1970, is referred to by the budget convention as FY70. A president elected in 1968 and taking office in January 1969 would submit a budget for FY70. The federal fiscal year was revised and now runs from 1 October to 30 September. The first full fiscal year on this new schedule began on 1 October 1976 and is noted as FY77.
6. These data are taken from the annual US Budgets, and from unpublished historical tables compiled by the Office of Management and

Budget. These tables are published as part of the US Budget documents beginning in FY86.

7. The fiscal Gross National Product (GNP) deflator is used to obtain real expenditure increases.
8. These acronyms stand for Old Age Assistance (OAA), Aid to the Blind (AB), and Aid to Dependent Children (ADC). The latter program was subsequently renamed Aid to Families with Dependent children (AFDC) when benefits were added for mothers.
9. Social Security benefits were increased 20 per cent just prior to the November 1972 election. For a discussion of election effects see Tufte (1978). See Derthick (1979) for an account of politics of Social Security financing and benefit increases.
10. Another state-federal program was also 'federalized' during the Nixon administration. Three public assistance programs (OAA, AB, APTD) were consolidated into Supplemental Security Income (SSI) in 1972.
11. Whether any of the programs enacted were 'really new programs' is an arguable point. Certainly many of the OEO programs were innovative. Programs such as Medicare, Medicaid, Food Stamps, or public housing were ideas which had been debated for some time or were programs which existed in previous periods.

References

ALTMEYER, A. J. (1966) *The Formative Years of Social Security* (Madison, Wisc.: University of Wisconsin Press).

BERKOWITZ, E. and MCQUAID, K. (1980) 'Welfare Reform in the 1950's', *Social Service Review*, March: 45–58.

BROWNING, R. X. (1986) *Politics and Social Welfare Policy in the United States* (University of Tennessee Press).

BURKHAUSER, R. V. and SMEEDING, T. M. (1981) 'The Net Impact of the Social Security System on the Poor', *Public Policy*, 29: 161–78.

CONGRESSIONAL QUARTERLY (1982) *Budgeting for America* (Washington, D.C.: Congressional Quarterly).

DANZIGER, S. H. and PLOTNICK, R. (1982) 'The War on Income Poverty: Achievements and Failures', in P. M. SOMMERS (ed.) (1982) *Welfare Reform in America*, 31–52 (Boston: Kluwer-Nijhoff).

DERTHICK, M. (1979) *Policymaking for Social Security* (Washington, D.C.: Brookings Institution).

GARFINKEL, I. and HAVEMAN, R. (1982) 'Income Transfer Policy in the United States: A Review and Assessment', Discussion Paper No. 701–82 (Madison, Wisc.: Institute for Research on Poverty).

GREIDER, W. (1981) *The Education of David Stockman and Other Americans* (New York: Dutton).

LAMPMAN, R. (1974) 'What Does it Do for the Poor? A New Test for National Policy', *Public Interest*, 34: 66–82.

LEVITAN, S. A. and TAGGART, R. (1976) *The Promise of Greatness* (Cambridge, Mass.: Harvard University Press).

McMILLAN, A. W. and BIXBY, A. K. (1980) 'Social Welfare Expenditures, Fiscal Year 1978', *Social Security Bulletin*, 43: 3–17.

PATTERSON, J. T. (1981) *America's Struggle Against Poverty 1900–1980* (Cambridge, Mass.: Harvard University Press).

PLOTNICK, R. D. (1979) 'Social Welfare Expenditures and the Poor: The 1965–1976 Experience and Future Expectations', *Policy Analysis*, 5: 271–90.

PLOTNICK, R. D. and SKIDMORE, F. (1975) *Progress Against Poverty* (New York: Academic Press).

RIPLEY, R. B. (1969) 'Legislative Bargaining and the Food Stamp Act, 1964', in F. N. CLEAVELAND, *et al.* (eds) (1969) *Congress and Urban Problems*, 279–310 (Washington, D.C.: Brookings Institution).

STEINER, G. Y. (1971) *The State of Welfare* (Washington, D.C.: Brookings Institution).

STOCKMAN, D. A. (1975) 'The Social Pork Barrel', *The Public Interest*, 39: 3–30.

TUFTE, E. (1978) *Political Control of the Economy* (Princeton: Princeton University Press).

US CONGRESS (1972) 'Handbook of Public Income Transfer Programs', Joint Economic Committee Studies in Public Welfare Paper, No. 2 (92nd Congress, 2nd Session, 16 October 1972).

US CONGRESS (1981) *Indexation of Federal Programs* Senate, Committee on the Budget (Committee print, 97th Congress, 1st session, May).

US DEPARTMENT OF HEALTH, EDUCATION AND WELFARE (1968) *Social Welfare Expenditures Under Public Programs in the United States, 1929–66*, Social Security Administration, Office of Research and Statistics, Research Report, No. 25 (Washington, D.C.: Government Printing Office).

WITTE, E. E. (1963) *The Development of the Social Security Act* (Madison, Wisc.: University of Wisconsin Press).

3 Recent Trends in Poverty and the Antipoverty Effectiveness of Income Transfers

Sheldon H. Danziger*

Poverty as officially measured by the Census Bureau declined from 22.4 per cent of all persons in 1959 to 11.1 per cent in 1973, remained in the 11 to 12 per cent range for the rest of the 1970s and then increased to 13.0 per cent in 1980, and 15.3 per cent in 1983 before dropping back to 14.4 per cent in 1984. While there are many valid criticisms of the official poverty series, the data presented in this chapter demonstrate that the higher incidence of poverty in the 1980s is not an artifact of the official measure. Poverty increased rapidly between 1978 and 1984 for each of a variety of alternative poverty measures. And, while poverty has been increasing, the antipoverty impact of income transfers has been declining. This is because a smaller percentage of poor households are receiving transfers whose average amounts have been declining in real terms.

ALTERNATIVE MEASURES OF POVERTY

The official measure of poverty provides a set of income cutoffs adjusted for household size, the age of the head of the household, and the number of children under age 18 (until 1981, sex of the head and farm-nonfarm residence were other distinctions). The cutoffs provide an absolute measure of poverty which specifies in dollar terms minimally decent levels of consumption. The official income concept, current money income received during the calendar year, is defined as the sum of money wages and salaries, net income from self-employment, Social Security income and cash transfers from

* The research reported here was supported in part by grants from the Graduate School Research Committee of the University of Wisconsin-Madison and the Alfred P. Sloan Foundation. Daniel Feaster and Christine Ross provided helpful computational assistance.

other government programs, property income (for example, interest, dividends, net rental income), and other forms of cash income (for example, private pensions, alimony). Current money income does not include capital gains, imputed rents, government or private benefits in-kind (for example, food stamps, Medicare benefits, employer-provided health insurance), nor does it subtract taxes, although all of these affect a household's level of consumption.

The official poverty cutoffs are updated yearly by an amount corresponding to the change in the Consumer Price Index so that they represent the same purchasing power each year. According to this absolute standard, poverty will be eliminated when the incomes of all households exceed the poverty lines, regardless of what is happening to average household income.

There have been numerous discussions over the past 20 years as to whether the official poverty thresholds and income concept are relevant to policy choices (US Department of Health, Education, and Welfare, 1976). Despite these controversies, the adoption of an official measure of poverty in the mid-1960s, and its use as a social indicator, became a symbol of this country's commitment to raising the standard of living of the poorest citizens.

Income poverty is a complex concept, and different types of poverty thresholds and income concepts are appropriate for different purposes. An absolute perspective, such as the official measure, focuses on those with incomes that fall short of a minimum (fixed) level of economic resources. On the other hand, relative poverty indicators emphasize not only the household's own level of resources, but how its position compares to that of others. A relative definition draws attention to the degree of inequality at the lower end of the income distribution. Those whose incomes fall well below the prevailing average in their society are regarded as poor, no matter what their absolute incomes may be. A relative poverty threshold, therefore, changes at about the same rate as average income.

Recent US Census Bureau technical papers (1982, 1985) on the valuation of in-kind transfers address only the issue of augmenting the official income concept, not the issue of changing the current poverty thresholds. However, just as the valuation of in-kind transfers reduces measured poverty, the use of a relative poverty threshold during a period of rising real incomes or an updating of the official thresholds would increase measured poverty (for example, see Fendler and Orshansky, 1979).

A matrix of poverty measures showing two income concepts and two types of poverty thresholds is presented in Table 3.1. The official income concept lies somewhere between pretransfer income and post-transfer–post-tax income on the first row. Census money income does not distinguish between income derived from market and private transfer sources (for example, wages, dividends, alimony) and income derived from government sources (for example, Social Security, public assistance income.) As such, it fails to separate the private economy's antipoverty performance from the performance of government cash transfer programs. Households that do not receive enough money income from private sources to raise them over the poverty lines constitute the pretransfer poor (a more exact title would be pre-government-transfer poor). Pretransfer poverty has received little attention, yet it reveals the magnitude of the problem faced by the public sector after the market economy and private transfer system (for example, private pensions, interfamily transfers) have distributed their rewards. This information is essential for analyzing the 'trickle-down' effects of economic growth and for assessing the extent to which public transfer programs reduce poverty.

Table 3.1 A matrix of poverty measures

	Income concept	
	Pretransfer income	*Post-transfer-post-tax income*
Absolute	I	II
Relative	III	IV

A related concept is prewelfare income. While pretransfer income does not count any money income from government programs, prewelfare incomes excludes only income from cash public assistance (that is, welfare) programs. Social insurance benefits (for example, Social Security, Unemployment Insurance) which are based on past earnings and tax contributions are included in prewelfare income along with private market income because they are generally perceived by the public as earned. For many, the 'real' poverty population, the one to whom antipoverty policy should be addressed, is the prewelfare poor.

The valuation of in-kind transfers in recent Census publications does provide a measure closer to the concept of post-transfer–post-tax income than does the official measure. This preferred measure would have been obtained if, in addition to adding in-kind government transfers received by the poor, the Census had also added

Table 3.2 The trend in the incidence of poverty among persons, selected years 1965–84

Type of measure (*year*)	*Pretransfer income* (*1*)	*Prewelfare income* (*2*)	*Post-transfer income (census money income)* (*3*)	*Adjusted income*[a] (*4*)
Official measure				
1965	21.3%	16.3%	17.3%	13.4%
1968	18.2	13.6	12.8	9.9
1972	19.2	13.1	11.9	6.2
1974	20.3	13.1	11.2	7.2
1976	21.0	13.1	11.8	6.7
1978	20.2	12.6	11.4	n.a.
1979	20.5	12.9	11.7	6.1
1980	21.9	14.1	13.0	n.a.
1981	23.1	15.0	14.0	n.a.
1982	24.0	15.9	15.0	n.a.
1983	24.2	16.1	15.3	n.a.
1984	22.9	15.3	14.4	9.2
% *Change*				
1965–78[b]	−5.2	−22.7	−34.1	−54.5
1978–84[b]	+13.4	+21.4	+26.3	+50.8
Relative measure				
1965	21.3%	16.3%	17.3%	n.a.
1968	19.7	15.3	14.6	n.a.
1972	22.2	n.a.	15.7	n.a.
1974	22.9	16.1	14.9	n.a.
1976	24.1	16.3	15.4	n.a.
1978	23.9	16.5	15.5	n.a.
1979	23.8	16.6	15.7	n.a.
1980	24.5	16.9	16.0	n.a.
1981	25.5	17.8	16.9	n.a.
1982	26.5	18.5	17.8	n.a.
1983	27.0	19.2	18.6	n.a.
1984	26.6	19.3	18.7	n.a.
% *Change*				
1965–78	+12.2	+ 1.2	−10.4	n.a.
1978–84	+11.3	+17.0	+20.6	n.a.

Source: Unless noted otherwise, the data are computations by the author from the Survey of Economic Opportunity (for 1965) and various March Current Population Surveys (for other years).

[a]Adjusted income data are from Timothy Smeeding (1982); figure for 1984 is an estimate based on US Bureau of the Census (1985). Smeeding's figures

in-kind private transfers (for example, employer-provided fringe benefits) and subtracted direct taxes paid. None the less, a recent study suggests that the results would not be significantly affected by these adjustments (Smeeding, 1983).

Table 3.2 presents seven different time series of the incidence of poverty for all persons for selected years between 1965 and 1984. Four series using the official poverty thresholds appear in the top panel; three series using a relative measure, in the bottom.

The relative measure is one developed by Robert Plotnick (Plotnick and Skidmore, 1975). In 1965, the first year for which detailed data is available, the relative poverty lines are set equal to the official (absolute) ones. (In 1965, the official lines were equal to about 44 per cent of the median income). In succeeding years the relative lines are changed at the same rate as the median income.[1] With this approach, trends in absolute and relative poverty are easily compared because they begin with the same base year value.

Consider first the four series in the top panel. Each shows that poverty declined over the 1965 to 1978 period and then increased rapidly in the 1978 to 1984 period. That the official data overstate poverty because of the failure to adjust for in-kind transfers can be seen by comparing columns three and four. None the less, poverty adjusted for in-kind transfers is higher than any point since the late 1960s. Also, column 1 shows that more than a fifth of all persons in 1984 live in households that do not receive market incomes high enough to take them out of poverty. This rise in poverty in the early 1980s results in part from a severe recession that raised unemployment rates and reduced pretransfer incomes, and in part from cutbacks in government spending on income support programs.

While the three series based on the official measure show a decline in the 1965–78 period and then an increase, the three series based on the relative measure are more stable.[2] They show no significant declines for the early period, and somewhat smaller increases for the later period. Because the relative poverty line has been about 10 to 15 per cent above the official line, it shows more poverty in every year.

continuation

include adjustments for selected in-kind transfers received, taxes paid, and income underreporting.

[b]Percentage changes for adjusted income data are from 1965–79 and 1979–84.

n.a. = not available

THE ANTIPOVERTY EFFECTIVENESS OF TRANSFERS

Between 1965 and the mid-1970s, the growth in real expenditures for cash and in-kind transfers per recipient household far exceeded the real increase in per household income. This growth, a major development in American social welfare policy, accounts for much of the observed declines in poverty over this period. Growth rates for transfers have slowed in recent years.

Table 3.3 measures the antipoverty effectiveness of major income transfer programs by the percentage of the pretransfer poor persons

Table 3.3 The antipoverty effectiveness of major income transfers, selected years, 1965–84

	Percentage of pretransfer poor persons removed from poverty by:			
Poverty measure	*Cash social insurance transfers*[a]	*Cash public assistance transfers*[b]	*In-kind transfers*[c]	*All transfers*
Absolute measure				
1965	23.5	3.3	16.4	43.2
1976	37.6	6.2	28.1	71.9
1978	37.6	5.9	n.a.	n.a.
1980	35.2	5.5	n.a.	n.a.
1982	33.8	3.8	n.a.	n.a.
1984	33.2	3.9	22.7[d]	59.8[d]
Relative measure				
1965	23.5	3.3	n.a.	n.a.
1976	32.4	3.7	n.a.	n.a.
1978	31.0	4.2	n.a.	n.a.
1980	31.0	3.7	n.a.	n.a.
1982	30.2	2.6	n.a.	n.a.
1984	27.4	2.3	n.a.	n.a.

[a]Cash social insurance transfers include social security, railroad retirement, unemployment compensation, workers' compensation, government employee pensions, and veterans' pensions and compensation.
[b]Cash public assistance transfers include AFDC, SSI (OAA, APTD and AB in 1965), and general assistance.
[c]In-kind transfers include Medicare, Medicaid, Food Stamps, and, for 1976, school lunch and public housing; this figure also adjusts for direct taxes paid and the underreporting of cash transfers.
[d]Based on estimate for adjusted income poverty for 1984.
n.a. = not available

removed from absolute or relative poverty by transfers.[3] The table divides all government transfers into cash social insurance transfers, cash public assistance transfers, and in-kind transfers (whether social insurance or public assistance).

For each type of transfer and for each measure of poverty, public transfers became increasingly effective until the mid-1970s.[4] The fraction of absolute pretransfer poor households receiving a cash transfer payment rose from less than 70 per cent in 1965 to over 80 per cent in 1978 and has declined slightly since then. The real value of recipients' transfers increased from 1965 to 1978, but declined thereafter. For example, outlays on all social programs grew at an annual rate (after inflation) of 10 per cent during the Nixon-Ford years, 4 per cent during the Carter Administration, and only 1.5 per cent during the first Reagan Administration. Whereas the Carter years mainly saw entitlements eroded by high inflation, under Reagan, some benefits were actively reduced (Danziger and Gottschalk, 1985). As a result, transfers removed about 43 per cent of the pretransfer poor from absolute poverty in 1965, over 70 per cent in 1976, and about 60 per cent in 1984.

Cash social insurance transfers remove more persons from poverty in all years and for all measures than do cash public assistance transfers, because a greater portion of the pretransfer poor receive them, and because the average social insurance benefit is higher. In-kind transfers – which include benefits from both social insurance and public assistance programs – have a smaller antipoverty impact than cash social insurance and a much larger impact than cash public assistance transfers.

POVERTY DEFICIT

The incidence of poverty reveals the percentage of persons whose incomes fall below the poverty threshold, but does not distinguish the degree of poverty. The 'poverty deficit', which measures the total amount of income required to bring every poor person up to the poverty threshold, does distinguish between poor persons who are very close to being non-poor and those who are farther away from the thresholds. Table 3.4 shows the pretransfer (column 1) and post-transfer (column 3) poverty deficits in billions of current dollars for selected years between 1967 and 1984. Cash transfers received by the pretransfer poor are shown in column 2. The fourth column shows the percentage reduction in the poverty deficit due to these cash

Table 3.4 Poverty deficit before and after cash transfers, selected years, 1967–84

Year	*Pretransfer poverty deficit*[a] (1)	*Cash transfers received by pretransfer poor households*[a] (2)	*Post-transfer poverty deficit*[a] (3)	*Percentage reduction in poverty deficit due to cash transfers* (4)	*Post-transfer poverty deficit as a percentage of GNP* (5)
1967	$23.5	$17.5	$10.6	54.9%	1.4
1974	44.1	57.3	14.2	67.8	1.2
1979	69.5	80.0	23.2	66.6	1.2
1980	87.5	95.9	30.3	65.4	1.4
1981	102.3	109.0	37.8	63.0	1.6
1982	113.2	118.1	43.9	61.2	1.7
1984	119.5	125.5	49.6	58.5	1.7
% Increase					
1979/1967[b]	195.7	357.1	118.9	–	–
1984/1979[c]	71.9	56.9	113.8	–	–

Source: Computations by author from various March Current Population Survey data tapes.
[a]Billions of current dollars.
[b]Between 1967 and 1979, the Consumer Price Index increased by 117 per cent.
[c]Between 1979 and 1984, the Consumer Price Index increased by 43 per cent.

transfers. The fifth column shows the post-transfer poverty deficit as a percentage of personal income. The bottom panel shows the percentage growth in current dollars for these concepts.

Between 1967 and 1979, total cash transfers to the pretransfer poor grew much faster than the pretransfer poverty deficit, so the post-transfer deficit grew more slowly. Between 1979 and 1984, the pretransfer deficit grew faster than did transfers. As a result, the post-transfer deficit grew more rapidly than the pretransfer deficit. This deficit declined from 1.4 per cent of aggregate personal income in 1967 to 1.2 per cent in 1979, and then increased rapidly until it was about 1.7 per cent of personal income in 1984.

The 1984 pretransfer poverty deficit of $119.5 billion means that the pretransfer income of the typical poor household is about $4700 below the poverty line; the post-transfer deficit of $49.6 billion, that the post-transfer poor are about $3500 below the line. These data reinforce the points made above – poverty has been increasing and the antipoverty impact of transfers has been decreasing in recent years.

DEMOGRAPHIC DIFFERENCES

Table 3.5 highlights the differences in poverty levels and trends for several major demographic groups for the 1967–84 period. It also shows the effect of in-kind transfers on each group in 1984. The largest reduction in poverty for the 17-year period and the largest impact of in-kind transfers in 1984 are for elderly persons. For example, between 1967 and 1984 poverty as officially measured declined by 24.2 per cent for all persons, but by 56.5 per cent for the elderly. And, in 1984, the addition of in-kind transfers reduced poverty for all persons by 31.9 per cent but by 75.8 per cent for the elderly. Adjusted poverty rates in 1984 for blacks, persons of Spanish origin, and female household heads remain above the official rates that existed for all persons in 1964, when in-kind transfers had little impact.

Table 3.6 shows the composition of pretransfer poor households in column (1) and post-transfer poor households in column (2). Each poor household has been placed into one of the eight categories shown. The four groups in the top rows are generally not expected to work, while those in the bottom four rows are so expected. That the direct effects of economic growth on poverty for all persons have not

Table 3.5 Alternative measures of the incidence of poverty: Official measure for 1964 and 1984 and money income plus the market value of in-kind transfers for 1984

Persons living in poverty, by type of household head	*Official measure 1964* (1)	*Official measure 1984* (2)	*Percentage change in poverty between 1964 and 1984* (3)	*Money income plus in-kind transfers at market value 1984*[a] (4)	*Percentage change in poverty due to in-kind transfers, 1984* (5)
All persons	19.0%	14.4%	−24.2%	9.8%	−31.9%
White	14.9	11.5	−22.8	8.1	−29.6
Black	49.6	33.8	−31.9	21.3	−37.0
Hispanic	n.a.	28.4	n.a.	20.2	−28.9
Female householder, no husband present	45.9	38.4	−16.3	24.3	−36.7
Elderly (65 and over)	28.5[b]	12.4	−56.5	3.0	−75.8
Children under 18	20.7[b]	21.5	+ 3.9	15.7	−27.0

Sources: For 1984, US Bureau of the Census (1985); For 1964, US Bureau of the Census (1983).
[a]In-kind transfers for food, housing, and medical care for non-institutionalized persons.
[b]Figures are for 1966 since none were published for 1964 or 1965.
n.a. = not available.

Table 3.6 Composition of households with incomes below the poverty line, official measure, 1984

Percentage of poor households where head is:	*Pretransfer poor* (1)	*Post-transfer poor* (2)
Over 65 years of age	43.21%	20.14%
Female, with children under six	7.69	12.83
Student	4.65	7.70
Disabled	10.56	12.28
Persons working full-time, full year	9.18	14.33
Single persons working less than full-time, full-year	10.48	14.54
Male family head, working less than full-time, full-year	8.95	10.50
Female family head, no children under six, working less than full-time, full-year	5.27	7.67
Total	100.00	100.00
Number of households (millions)	25.2	14.2

Source: Computations by author from March 1985 Current Population Survey data tape.
Note: Classification is mutually exclusive and is hierarchical: Any household head who fits in more than one category has been classified only in the one closest to the top of the table.

been large in recent years should not be surprising, as only about one-third of those who are poor before the receipt of transfers can be expected to work (see Gottschalk and Danziger, 1984). The remaining two-thirds – the aged, female-headed households with children under six, students and the disabled – are not directly affected much by growth in market incomes and are thus likely to remain in need of government assistance.

A comparison between the pretransfer and post-transfer poor shows the relative success of cash transfers in relieving poverty among the aged, who are about 43 per cent of the pretransfer poor and only about 22 per cent of the post-transfer poor. There are also significant differences in the composition of the poor by race. The major difference is that while 12.83 per cent of all post-transfer poor households are headed by women with children under six, the corresponding percentage for blacks is 21.68 (data not shown).

CONCLUSION

Poverty, no matter how measured, has increased in recent years. And, while the antipoverty impacts of income transfers have declined, they still significantly reduce poverty.[5] Transfers also protect against income losses due to unemployment, retirement, disability and death and guarantee access to minimum levels of food, shelter, and medical care. The growth in transfers has been accompanied by some declines in work effort and savings that may have contributed somewhat to the sluggish economic performance of the post-1973 period. But the magnitude of these declines is estimated to be small (see Danzinger, Haveman and Plotnick, 1981). While reductions in poverty through increased market incomes has always been the primary stated goal of antipoverty policy, increased cash and in-kind transfers have been major factors in the reductions in poverty that have occurred since the declaration of the War on Poverty.

Recent projections of the prospects for significantly reducing poverty in the late 1980s as a result of the growth that is expected (Gottschalk and Danziger, 1984) provide little grounds for optimism. This results because the antipoverty effects of growth in the recent past have been partially offset by demographic changes (the increased proportion of households headed by women without husbands and by the young) and by increased inequality in earnings. Only if these trends are reversed or if significantly greater government assistance is provided will poverty be as low in the late 1980s as it was in the early 1970s.

Notes

1. The specifics of this measure are as follows. Each family's current money income is divided by its official poverty line. This yields a 'welfare ratio' that indicates the fraction by which the family's income exceeds or falls below the official poverty line. Families with the same welfare ratio are assumed to be equally well-off. The relative poor are defined as those families with welfare ratios below 0.44 of the median ratio.

   The fraction 0.44 was not an arbitrary choice. In 1965, the base year for this analysis of changes in poverty, the median welfare ratio was 2.25. All living units with incomes below the official poverty lines had, of course, welfare ratios less than one. Thus, any household that in 1965 was poor under the official definition necessarily had a welfare ratio less than 1.00/2.25 of the median. Defining the relative poor as those with welfare ratios below 1.00/2.25 = 0.44 of the median yielded, in 1965, the same group of households as were poor from the absolute perspective.

2. The adjusted income data are not compared to the relative poverty line. Estimating in-kind income from private sources (for example, fringe benefits) and taxes paid by the non-poor poses measurement problems that have not yet been solved. Thus, we could not compute a relative measure based upon the median adjusted income.
3. The antipoverty impacts of seven cash and three in-kind transfer programs are assessed here. They are (1) Social Security and Railroad Retirement, (2) federal, state and local government employee pensions, (3) unemployment insurance, (4) workers' compensation, (5) veterans' compensation and pensions, (6) Supplemental Security Income (prior to 1974, OAA, APTD, and AB), (7) public assistance (AFDC, AFDC-U, General Assistance), (8) Food Stamps, Medicare, and Medicaid. While several in-kind transfer programs and all expenditures on public education have been omitted, Food Stamps, Medicare, and Medicaid alone account for over 80 per cent of all federal in-kind transfers. For 1976, and the estimate for 1984, school lunch and public housing benefits are also included.
4. Pretransfer income is calculated by subtracting government transfers from post-transfer income. While this definition assumes that transfers elicit no behavioral responses, transfers do induce labor supply reductions. As a result, recipients' net incomes are not increased by the full amount of the transfer and the pre/post comparisons made here will provide upper-bound estimates of the antipoverty effects of transfers.
5. For more detailed discussion of the causes of recent trends in poverty and the roles of other government programs (for example, education, employment and training) see Danziger and Weinberg (1986).

References

DANZIGER, S. H. and GOTTSCHALK, P. (1985) 'The Impact of Budget Cuts and Economic Conditions on Poverty', *Journal of Applied Public Policy and Management*, 5: 587–93.

DANZIGER, S. H., HAVEMAN, R. and PLOTNICK, R. (1981) 'How Income Transfer Programs Affect Work, Savings, and the Income Distribution: A Critical Review', *Journal of Economic Literature*, 19: 975–1028.

DANZIGER, S. H. and WEINBERG, D. (eds) (1986) *Fighting Poverty: What Works and What Doesn't* (Cambridge, Mass.: Harvard University Press).

FENDLER, C. and ORSHANSKY, M. (1979) 'Improving the Poverty Definition', *Proceedings of the Social Statistics Section of the American Statistical Association*: 640–645.

GOTTSCHALK, P. and DANZIGER, S. H. (1984) 'Macroeconomic Conditions, Income Transfers and the Trend in Poverty', in D. L. BAWDEN (ed.) (1984) *The Social Contract Revisited* (Washington, D.C.: Urban Institute Press).

PLOTNICK, R. and SKIDMORE, F. (1975) *Progress Against Poverty* (New York: Academic Press).

SMEEDING, T. (1982) 'The Antipoverty Effects of In-Kind Transfers', *Policy Studies Journal*, 10: 499–521.

SMEEDING, T. (1983) 'The Size Distribution of Wage and Nonwage Compensation', in J. TRIPLETT (ed.) (1983) *The Measurement of Labor Cost* (Chicago: University of Chicago Press).

US BUREAU OF THE CENSUS (1982) *Alternative Methods for Valuing Selected In-kind Transfer Benefits and Measuring Their Effects on Poverty*, Technical Paper, No. 50 (Washington, D.C.: Government Printing Office).

US BUREAU OF THE CENSUS (1983) Money Income and Poverty Status of Families and Persons in the United States: 1982, *Current Population Reports*, Series P–60, No. 140 (Washington, D.C.: Government Printing Office).

US BUREAU OF THE CENSUS (1985) *Estimates of Poverty Including the Value of Noncash Benefits: 1984*, Technical Paper, No. 55 (Washington, D.C.: Government Printing Office).

US DEPARTMENT OF HEALTH, EDUCATION, AND WELFARE (1976) *The Measure of Poverty*, A Report to Congress (Washington, D.C.: Government Printing Office).

4 Reagan, the Recession, and Poverty: What the Official Estimates Fail to Show

Timothy M. Smeeding*

INTRODUCTION

The measurement of poverty in advanced post-industrial countries is not easily accomplished. In the United States poverty has been 'officially' measured for the past 20 years by comparing pre-tax cash money income to a poverty line designed by Mollie Orshansky (1965). Although the measurement of poverty in the United States was extensively researched in the 1970s (for example, US Department of Health, Education, and Welfare, 1976), there have been no official changes in this measurement procedure. However, as the Reagan Administration, Congress and the public have become increasingly dissatisfied with this index of deprivation, several 'alternative' measures of poverty have appeared. These measures generally deal with at least one of three major items which substantially affect the level of poverty in the United States but which are not taken into account in the official poverty figures. In order of importance, they are:

1. Failure to include the impact of benefits from in-kind or non-money income transfers such as Food Stamps, public housing, and Medicaid in the incomes of the poor.
2. Failure to subtract federal and state income and payroll taxes before comparing incomes to poverty levels.
3. The problem of underreporting, non-reporting, and misreporting in the income survey used to measure poverty.

* The author would like to thank the Division of Social Science Research at the University of Utah, and the Institute for Research on Poverty for support. The analysis, statements of fact, conclusions, and opinions contained in this paper are those of the author and do not represent the position or opinions of the Division of Social Science Research, the University of Utah, or the Institute for Research on Poverty.

In this paper I will first treat these shortcomings in this order, explaining my estimates of their individual impacts on poverty. Secondly, I will relate these shortcomings to the recent changes in the official poverty count, attributable in large part to the recession and to President Reagan's economic program. Finally, I will present estimates of the net impact of these judgements on the extent and trend in poverty in the US.

ACCOUNTING FOR IN-KIND BENEFITS, TAXES, AND UNDERREPORTING

In 1980 the US Senate (1980) tied the US Department of Commerce budgetary appropriations for fiscal year 1982 to the production of a report on the effect of federally-funded in-kind benefit programs on poverty in the US. This report was prepared by the author (Smeeding, 1982a). Earlier work by the author not included in this particular report concentrated on the effects of taxes and underreporting as well as that of in-kind benefits (Smeeding, 1975, 1977, 1982b). This section of the paper summarizes this research as it concerns the major problems and the controversies encountered when assessing the impacts of in-kind transfer benefits, taxes, and underreporting on the level of poverty. The earlier work is also extended to reflect recent economic and policy developments, especially in federal tax policy arena.

Measuring and valuing in-kind transfers and assessing their impact on poverty

The Census Bureau report to Congress (Smeeding, 1982a) and its recent successor (US Bureau of the Census, 1984) describe three different strategies for valuing in-kind transfers and develop the estimating procedures to implement them:

1. The *market value* is equal to the purchase price in the private market of the goods received by the recipient, for example, the face value of food stamps; or the government cost of particular goods, for example, the insurance value of Medicare and Medicaid.
2. The *recipient or cash equivalent value* is the amount of cash that would make the recipient just as well off as the in-kind transfer; it,

therefore, reflects the recipient's own valuation of the benefit. The recipient or cash equivalent value is usually less than the market value. Even though cash equivalent value is the theoretically preferred measure, it is quite difficult to estimate, especially for medical care.

3. The *poverty budget share value*, which is tied to the poverty concept, limits the value of food, housing, or medical transfers, to the proportions of income spent on these items by persons at or near the poverty line in 1960–61, when in-kind transfers were minimal. It assumes that in-kind transfers in excess of these amounts are not relevant for determining poverty status because an excess of one type of good (for example, medical care) does not compensate for a deficiency in another good (for example, housing).

Because of the importance of medical benefits, which constitute over 80 per cent of the total market value of in-kind transfers, and because of the problematic nature of valuing these benefits, three alternative definitions of in-kind benefits to be included as income were also presented in these reports. These definitions were: food and housing alone; food, housing, and medical care excluding institutional care (nursing home) benefits; and food, housing, and medical care including institutional care. In summary, the report contains nine basic alternative measures of poverty, each alternative incorporating one of the three valuation strategies and one of the three definitions of in-kind benefits to be counted in income. Each of these measures can be compared to the poverty rate based on census money income – the official measure of poverty.

Table 4.1 summarizes these results for the 1979–84 period. It should be noted that each of these different income definitions and valuation strategies are separable. Thus it is possible to combine them in any way that policy-makers deem relevant. From an economist's perspective, the cash equivalent value approach is the most appropriate over-all strategy. But cash equivalents are difficult to measure. Taking into account difficulty of estimation, protecting against medical benefit overvaluation, and finally the logistics of providing annual estimates of poverty including these benefits in a timely fashion, a mixture of all three valuation strategies might be recommended: the market value strategy for food benefits; recipient or cash equivalent value for housing benefits; and poverty budget share value for medical benefits. With no other changes, for example,

Table 4.1 Comparison of the number of poor and poverty rates for persons using alternative income concepts and valuation techniques: 1979–84

A. Number (thousands) of persons in poverty

Type of measure	*1979*	*1980*	*1981*	*1982*	*1983*[r]	*1984*
Official definition	26 072	29 272	31 822	34 398	35 515	33 700
Market value approach:						
Including food and housing	21 698	25 042	27 932	30 688	32 123	30 103
Including food, housing, and medical care for noninstitutionalized persons	15 696	18 221	21 046	23 563	24 512	23 019
Including food, housing, and all medical care	15 099	17 706	20 500	22 885	23 911	22 602
Recipient value approach:						
Including food and housing	22 270	25 633	28 651	31 365	32 718	30 909
Including food, housing, and medical care for noninstitutionalized persons	20 478	23 895	26 784	29 407	30 720	28 917
Including food, housing, and all medical care	20 152	23 512	26 500	29 058	30 332	28 623
Poverty budget share value approach:						
Including food and housing	22 409	25 602	28 317	31 111	32 458	30 455
Including food, housing, and medical care for noninstitutionalized persons	20 186	23 299	26 175	28 720	30 137	28 296
Including food, housing, and all medical care	20 184	23 299	26 175	28 713	30 137	28 296

B. Poverty rate

Type of measure	*1979*	*1980*	*1981*	*1982*	*1983*[r]	*1984*
Official definition	11.7	13.0	14.0	15.0	15.3	14.4
Market value approach:						
Including food and housing only	9.7	11.1	12.3	13.4	13.9	12.9
Including food, housing, and medical care for noninstitutionalized persons	7.0	8.1	9.3	10.3	10.6	9.8
Including food, housing, and all medical care	6.8	7.9	9.0	10.0	10.3	9.7
Recipient value approach:						
Including food and housing only	10.0	11.4	12.6	13.7	14.1	13.2
Including food, housing, and medical care for noninstitutionalized persons	9.2	10.6	11.8	12.8	13.3	12.4
Including food, housing, and all medical care	9.0	10.4	11.7	12.7	13.1	12.2
Poverty budget share value approach:						
Including food and housing only	10.1	11.4	12.5	13.6	14.0	13.0
Including food, housing, and medical care for noninstitutionalized persons	9.1	10.4	11.5	12.5	13.0	12.1
Including food, housing, and all medical care	9.1	10.4	11.5	12.5	13.0	12.1

Source: US Bureau of the Census, 1985a: Tables C and D.
r = revised after initial publication by the Census.

those for taxes or reporting, such a combination would have produced a poverty rate of about 12.3 per cent in 1984, a reduction of 2.1 percentage points or 14.6 per cent from the 'official' money income only poverty rate of 14.4 per cent, and very close to the theoretically preferred 12.4 per cent obtained by the cash equivalent value approach. The rationale for these choices needs some explanation.

The recipient or cash equivalent value of food stamps (and school lunch) subsidies is virtually identical to their market value. In other words, recipients spend at least as much on food (and school lunch) as these benefits afford. In particular, food stamps are virtually as good as cash. The face value of food stamps is already reported in the March *Current Population Survey* (CPS) and the market value of school lunch subsidies are easily calculated. There is no need to move to alternative valuation strategies in this case; the market value is sufficient.

The recipient or cash equivalent value of public housing subsidies averages 80 per cent of their market value, and averages 60 per cent of market value for the lowest income groups. Thus market value overstates the true welfare gain, as measured by the recipient value of housing subsidies, by a substantial amount. In calculating recipient value, good up-to-date information on housing expenditures among non-public housing/low income families is a necessity. The Census Bureau *Annual Housing Survey* provides all of the data that is needed to annually update these estimates of recipient value with a reasonable degree of accuracy. The Census Bureau has developed an easily replicable methodology which will allow them to carry out this task. In the case of housing benefits then, market value clearly overstates the true welfare gain of the poor, while a reasonably good estimate of cash equivalent value is available and should be used.

Medical care is much more problematic. On average the recipient value of Medicare and Medicaid is only 47.3 per cent of the market value. Clearly market value overstates true welfare gain in this case. However, calculating the recipient value of medical benefits is fraught with difficulty (see Smeeding, 1982a). In addition, the problem of whether or not to include institutional care expenditures in medical benefits remains.

Because of their enormous market value, the treatment of medical benefits is the crucial element in assessing the impact of in-kind benefits on poverty. Unless one assumes that medical benefits can be used to heat homes or to feed people, there is a distinct danger of overvaluation by assigning medical benefits at their market value, particularly for the elderly. Medicare benefits have grown at a 17 per cent annual rate over the past decade, roughly doubling in value every three and a half years. The market value of Medicare as insurance has thus increased from about $900 in 1979 to over $1650 per elderly person in 1982. When combined with Medicaid (including institutional care benefits) these insurance values are truly enormous, totaling over $5700 per elderly person in 1984. At such benefit levels there would be virtually no poverty among the elderly based on these benefits alone! While the recipient value estimates adjust for this problem and are therefore preferable to the market value approach, they are highly speculative. The poverty budget share approach, which limits the value of medical benefits to the amount needed to fulfill an estimated fraction of the over-all poverty budget, seems to be the best choice for measuring the antipoverty effect of medical benefits.

The poverty budget share approach for medical care has several advantages, both conceptual and practical. Viewed from one perspective, the poverty line budget presents the dollar costs of a person's basic human needs. Certain amounts are thus implicitly budgeted for specific needs, for example, food and medical care. If a person receives more medical care than is budgeted, these needs are met, but other basic needs, for example, food, are *not* met by excessive medical benefits. As such, the poverty share approach guards against the overvaluation problem and is free of the recipient value estimation vagaries. Moreover, the antipoverty effect of medical transfers under this approach is exactly the same whether or not institutional care benefits are included. Since the poverty budget shares have already been calculated, it is a simple procedure to implement this approach on an annual basis. In cases where market value is close to recipient value (food) benefits or, in cases where the cash equivalent value can be reasonably estimated (for example, housing), the poverty budget share approach makes little sense. But, in terms of accuracy in measurement, fairness, and efficiency in being able to rapidly calculate the impact of medical benefits on an annually updated basis, the poverty budget share strategy for medical care is the most appropriate choice.

The treatment of taxes

The current poverty line is based on the ratio of food expenditures to after-tax income, but Census money income does not subtract out the taxes paid by families before determining their poverty status. If we interpret the poverty line as an expenditure needs standard, fairness and common sense demand such an adjustment. The poverty budget cannot be bought with tax dollars. According to my estimates, subtracting federal income and payroll taxes would have decreased the income of many borderline poor families and thus would have increased the poverty rate by about 8 per cent in 1979 and by about 10 per cent in 1984. Earlier estimates for 1972 and 1974 indicate increases in poverty of 6 to 7 per cent.[1]

Moreover, a recent Census Bureau (1985a, Table D) report indicates that in 1983 7.6 per cent of officially (money income) poor households paid federal income taxes, pre-tax, while 44 per cent paid payroll taxes. The report also indicates that the percentage of poor households paying each type of tax increased between 1982 and 1983.

It is important to note that the *Economic Recovery and Tax Act* (ERTA) of 1981 did not adjust personal exemptions or the standard deduction (zero bracket amount) to account for their erosion by inflation. Since these were the two major progressivity features which prevented most poor families from paying federal income taxes, their ignorance by ERTA, coupled with scheduled Social Security payroll tax increases, has recently magnified the poverty-increasing impact of personal taxes, and will continue to do so over the foreseeable future. Based on recent trends in poverty, the impact of subtracting state and federal income and payroll taxes would increase the poverty count by about 10 per cent today.

Tables 4.2 and 4.3 suggest the growing burden of federal income and payroll taxes on families near the poverty line.[2] In Table 4.2 we compare the income tax threshold, the level at which income taxes become positive, after netting out the Earned Income Tax Credit (EITC),[3] to the poverty threshold for a four-person family. Before the EITC came into effect in 1975, the tax level was generally below, but close to, the poverty line. Low income families with earned income as their primary means of support were thus liable for small amounts of income taxes. All earnings were also subject to payroll tax liability, but payroll taxes were relatively low (about 5 per cent in 1970). When the EITC came into being (1975), the small positive income tax liabilities were more than made up for by EITC benefits. The income level at which taxes were due rose to 21.7 per cent above the poverty level for families with children during 1975. In fact, because of EITC refundability, income taxes were actually negative at poverty line income levels and below. However, as the 1970s

Table 4.2 Poverty lines for four-person families *v*. the income tax threshold for a four-person family: 1970–84

Year	*Tax threshold*[1] $	*Poverty line* $	*Tax threshold minus poverty line* $	*Tax threshold as a percentage of poverty line*
1970	3 750	3 968	–218	94.5
1975	6 692	5 500	1 192	121.7
1976	6 892	5 815	1 077	118.5
1978	7 533	6 662	871	113.1
1979	8 626	7 412	1 214	116.4
1980	8 626	8 414	212	102.5
1981	8 634	9 287	–653	93.0
1982	8 727	9 860	–1 133	88.5
1983	8 783	10 178	–1 395	86.3
1984	8 783	10 609	–1 826	82.8

Note: 1. Assumes all income in the form of earnings and accounts for the effect of the Earned Income Tax Credit (EITC) on federal income tax liability.
Sources: US Congress (1983), Joint Committee on Taxation.
US Bureau of the Census (1985a).

progressed, the difference between the income level where income taxes were due and the poverty line decreased constantly. The last increase in personal exemptions and the zero bracket amount took place in 1979. Since 1980 the income level at which taxes are due has changed only slightly.[4] However, inflation has driven the poverty line increasingly higher, to the point where a family of four with poverty line earnings in 1983, even counting the EITC, had nearly $1400 of federally taxable income. For 1984 this amount increases to $1830.

Table 4.3 indicates the amount of income, payroll, and combined taxes that would be due for families of two, four, and six persons with earnings equal to the poverty line from 1979 through 1984. These figures bring out several important points. First of all, payroll taxes are a much heavier burden on low income earners than are income taxes. Secondly, these tax burdens are not insubstantial. Even though state income taxes are ignored, *a poverty line family of four was liable for $1076 in income and payroll taxes in 1982. Average food stamps benefits for working families at this income level in that year was about $980*. Thus for this family, the net effect of taxes and food stamps (the in-kind program which they are most likely to benefit from) was to

Table 4.3 Income tax liabilities at poverty line income levels: 1979–84 ($)

Measure	*Family size*	*1979*	*1980*	*Year* *1981*	*1982*	*1983*	*1984*
1. Poverty level	2	4 727	5 363	5 917	6 281	6 483	6 762
	4	7 412	8 414	9 787	9 862	10 178	10 609
	6	9 892	11 269	12 449	13 207	13 630	14 207
2. *Income tax*	2	0	0	74	106	118	150
	4	4	144	263	285	318	365
	6	74	263	442	491	507	570
3. *Payroll tax*	2	290	329	393	421	434	453
	4	454	516	618	661	681	711
	6	606	691	828	885	913	953
4. *Combined tax*	2	290	329	467	527	552	603
	4	458	660	881	946	999	1076
	6	680	954	1270	1376	1420	1523
5. *Combined tax as percentage of poverty level*	2	6.1	6.1	7.9	8.4	8.5	8.9
	4	6.2	7.8	9.0	9.6	9.8	10.1
	6	6.9	8.5	10.2	10.4	10.4	10.7

Assumption: All income from earnings, families of size 4 and 6 are eligible for the EITC.
Sources: US Congress (1983), Joint Committee on Taxation.
US Bureau of the Census (1985a).

reduce their net income by $96! Finally, we note that combined income and payroll tax rates are higher for larger families, and that they have steadily increased since 1979 for all family size groups. Clearly there are poor and near-poor people in America today who are paying insignificant amounts of income and payroll tax. Perhaps the largest single benefit from recent federal tax reform proposals would be to exempt poor families from federal income taxation.

Underreporting

The final major problem with current poverty estimates is their failure to deal with survey income underreporting. The report which was prepared for the Census Bureau (Smeeding, 1982a) and its recent update (US Bureau of the Census, 1985a) did not adjust for this problem because the Census Bureau does not believe that a reasonable methodology for making such adjustments is currently available. Unfortunately this is a very defensible position; underreporting adjustments are difficult to carry out. Still, recent experience with the Current Population Survey (CPS), upon which poverty estimates are based, indicates that only about 90 per cent of the money income amounts for the previous year which should have been reported are actually reported each March. In-kind benefit recipiency and consequently in-kind income, is underreported as well, though to a lesser extent. For instance, about 93 per cent of all Medicaid beneficiaries, and 93 per cent of public housing recipients reported coverage in 1982. Among programs targetted to the poor, only about 77 per cent of the administrative dollar total for Aid to Families with Dependent Children (AFDC) and Supplemental Security Income (SSI) was reported in 1983, while only 72 per cent of the face value of food stamps was recorded on the CPS in 1982 (US Bureau of the Census, 1985a). Faced with these anomalies it is fair to ask, why won't the Census Bureau make any adjustment?

First of all, the issue of how to deal with money income underreporting is quite complex. While on average only 9 out of every $10 is reported, this figure differs considerably by income type. Wage and salary income is 98 per cent reported, while some reported transfer and property income amounts are 75 per cent or less of the benchmark amount. Once specific types of income (for example, interest or AFDC benefits) are singled out, the problem of misreporting (that is, reporting one type of income as another type) need also be considered. For instance, one recent study (Goudreau, Oberheu, and Vaughn, 1981) indicates that misreporting of AFDC as general assistance or child support is more prevalent than either underreporting dollar amounts of AFDC or failing to report AFDC altogether. Moreover, of those reporting AFDC in that study, only 70 per cent reported the correct amount. Twenty-one per cent underreported the correct amount by an average of 26 per cent. Nine per cent overreported the correct amount by an average of 37 per cent. Adjustments for underreporting which merely 'blow up' reported amounts of AFDC to reach aggregate benchmark income totals ignore both of these problems.

Additional research in this area is sorely needed. However, until underreporting adjustment methodologies are improved upon, one can get a rough idea of how much difference such changes might make by looking at the results of the several research efforts which adjust for cash and in-kind income cash underreporting and misreporting using various methodologies (including at least one study which directly matched tax and social security administrative records to reported survey income amounts). These studies (Budd and Radner, 1975; Smeeding, 1975; Paglin, 1979; Plotnick and Smeeding, 1979; Hoagland, 1980) indicate a net reduction in poverty ranging from 14 to 26 per cent from such adjustments. Until better estimates are developed, a 20 per cent reduction for reporting errors in the poverty estimates presented in Table 4.1, may not be too far off the mark.

RECENT CHANGES IN POVERTY: THE OFFICIAL POVERTY RATES

When the Census report on in-kind benefits to Congress was prepared, the official poverty rate for 1979 (the year on which the report was based) was 11.7 per cent. Since then it has risen to 13.0 per cent (1980), 14.0 per cent (1981), and finally to 15.3 per cent in 1983 before declining slightly to 14.4 per cent in 1984 (US Bureau of the Census, 1985a). Some of this poverty increase was due to the growing problem of relatively more persons living in younger female-headed families, the so-called feminization of poverty. If we held the share of persons in female-headed families with related children under age 18 at their 1970 per cent of the total population but used the 1984 poverty rate, we would find 1230 less poor persons in these families. All else equal, this would have reduced the 1984 poverty rate from 14.4 per cent to 13.9 per cent. Thus the increase in this family type alone (relative to the rest of the population) has increased poverty rates by 0.5 percentage points. Poverty rates among these types of persons increased only marginally from 53.0 to 54.0 per cent between 1970 and 1984 (US Bureau of the Census, 1985c: Table 15). Thus the increasing proportion of poor persons in poor female-headed families with children under 18 is mainly due to the increasing proportion of all persons which are living in this type of unit. Still, despite this growth, poor persons in these female-headed families declined from 21.7 per cent of the poor in 1979 to 20.1 per cent in 1984 (US Bureau of the Census, 1985c: Table 15). As officially measured, poverty among the elderly is still a problem, though a less pressing one than earlier believed. In 1979 14.1 per cent of the poor were over 65, while in 1984, 9.9 per cent of the poor were elderly. Poverty rates among persons age 65 and over fell from 15.2 to 12.4 per cent between 1979 and 1984.

I single female-headed families with children and the elderly out because they are the groups whose poverty status is most affected by in-kind transfers (especially medical care benefits), least affected by income and payroll taxes (because most of their income is from transfer payments), and most affected by income underreporting (because the types of income they receive are most subject to underreporting). Because of large in-kind and underreporting adjustments (which tend to lower poverty) and a small tax effect (which tends to increase poverty) these are precisely the groups whose poverty status would undergo the greatest downward change were these adjustments made. Yet together they have shrunk from 35.8 per cent of the poor in 1979 to 30.0 per cent in 1984. Who has taken their place?

I would argue that the major increases in poverty experienced during the past six years have been in persons, adults but especially children, living in traditional husband-wife families. In 1979 these persons constituted 16.7 per cent of the poor, while in 1984 they comprise 18.3 per cent of the poor. In this case, demographic change works in the opposite direction. Had persons in husband-wife families with children under age 18 remained at their 1970 per cent of the total population, and had poverty rates increased to their 1984 levels for this group, we would have found an *additional* 2.584 million poor persons in 1984, bringing the over-all poverty rate up from 14.4 per cent to 15.5 per cent, all else being equal. Thus the change in the fraction of persons in female-headed families from 1970 to 1984 which contributed to higher over-all poverty rates in 1984 needs to be counter-balanced with the decrease in the fraction of persons in traditional families which helped hold poverty down in 1984. In 1970 the poverty rate for younger male-headed families with children was 9.2 per cent as compared to the 1984 rate of 12.5 per cent.

We single this group out for precisely the *opposite* reason. These families are least likely to be affected by in-kind benefits (because of ineligibility or low benefit amounts), most likely to pay taxes, and least likely to be affected by underreporting (both being due to the heavy reliance on heavily taxed, but also well reported, earned income in these families).

For instance, in 1984 43 per cent of all poor households had at least one member who received food stamp benefits, 16 per cent lived in public housing, and 42 per cent benefited from Medicaid (US Bureau of the Census, 1985d). In contrast, only 36 per cent of poor husband-wife families got food stamps, only 6 per cent lived in public housing, and only 28 per cent were eligible for Medicaid benefits. The point of this discussion is to argue that the increasing numbers of poor families of this type are least likely to be reduced by adjusting for in-kind income and reporting, but most likely to be increased by adjusting for taxes. Given these trends, not much of a reduction in poverty for these families should be expected once the adjustments for income in kind, taxes, and reporting are made.

Reagan's budgetary policies

It is just this group of low earners in two parent families and their children who have been most adversely affected by the Reagan Administration's taxation and social policies. These individuals increasingly became poor because of recession-induced job loss, and subsequent declines in earned income; because less than 40 per cent of the unemployed were covered by unemployment insurance in 1983 (as compared to over 75 per cent during the 1975 recession); because the 1981 ERTA did not provide them with any over-all direct tax relief (but instead with large effective tax increases); and finally, because cutbacks in food stamps and other social programs have most negatively affected precisely these low-earnings people. Unfortunately this group has fallen through the administration's safety net, even after the 1984 economic recovery.

A SUMMING UP

It remains to put these pieces of information together to attempt to update the net impact of in-kind benefits, taxes, and income underreporting on the recent post 1979 changes in poverty. All of the figures in Table 4.4 other than those in the last column for 1982–4 are based on sophisticated income microdata modeling and imputation procedures. The Census Bureau has updated their 1979 base year report on in-kind benefits through 1984, but the net effects of income underreporting and taxes on poverty has not yet been estimated using income microdata. Thus this last set of figures (superscripted with an 'e') are only a rough estimate.

Table 4.4 indicates that poverty in the US is on the rise even after adjustments for in-kind benefits, underreporting and taxes are carried out. The Census update of my earlier report indicated an increase from 9.0 per cent to 13.1 per cent in 1983, and then a drop to

Table 4.4 Percentage of persons with incomes below the poverty line: 1965–84

Year	*Official census money income*[1]	*Adjusted income: in-kind only*[2]	*Adjusted income: Taxes, reporting and in-kind*[3]
1965	17.3	–	12.1
1968	12.8	–	9.9
1970	12.6	–	9.3
1972	11.9	–	6.2
1974	11.2	–	7.2
1976	11.8	–	6.7
1979	11.7	9.0	6.1
1982	15.0	12.7	10.0–11.0[4]
1983	15.3	13.1	10.2–11.2[4]
1984	14.4	12.2	9.8–10.8[4]

Notes: 1. Census figures for 1965–76 are taken from various issues of the *Current Population Reports* P–60 series (figures for 1979 to 1984 are taken from Table 4.1).

2. This estimate adjusts Census money income by adding food, medical (excluding institutional care benefits) and housing in-kind transfers at their cash-equivalent value (see US Bureau of the Census, 1985a, and Table 4.1).

3. Adjusted income adjusts Census money income for underreporting, measures poverty on a household income basis, adds in-kind public transfers at their cash equivalent value, and subtracts federal payroll and income taxes. The data for 1965–79 are as in Smeeding (1982b).

4. Author's estimate.

12.2 per cent in 1984, adjusting only for in-kind benefits (measured at their cash equivalent value) and ignoring taxes and reporting problems, as was the case with the earlier report. Recent cutbacks in in-kind transfer income support systems and growing numbers of poor husband-wife families who benefit least from such programs explain this increase.

In 1979 once adjustments for taxes and income underreporting were made as well, poverty fell to about 6.1 per cent. However, taxes had a larger poverty increasing effect in 1982–4 than in 1979. Thus, assuming that underreporting had as substantial an effect in reducing poverty in 1982 as in earlier studies, we still end up today with a 1984 poverty rate of somewhere between 9.8 and 10.8 per cent after all adjustments have been made.

Implications for policy and research

Such figures have far-reaching policy implications. They indicate that Reagan Administration statements were correct in that in-kind benefits reduced poverty below the official figures. This was obvious all along. But what the administration didn't tell us was that: (a) a 9.8 to 10.8 per cent poverty rate means over 23 million poor and needy Americans, even after counting these benefits; and (b) that the income and payroll tax burden on the working poor is substantial and growing at a rapid rate; and (c) that the poverty rate including in-kind benefits, taxes, and reporting adjustments is now as high or higher than it was in 1968.

In case there was any doubt, America still has a serious poverty problem and, all the in-kind benefit rhetoric aside, that problem is not going away. The considerable doubts that the recovery from the 1981–3 recession would not lead to very large decline in poverty have now been justified (Gottschalk, 1983). The latest 1984 poverty rates after in-kind benefits, taxes and reporting are near the 1982 levels and far above 1979 estimates. Moreover, unemployment in 1985 was not much changed from 1984, thus indicating relatively little change in poverty rates once the 1985 figures are released. If we are to reduce poverty further, the policy agenda should again consider reforming and revamping programs to reduce poverty in America.

Anti-poverty policy aside, further research and annually updated estimates of the effect of in-kind benefits (and taxes) on poverty should continue to be carried out. To their credit, the Census Bureau convened a group of experts to recommend a strategy for integrating the value of noncash benefits into the measure of poverty and of income distribution more generally in December 1985. The conferees recommended that the Census Bureau adjust their procedures to account for direct tax liability in measuring poverty. Much additional work on income reporting adjustments and on in-kind transfer valuation, especially for medical transfers, was also called for. Now, perhaps more than ever before, policy-makers need an accurate and up-to-date estimate of poverty in America. By continuing to work on and to improve these estimates, policy-makers should have this need fulfilled.

Notes

1. See Smeeding (1975), Plotnick and Smeeding (1979). A recent Census report (US Bureau of the Census, 1983a) indicates an increase in poverty

of 1.2 per cent among households in 1980 accounting for income taxes and the Earned Income Tax Credit (EITC) only. Payroll taxes, which are quite a bit larger at poverty line income levels than are income taxes, were not counted.
2. State income taxes are not included in these calculations, despite the fact that 13.1 per cent of poor households paid state income taxes in 1983 (US Bureau of the Census, 1983a: Table D).
3. The EITC applies only to families with children and only to families with money incomes below $10 000. For those earning $5000 or less, a subsidy equal to 10 per cent of earnings is paid. The subsidy maximum is therefore $500 after $6000 of earnings. The subsidy is reduced $12.50 for each additional $100 in earnings, thus phasing out at $10 000 at which point the regular federal income tax is levied.
4. These changes are due to the effect of slightly lower income tax rates as a result of ERTA, and their interaction with the EITC.

References

BUDD, E. and RADNER, D. (1975) 'The BEA and CPS Size Distributions: Some Comparisons for 1964', in J. D. SMITH (ed.) (1975) *The Personal Distribution of Income and Wealth* (New York: Columbia University Press).

GOTTSCHALK, P. (1983) 'Will a Resumption of Economic Growth Reverse the Recent Increase in Poverty?' Testimony before US House of Representatives, Ways and Means Committee, 18 October.

GOUDREAU, K., OBERHEU, H. and VAUGHN, D. (1981) 'An Assessment of the Quality of Survey Reports of Income from the AFDC Program', *Proceedings of the American Statistical Association*: 377–82.

HOAGLAND, G. W. (1980) 'The Effectiveness of Current Transfer Programs in Reducing Poverty', presented at Middlebury College Conference on Economic Issues, 19 April.

ORSHANSKY, M. (1965) 'Counting the Poor: Another Look at the Poverty Profile', *Social Security Bulletin*, 28 (1): 3–29 January.

PAGLIN, M. (1979) *Poverty and Transfers In Kind* (Palo Alto: Hoover Institution Press).

PLOTNICK, R. and SMEEDING, T. M. (1979) 'Poverty and Income Transfers: Past Trends and Future Prospects', *Public Policy*, 27 (3): 255–72.

SMEEDING, T. M. (1975) 'Measuring the Economic Welfare of Low Income Households and the Anti-Poverty Effectiveness of Cash and Noncash Transfer Programs', Unpublished PhD dissertation, University of Wisconsin-Madison.

SMEEDING, T. M. (1977). 'The Anti-Poverty Effectiveness of In-Kind Transfers', *Journal of Human Resources*, 12: 360–78.

SMEEDING, T. M. (1982a) 'Alternative Methods for Valuing Selected In-Kind Transfer Benefits and Measuring Their Effect on Poverty', *U.S. Bureau of the Census*, Technical Paper, No. 50 (Washington, D.C.: Government Printing Office).

SMEEDING, T. M. (1982b) 'The Anti-Poverty Effects of In-Kind Transfers:

A 'Good Idea' Gone Too Far?' *Policy Studies Journal*, June, 10: 491–521.
US BUREAU OF THE CENSUS (1983a) 'Estimating After-Tax Money Income Distributions Using Data from the March CPS', *Current Population Reports*, Series P-23, No. 126.
US BUREAU OF THE CENSUS (1985a) *Estimates of Poverty Including the Value of Noncash Benefits: 1984*, Technical Paper No. 55 (Washington, D.C.: Government Printing Office).
US BUREAU OF THE CENSUS (1985b) 'After-Tax Money Income Estimates of Households'; *Current Population Reports*, Special Studies, Series P-23, No. 143.
US BUREAU OF THE CENSUS (1985c) 'Money Income and Poverty Status of Families and Persons in the United States: 1984', *Current Population Reports*, Series P-60, No. 149.
US BUREAU OF THE CENSUS (1985d) 'Selected Characteristics of Families and Persons Receiving Noncash Benefits: 1984', *Current Population Reports*, Series P-60, No. 150 .
US CONGRESS (1983) 'Tabulations Comparing Poverty Level with Tax Liability Starting Point', Joint Committee on Taxation (Washington, D.C., 5 August).
US DEPARTMENT OF HEALTH, EDUCATION AND WELFARE (1976) *The Measure of Poverty* (Washington, D.C.: Government Printing Office).

Part II
Distributional Impacts of Public Policy Reforms

5 Alternative Child Support Regimes: Distributional Impacts and a Crude Benefit-Cost Analysis*

Donald T. Oellerich and Irwin Garfinkel

INTRODUCTION

Child support is a transfer of income from a noncustodial parent to a custodial parent and child. In this paper we examine the effects of current child support payments on the incidence of poverty and the poverty gap among children with living noncustodial fathers. In addition, we simulate the effects of both increased child support orders and increased child support collection effectiveness on the economic well-being of these children.

In 1983 there were 13.3 million children below the age of 21 living in 7.7 million families who were potentially eligible to receive child support from a noncustodial father.[1] That is, they had a living noncustodial father. These children represent one out of every five children in the United States today (Garfinkel and Melli, 1982). Estimates indicate that nearly one out of every two children born today will become eligible for child support before reaching the age of 18 (Moynihan, 1981). Hence, the quality of our child support institutions is of great concern to the nation.

In this paper we will examine four important questions: (1) How many more children eligible for child support would be poor and how much larger would the poverty gap be in the absence of the present child support system? (2) What is the best the present child support system could do in reducing both of these poverty indicators, that is, what would be the effects if present child support obligations were paid in full? (3) What effect could a reformed child support system

* This research was supported by a grant from the Graduate School–University of Wisconsin-Madison (Grant No. 1353053).

have on the poverty rate and poverty gap for eligible families? and (4) What would be the costs of a reformed child support system?

In the next section we will describe the present child support system and a proposal for reforming that system. The third section will describe our data source and our methodology. The fourth section will present our results. The last section will present a summary of our work.

A DESCRIPTION OF THE PRESENT CHILD SUPPORT SYSTEM AND A REFORM PROPOSAL

The present system

Child support is principally a function of state and local government. Most states have codified the right of a child to the support of both parents (Krause, 1981). Within each state the operation of the child support system is mostly a local matter.

Child support is the province of the judiciary. In order to be eligible to receive child support there must be a court order or a stipulation (that is, a voluntary agreement approved by the court). The level of the support obligation is set by the judge, and the enforcement of the support obligation is in the court's domain.

Each part of the support process is problematic and, with the exception of welfare families, recipient activated. The first part that is problematic is securing a legally enforceable court order. Some 48 per cent of demographically eligible child support families do not have a legally enforceable order. Over 87 per cent of never-married women, 66 per cent of separated women, and 28 per cent of divorced women are therefore not eligible for support payments.

The second part of the present child support system that is problematic is setting the level of child support obligations. The methods of setting the level of child support obligations result in inadequacies and inequities. A study of California divorce cases indicates that, even after child support awards are counted, on average the standard of living, adjusted for family size, of divorced men increased by 43 per cent after divorce, while the standard of living of the women and children decreases by 73 per cent (Weitzman, 1981). Guidelines to assist the judge or family court commissioner in setting support levels are often nonexistent. Those guidelines that are available in many jurisdictions are vague and often ignored. Judicial discretion reigns supreme in setting obligation levels.

The enforcement of past due child support is the third problematic part of the system. It requires that the custodial parent initiate court action. Once the custodian has initiated action the courts have a number of enforcement tools available, which vary from state to state. They include civil and criminal contempt citations, garnishment, seizure of property, wage assignments, and the ultimate sanction – jail.

In the usual scenario, the custodian brings court action; the noncustodial parent receives a contempt citation and makes a promise to pay. When the noncustodian fails to pay, the custodial parent must again initiate action. The process is time consuming and costly. Not infrequently these costs outweigh the return; the noncustodian is no longer pursued. Of those with child support awards in 1983, only 51 per cent received the full amount, and 24 per cent received nothing (US Department of Commerce, 1985)

Federal involvement in child support, though hampered by the traditional role of the states in areas of family law, has been growing. Federal interest in child support has been sparked by rising welfare costs. Therefore, the main thrust of the federal government has been to collect child support for families receiving Aid to Families with Dependent Children (AFDC).

In 1950 Congress enacted the first federal child support legislation. This required state welfare agencies to notify law enforcement officials when a child receiving AFDC benefits had been deserted or abandoned. Further legislation, enacted in 1965 and 1967, allowed states to request addresses of noncustodial parents from the Department of Health, Education and Welfare (HEW) and the Internal Revenue Service (IRS) and required states to establish a single organizational unit to enforce child support and establish paternity.

The most significant legislation was enacted in 1975, when Congress added Part D to Title IV of the Social Security Act, thereby establishing the Child Support Enforcement program sometimes referred to as the IV-D program. Responsibility for running the program rests with the states. They are reimbursed by the federal government for 75 per cent of their costs for running the program. In 1980 the law was amended to provide 90 per cent federal funding for computerizing the program. The IV-D program is supposed to serve nonwelfare as well as welfare cases. As of 1981 about 17 per cent of the IV-D caseload was attributable to non-AFDC cases.

Use of the IRS to collect child support owed to AFDC beneficiaries was authorized by the 1975 law. In 1980 use of the IRS extended to non-AFDC families. In 1981 legislation required the IRS to withhold tax refunds in cases where states certified that the individual owed child support which was overdue.

The most recent, and far-reaching, federal initiative is contained in the 1984 Social Security Amendments. This initiative requires states to withhold child support obligations from the wages/salary of delinquent noncustodians. In addition, this legislation requires states to appoint commissions to recommend normative standards to set levels of child support awards.

The performance of these federal initiatives, although noteworthy, is not impressive. IV-D collections in 1983 showed nearly a threefold increase over 1977 child support collections, amounting to 2 billion in 1983 (US Department of Health and Human Services, 1984). Despite the fact that the IV-D program had an average monthly non-AFDC caseload of 1.7 million compared with an average monthly AFDC caseload of 5.8 million, collections for the non-AFDC caseload totaled $1.1 billion compared to $0.88 billion for the AFDC caseload. AFDC benefit expenditures for this same period totaled $14 billion.

Yet more than half of the families potentially eligible to receive child support received nothing. Further, of all the children eligible to receive child support, 38 per cent, or 5.8 million, live in poverty.[2] The incidence of poverty for those eligible children who live in female-headed households was 48 per cent.[3] The fact that so many of these children live in poverty calls for public attention.

In summary, the present child support system fails. It fails to get support obligations for many who are demographically eligible. It fails to provide adequate and equitable levels of support for those with support awards. And it fails to collect much of what is due.

A new child support system

In view of these problems with the present child support system, a research team from the Institute for Research on Poverty, under contract with the Wisconsin Department of Health and Social Services, has developed a proposal for a new child support benefit and tax system (Garfinkel and Melli, 1982). The purpose of this paper is not to convince the reader that this proposal is the best possible reform, nor even that it is necessarily superior to the current system – though we are pretty confident of at least the latter. Rather, our purpose is to illustrate the effects of some such reform.

The basic goals of the proposed reform are: (1) assurance that those who parent a child share their income with that child;

(2) establishment of equitable support obligations; (3) collection of those obligations effectively and efficiently; and (4) increase in the economic well-being of eligible children. It is believed that these goals would best be met by enacting legislation which would create a new system of establishing, collecting, and distributing child support payments.

The child support tax system as proposed, would operate through the wage-withholding system. The tax rate will be proportional based solely on the number of eligible children. For example, the rate would be 17 per cent for one child, 25 per cent for two children and 29 per cent for three, 31 per cent for four and 32 per cent for five children. The tax base is the noncustodial parent's gross income.

The child support benefit side of the proposed system would entitle all children with a living noncustodial parent to benefits equal to either the child support tax paid by the absent parent, or a minimum benefit, whichever is higher. Should the noncustodian pay less than the minimum, the custodial parent would be subject to a small surtax up to the amount of the public subsidy. Should the sum of the noncustodial and custodial parent taxes be less than the minimum, the difference would be financed out of general revenues.

The proposed child support system would be administered by either the federal or state government. Access would be gained by the custodial parent making application to the agency. The amount of child support, a percentage of the noncustodial parent's income, would be determined administratively. The child support tax would be withheld from wages and salary by the noncustodial parent's employer. The employer would forward the money to the designated agency. Those self-employed and persons whose chief source of income is non-employment income would be required to make the transfer to the agency themselves. Year-end accounting, employing the income tax return, would be used to balance the account for unpaid child support on unearned income. The receiving agency would forward all monies collected to the custodial parent.

DATA AND METHODOLOGY

Data

The 1982 Current Population Survey – Child Support Supplement (CPS-CSS) provides the data for our analysis. The CPS-CSS is a match file containing the records of 4154 women who were eligible to receive child support because they had children under 21 years of age in their home whose father was absent from the home. The match file contains data from both the April child support supplement and the March Annual Demographic Survey; it provides a wealth of data. In fact, the CPS-CSS is unique in that it provides a nationally representative sample of women eligible for child support with detailed microdata on the amounts of child support due and the amounts of support actually received. In addition, detailed information is included on the method of payment, reasons for irregular payments, alimony payments and property settlements. The CPS-CSS provides the most current and complete data source for our analysis.

Although the CPS-CSS provides the best available information on child support, it does have several weaknesses. First, the sample is restricted to mothers 18 and older, thereby excluding a small portion of the eligible population. Secondly, the data collected were for the most recent divorce or separation only, thereby excluding child support information from prior unions. Both of these weaknesses result in under-counting the number of eligible children and the amount of child support obligations and collections.

The third weakness results from the annual reporting of both AFDC benefits and child support payments. Annual reporting creates a problem when trying to adjust family income for increases in child support and concomitant decreases in AFDC payments, because AFDC uses a monthly rather than an annual accounting period. The fourth and last weakness is underreporting of child support by AFDC recipients. This may have two causes. First, child support for an AFDC recipient is paid directly to the state and the recipient may be unaware of the amount received. Secondly, child support received directly by the AFDC recipient is likely to go unreported for fear that its disclosure would subject their AFDC benefit to the 100 per cent benefit reduction rate for child support received. This underreporting will result in an underestimate of the impacts of the present system.

Methodology for the present system

To measure the actual and potential impacts of the present child support system on the poverty rate and poverty gap we use the following data: (1) total family income from all sources including welfare and child support; (2) total welfare income; (3) total child support income received; (4) total child support income due; and (5) the official poverty lines appropriate for each family size. The poverty lines and all incomes are in 1983 dollars.

Calculation of the poverty rate

The denominator of the poverty rate is the number of children less than 21 years of age who have a living noncustodial father; the numerator is the number of such children who are poor. The income of interest varies by what we are trying to measure. We simply use the total family income to measure the actual impact of the present system. Measuring impacts for both the absence and potential of the present system requires that we make some assumptions about the response of the AFDC system. We assume that, in the absence of any child support, those families who are currently non-AFDC recipients will remain nonrecipients. Because some of these families would lose sufficient income to become eligible for AFDC, this assumption underestimates the effect of AFDC. We also assume the AFDC benefits will rise (or decline) dollar for dollar in response to the reduction (or increase) in child support.

Calculation of the poverty gap

The poverty gap is the amount of income required to raise the incomes of all poor families up to the poverty level. The poverty gaps are calculated by summing the difference between income and the official poverty line for those families who are below that line.

Methodology for the reform system

The methodology for measuring the two poverty indicators for the proposed reform system is more complex. We need to determine the noncustodial father's child support liability, which under the proposed reform would depend upon the noncustodial father's ability to pay. To do this we must do two things. First, we need to know the income of the noncustodian. Secondly, we need to apply a tax to his income equal to a normative standard: how much he should pay in child support.

Information on the noncustodial father's income and characteristics is not available. Therefore, we utilize an indirect method for estimating his income. The method employs the custodial mother's characteristics and other demographic information as proxies for those of the noncustodial father. The methodology is based on the assumption that the relationship of a wife's characteristics to husband's income is the same as that of the custodial mother's characteristics to the noncustodial father's income.

The methodology can be broken down into three steps. The first step is to estimate the relationship between a woman's characteristics and her mate's income. To do this we estimate a regression equation employing a sample of currently married couples with children under 18 years of age. The dependent variable is the income of the man from all earned and unearned sources excluding welfare income.[4] The independent or explanatory variables include the characteristics of the woman: age, education, number of children, residence in a central city, or outside of a Standard Metropolitan Statistical Area (SMSA), and interaction terms.[5] The independent variables are chosen to be proxies for the variables normally included in human-capital regressions. In this and subsequent regressions there are two sets of regressions, one for whites and another for nonwhites, to control for the interaction of race and the other explanatory variables. The estimation method is ordinary least squares regression (OLS).[6] The results of these regressions are presented in Appendix Table 5.A1.

The second step is to impute income estimates for the noncustodial fathers. To do this we use the characteristics of the custodial mother, and the coefficients estimated in step one.

The third and last step is to adjust our income estimates to take account of the fact that divorced, separated, and never-married men have lower incomes than married men with the same characteristics. To correct for the overestimate that arises from basing an estimation on the relationship of married men's earnings to married women's characteristics, we reduce the estimated incomes by the ratio of divorced or separated or never-married men's income to married men's income, controlling for the men's characteristics (see Appendix Table 5.A2). For example, if the marital status of the custodial parent is never married, we assume that the father is a never-married man and reduce the imputed income by the ratio of never-married to married men's income. This will lead to some over-correction of the bias, because many noncustodial fathers of both never-married and divorced women are married.

So far we have a point estimate of noncustodial-father income for each woman in the sample. Each woman represents many women in the population. Not all of these absent spouses have the same income, but rather they make up a distribution of income which we are summarizing by the point estimate. To further define these distributions we use the mean square error of the Step 1 regression as an estimate of the variance. We can now define our distributions of income by two parameters: the mean estimated by the point estimate and the variance. In addition, we assume that income is distributed log normal. The distributions allow us to simulate a nonlinear normative standard which incorporates an income exemption or set-aside.[7]

Estimates of the income of the noncustodial fathers are necessary but not sufficient for determining their ability to pay child support. A tax equal to a normative standard must be applied to the income. Normative standards are value judgements made by people about how much noncustodial parents can afford to pay in child support.

The Wisconsin Reform Proposal provides the normative standard for the first reform support regime. The child support tax is a proportional tax rate based on the number of children; it is applied from the first dollar of income. The proposed tax rates are 17 per cent of gross income for the first child, 25 per cent for two children, and 29 per cent for three, 31 per cent for four and 32 per cent for five or more children. Some people believe that the noncustodial father should be permitted an exemption to cover his own basic needs. Our second support regime will incorporate this by using the same tax rates as the first regime but will exempt $5765 (poverty level for a one-person household) from the tax. Estimates of ability to pay are calculated by taxing the income estimates by each of the normative standards. The result is a point estimate of child support for each sample family and the variance.[8] Finally, in the simulations of the full reform regime, if the child support payment from the noncustodial father is less than the minimum, the child support benefit is equal to the minimum.

Calculating the poverty rate

Poverty rates are calculated for the reformed child support regimes by using the following variables: total family income, child support payments, AFDC income, Census family weight, official poverty lines, and the estimated distributions of the noncustodial father's ability to pay (child support).

The impacts of each support regime are determined by calculating the probability that each family will be below the poverty line given their distribution of child support plus their family income. Family income for AFDC recipients is total nonwelfare family income plus the larger of AFDC income or child support income. The probabilities are multiplied times the Census family weight to obtain a count of families below poverty.[9]

Calculation of the poverty gap

The poverty gap remaining after the transfer of child support employing each support regime is calculated by summing the weighted difference between the total family income after the child support transfer and the official poverty line. This is done for all families who are left poor following the support transfer. The family income for those below the poverty line is the mean of a truncated distribution.

Calculation of the cost or savings of the new system

The cost of the new child support system is equal to total child support benefits paid to children minus the sum of revenues raised from both the noncustodial and custodial parent taxes and savings from the AFDC program. Savings from the AFDC program for each family are equal to AFDC benefits minus child support benefits. To account for underreporting of AFDC benefits, the sum of the savings is then multiplied by the ratio of total AFDC benefits paid out according to official government statistics to the total AFDC benefits reported in the CPS.

THE BENEFITS AND COSTS OF A SOCIAL CHILD SUPPORT PROGRAM

The benefits: reductions in the poverty gap

The results of our analysis of the antipoverty effectiveness of alternative child support regimes are presented in Table 5.1. Antipoverty effectiveness is measured by three indicators: (1) the number of poor US children under age 21 who are eligible for child support (number poor); (2) the percentage of these children who are poor (poverty rate); and, most important for our benefit-cost analysis, (3) the aggregate income needed to bring poor children who are eligible for child support up to the poverty line (poverty gap). These three measures are presented in three sets of columns. The first panel of columns is for all races combined. The next two are split into nonwhites and whites.

Each row presents the effects of a different child support regime on these alternative indicators of antipoverty effectiveness. Row 1 indicates how much poverty there would be under a regime in which there were no private child support transfers. Each successive row presents estimates for increasingly effective regimes. Following the no system regime is the current regime (row 2). Next (row 3) comes a reformed version of the current regime in which no changes in support awards are made, but all amounts are perfectly enforced so that 100 per cent of every award is paid (perfect collection regime). The next two rows (4 and 5) add to perfect collection the effects of universal application of a normative standard in setting child support awards. In both standards child support awards are equal to 17 per cent of gross income for one child, 25 per cent for two children, 29 per cent for three, 31 per cent for four and 32 per cent for five or more children, except that in the first standard (row 4) only income in excess of $5765 per year is taxed at these rates. The exempted income in the 'Standard with exemption regime' equals the poverty level for a single person. The 'Standard without exemption regime' presented in row 5 has no exemption. The last two rows present the antipoverty effects of adding to the 'Standard without exemption regime' a national minimum child support benefit. The minimum in row 6 is equal to $3000 per year for the first child, and $1000 for the second child and $500 per year for each subsequent child up to $6000 per year. In row 7, the minimum equals $4000 per year for the first child and $1000 per year for the second child and $500 each subsequent child up to a maximum of $7000.

Perhaps the single most striking fact presented in Table 5.1 is that virtually two of five American children potentially eligible for child support is poor. This astoundingly high number is explained by several factors. First, many children who are potentially eligible for support live with single mothers. Secondly, nearly half of all children in female-headed families are poor. Whatever the causes, the fact that two of five children potentially eligible for child support is poor suggests that the quality of our child support system should be an important social concern.

Nearly as stunning is the fact that the number of poor nonwhite (mostly black) children is as large as the number of poor white children, even though there are more than eight whites for every

Table 5.1 The antipoverty effectiveness of alternative child support regimes

	All races			*Nonwhite*			*White*		
Alternative child support regimes	*No. Poor (millions)*	*% poor*	*Poverty gap (billion $)*	*No. Poor (millions)*	*% poor*	*Poverty gap (billion $)*	*No. Poor (millions)*	*% poor*	*Poverty gap (billion $)*
1. No child support	5.5	42.2	13.2	2.6	63.1	6.7	2.9	32.5	6.5
2. Current system	5.2	40.0	12.4	2.6	62.5	6.5	2.6	29.6	5.8
3. Perfect collection regime	5.1	39.0	12.0	2.6	62.4	6.4	2.5	28.2	5.6
4. Standard with exemption regime	4.8	36.8	11.1	2.5	60.9	6.4	2.3	26.1	4.6
5. Standard without exemption regime	4.3	32.9	9.3	2.3	56.3	5.6	2.0	22.4	3.7
6. Minimum benefit regime $3000/1000/500[a]	4.0	30.7	7.1	2.2	52.6	4.2	1.8	20.5	2.9
7. Maximum benefit regime $4000/1000/500[b]	3.7	28.3	5.7	2.0	48.5	3.4	1.7	19.1	2.3

[a] This is referred to as Plan I below.
[b] This is referred to as Plan II below.

nonwhite in the population. There are several explanations for this. First, blacks are poorer than whites. Secondly, a greater percentage of black than white children live in female-headed families. Thirdly, the percentage of blacks who are children is higher than the percentage of whites who are children.

Over 62 per cent of black children are poor. This is more than twice the rate for whites. In short, the quality of our child support institutions is of particular interest to the black community. We therefore turn now to the main purpose of constructing Table 5.1, to examine one aspect (antipoverty effectiveness) of the quality of alternative child support regimes.

A comparison of rows 1 and 2 in Table 5.1 shows that the present child support system does little to alleviate poverty. Only 300 000 children are removed from poverty by the present system. This amounts to a mere 2 percentage points over what it would be in the absence of the system. Finally, and most important, the poverty gap is reduced by only 0.8 billion dollars.

The effects of collecting 100 per cent of present child support obligations can be gleaned by comparing rows 2 and 3. The results are not very encouraging. For the total population of children eligible for child support, poverty is reduced by just one percentage point over the present system or 3 percentage points over the absence of the system. Similarly, the poverty gap is reduced by only another $0.4 billion. In other words, if all that was owed were paid, the system would do twice as well. But doing twice as well from such a low base still means that little is achieved.

In sum, the present system fails to transfer enough money from the noncustodial father to the custodial family to substantially reduce the poverty rate and poverty gap for eligible children. Even at peak effectiveness – collecting 100 per cent of current obligations, the present system can do little to alleviate poverty for eligible children.

The reductions in poverty which would accrue from the universal application of a normative standard are more impressive. On the most sensitive indicator, the poverty gap, even the standard with an exemption reduces the gap by 1.3 billion, or three times the effect of the perfect collection regime. The standard without an exemption cuts the poverty gap by another 0.9 billion. *Vis-à-vis* the absence of any child support program, the 'Standard without exemption regime' cuts the poverty gap by nearly 30 per cent. Although the results for the less sensitive poverty indicators are not quite so dramatic, they are nevertheless impressive.

The full social child support regimes, which include the minimum benefit, reduce poverty even more. In the first, less generous, plan the number of poor children is cut to 4 million, the incidence of poverty to 28 per cent, and the poverty gap to 7.1 billion. Relative to the current system, the poverty gap is reduced by nearly 43 per cent. The more generous plan reduces the poverty gap by 55 per cent to 5.7 billion.

Note that the results by race are again interesting. Whereas reforms on the collection side do more in percentage terms for whites than nonwhites (compare rows 2 and 5), the opposite is true for the minimum benefit. This is not surprising in view of the fact that nonwhites have less income.

To reiterate the main finding of this subsection: Compared to the status quo, the benefits of a social child support system like the one described in this section are large. The poverty gap is reduced by approximately 43 to 55 per cent. The following subsection considers costs.

The costs: public subsidy costs or saving

How much this new social child support system would cost or save depends upon (1) the tax rate on noncustodial and custodial parents; (2) the level of the child support minimum benefit; and (3) the effectiveness of child support collections. Estimated benefits, costs, and savings in the United States of two alternative social child support plans are given in Table 5.2. The first three columns describe the different plans: both the tax rate on the noncustodial father (as a percentage of his gross income up to $50 000), given in column (2), and the minimum benefit, given in column (3), depend upon the number of children owed support, given in column (1). Column (4) is the total cost of the benefits paid to these children. Column (5) is the total amount collected from noncustodial parents. Column (6) is the total amount collected from custodial parents. This tax is imposed only when the tax on the noncustodial parent is not sufficient to cover the minimum benefit. The tax rate on the custodial parent is half the tax rate on the noncustodian, up to the amount of the minimum benefit. Column (7) is the reduction in the cost of AFDC that will result from implementing each child support plan. In most AFDC cases, child support benefits will be less than AFDC benefits. In these cases AFDC savings equal the child support benefit.[10] In cases where the child support benefit exceeds the AFDC benefit, the AFDC

Table 5.2 Estimated cost and savings of alternative social child support plans in the USA, 1983 (assuming noncustodial parents pay 100 per cent of their child support obligation and no labor supply response for the custodial parents)

Description of plan			*Costs and savings (billion $)*				
No. of children (1)	*Tax rate on absent parent* (2)	*Minimum benefit* (3)	*Total benefits* (4)	*Total revenue from absent parents* (5)	*Total revenue from custodial parents* (6)	*Savings from reduction in cost of AFDC* (7)	*Net savings* (5) + (6) + (7) – (4) (8)
Plan 1							
1	17%	$3 000					
2	25	4 000					
3	29	4 500					
4	31	5 000					
5	32	5 500					
6+	33	6 000	37.2	28.9	2.4	6.9	1.0
Plan 2							
1	17%	$4 000					
2	25	5 000					
3	29	5 500					
4	31	6 000					
5	32	6 500					
6+	33	7 000	42.1	28.9	3.6	7.6	–1.9

savings equal the AFDC benefit. Column (8) gives the net savings for each of the three plans: the cost of benefits is subtracted from the total collected in taxes and the savings from AFDC. Net savings gives what is commonly referred to as 'the bottom line'.

These estimates indicate that if the United States had a social child support system in effect in 1983 with tax rates on noncustodial parents equal to 17 to 33 per cent of gross income depending upon the number of children (Plan 1), the government could have afforded to pay a minimum child support benefit of $3000 for the first child, $4000 for two, $4500 for three, $5000 for four, $5500 for five and $6000 for six or more children and still saved $1.0 billion – provided that the government collected 100 per cent of what noncustodial parents owed. That is to say, with what many people would consider to be reasonable child support tax rates, the government could provide a low but hardly negligible minimum benefit, reduce the poverty gap by over $5 billion, and still save 37 per cent of current AFDC costs devoted to child support eligible children.

Of course, with a different set of parameters total public subsidy costs could increase rather than decrease. Plan 2 in Table 5.2 illustrates this point. With the same tax rates but higher minimum benefits, a savings of $1.0 billion turns into a cost of $1.9 billion (see column 8). However, some of these extra costs further reduce the poverty gap. The gap for Plan 2 is 1.3 billion lower than that for Plan 1 (Compare rows 6 and 7 in column 3 of Table 5.1).

The estimates in Tables 5.1 and 5.2 are overoptimistic in that no matter how much enforcement is improved, we will not be able to obtain awards in 100 per cent of cases nor collect 100 per cent of the obligation. On the other hand, the estimates are too pessimistic in that they take no account of the increases in work effort of female heads of welfare families that will result from the improvement in work incentives. Despite these weaknesses, the results suggest that small-scale experimentation with adding social child support to our menu of social security programs is warranted. As the very least these results suggest that measurement of the as yet unmeasured benefits and costs of a social child support program is a very high research priority.

SUMMARY

The intent of government child support policy is that noncustodial parents should share the cost of raising their children. The performance of the present child support system fails to meet this goal and concomitantly leaves many children poor. Our estimates show that the antipoverty effect of the present child support system is minimal. It results in a 2 percentage point reduction in the poverty rate over the rate in the absence of a child support system.

We show, utilizing simulations, that the potential of noncustodial fathers to support their children far outweighs the performance of the present system. Our estimates show that the increased transfers possible under an alternative child support system would substantially reduce poverty for eligible children. This could result in a 57 per cent reduction in the poverty gap.

An important question left unaddressed by our analysis is the impact of an improved child support system on the economic status of noncustodial fathers. Present data do not permit the evaluation of this question, but we are developing a methodology to estimate the impact on noncustodial fathers.

Appendix

Table 5.A1 Results of OLS regression for whites and nonwhites

Dependent variable: log of annual income of husband	*Whites*	*Nonwhites*
Explanatory variables		
Age	.0621	.08476
	(.0006)	(.01829)
Age^2	−.0008707	−.00111
	(.0000808)	(.00022)
Age × Education	.00116	.00563
	(.00015)	(.00038)
Education < 9	−.1799	−.09772
	(.0438)	(.1147)
Education 9–11	−.08367	−.12788
	(.0236)	(.0647)
Education > 12	.10191	.16861
	(.02285)	(.0669)
Non-central city	.09671	.05817
	(.01961)	(.05162)
Non-SMSA	−.22725	−.16827
	(.0159)	(.0592)
2 children	.05064	.03103
	(.01693)	(.05175)
3+ children	.06684	−.04254

continued on page 84

Table 5.A1 *continued*

Dependent variable: log of annual income of husband	*Whites*	*Nonwhites*
	(.01943)	(.05567)
Northeast region	−.01481	−.17811
	(.0201)	(.0705)
South region	−.03063	−.20191
	(.01846)	(.06094)
West region	−.00087	.00297
	(.0212)	(.07271)
Income dummy	−5.5793	−5.533261
	(.06811)	(.1444)
Intercept	8.04844	7.71464
R^2	.4362	.5759
F test	605.83	116.41
Number of observations	10590.	1214.
Mean squared error	.54216	.54369
Mean of dependent variables	9.543	9.212

Note: Standard errors are in parentheses.

Table 5.A2 Regression adjusted means for marital status adjustment

	Whites	*Nonwhites*
Never married	−.68797 (50.3)	−.91063 (40.2)
Separated	−.23966 (78.7)	−.51656 (59.7)
Divorced	−.26646 (76.6)	−.37883 (68.5)

Note: Numbers in parentheses show the income of that group as a percentage of that of married men.

Notes

1. The 1982 March/April Current Population Survey provides the sample for our analysis. The April Child Support Supplement contains data representing 8.7 million families potentially eligible for child support. We excluded from our analysis 1 million families who had a child support award but were not supposed to receive child support payments in 1981. The number of potentially eligible children was tabulated by the authors from the Survey.

2. Tabulated by the authors from the US Bureau of the Census (1985) Table 1.
3. Tabulated by the authors from the US Bureau of the Census (1985) Table 1.
4. Income is assumed to be distributed log normal. Examples of earned income include wages, salary, and farm income; while examples of unearned income include pensions, workman's compensation, interest, and dividends.
5. The use of the log transformation of income creates a problem for 0 and negative incomes. Rather than exclude those cases we assigned them a small positive income ($50). A dummy variable is included to capture the effect of this.
6. A more complicated methodology was employed early on in our research which employed probit and OLS to account for selectivity bias, but the results do not differ significantly between the two methods. Therefore, we prefer the simpler OLS method. See Donald T. Oellerich, 'Regression Analysis in the Case of Non-Random Missing Data on the Dependent Variable: The Estimation of Absent Fathers' Income', in Garfinkel and Melli (1982), vol. III.
7. Consider the following simple example. Suppose we say a noncustodial father's ability to pay child support is equal to 20 per cent of his income in excess of $3000. Suppose further that we had three noncustodial fathers whose predicted mean income is $10 000, but whose individual incomes are $0, $10 000 and $20 000, respectively. If we assign each the mean, we will estimate that the three together can pay 0.2 × (10 000 − 3000) = $1400 × 3 = $4200. If we allow for variance around the mean, the first can pay nothing, the second can pay $1400 and the third can pay $3400, for a total of $4600. This problem arises whenever the normative standard used for ability to pay is a nonlinear schedule.
8. Since our tax schedules are linear in log dollars the variance of child support is equal to the variance of income. An exception is the standard with exemption regime, where we recompute the variance of the truncated distribution.
9. For example, 35 families are below poverty if the probability that a particular family is poor is 0.35 and the Census family weight is 100 (0.35 × 100 = 35). The poverty rate is calculated by summing the number of families below the poverty cutoffs and dividing by the total number of families.
10. Many of those on AFDC will leave welfare because, when combined with a bit of earnings, the child support benefit will provide them with higher income than they could achieve on welfare. Our estimates of AFDC savings are conservative in that we do not try to incorporate this work incentive effect.

References

GARFINKEL, I. and MELLI, M. (1982) *Child Support: Weaknesses of the Old and Features of a Proposed New System*, vols I, II, III (Madison, Wis.: Institute for Research on Poverty).

KRAUSE, H. O. (1981) *Child Support in America: The Legal Perspective* (Charlottesville, Va.: The Miche Co.).
MOYNIHAN, D. P. (1981) 'Welfare Reform's 1971–72 Defeat, A Historical Loss', *Journal of the Institute for Socioeconomic Studies, 6*: 1–20.
US BUREAU OF THE CENSUS, (1985) 'Child Support and Alimony: 1984', *Current Population Reports* Series P-23, No. 112.
US DEPARTMENT OF HEALTH AND HUMAN SERVICES (1984), Office of Child Support Enforcement, *Child Support Enforcement Statistics-Fiscal 1983* (June).
WEITZMAN, L. J. (1981) 'The Economics of Divorce: Social and Economic Consequences of Property, Alimony and Child Support Awards'. *UCLA Law Review, 28* (6): 1251.

6 Cost-of-Living Adjustments for Social Security Benefits: Their Impact on the Incomes of the Elderly

Sandra R. Baum and Jane Sjogren*

In 1973 Congress passed legislation requiring that Social Security benefits be adjusted annually according to changes in the Consumer Price Index (CPI). The intent of this provision was to insure that adjustments in benefits would be made on a regular basis and that Social Security recipients, most of whom were elderly and retired, would not suffer a decrease in real benefits during inflationary periods. Since 1973 the combination of rapid inflation, slow growth in real wages, unemployment and an increased elderly population has strained the Social Security system's financial resources to the point where the solvency of the Social Security system has been threatened. Recent reforms have included a one-time six-month postponement of the cost-of-living adjustment.

Concern over the system's financial status has led to consideration of several alternative means of adjusting Social Security benefits to reflect changes in the cost of living. Critics of the current system charge that the Consumer Price Index overstates increases in the cost of living for the elderly, so that the current system overcompensates them for inflation and puts an undue burden on the wage-earners whose taxes finance Social Security. Some argue that the rate of increase in Social Security benefits should simply be slowed in order to reduce the system's costs. Others argue that an index based specifically on the living costs of the elderly should be used. Another recommendation is that changes in Social Security benefits be tied to the wages of the system's working contributors.

* This research was funded by the Braitmayer Foundation and Wellesley College. The authors are indebted to Irene Walborsky and Julia Lowell for expert research assistance. We are also grateful to Saul Schwartz and the anonymous referees for valuable suggestions. Any remaining errors are our own.

Whether one views the Social Security system as a social insurance program, a mandatory retirement savings program, an earnings replacement program, or an income redistribution program, it is important to consider the impact of any modifications in the benefit determination scheme not just on the solvency of the system, but also on the over-all income distribution and incidence of poverty among the elderly. In this paper, we focus on the latter concern. We estimate the effects of alternative indexing schemes for Social Security benefits on the incomes of the elderly, giving particular attention to income distribution and poverty rates under different indexing schemes.

Briefly summarizing our findings, we conclude that proposed minor modifications in the indexing scheme for Social Security benefits would not have a large impact on the distribution of income among recipients. A relatively large decline in real benefits resulting from a significant slowdown in benefit increases would, however, measurably increase income inequality among the elderly. More striking is the finding that even a small decline in the rate of indexing would have a substantial impact on official poverty rates among the elderly. A tradeoff clearly exists between reducing the growth of the Social Security system's expenditures by slowing benefit increases and the prevalence of poverty among the elderly.

This paper consists of three sections. The first describes the incomes of older Americans in the period from 1970 to 1976, using data from the Retirement History Survey conducted by the Social Security Administration. In the second section we use these data to make quantitative estimates of the impacts of alternative indexing schemes for Social Security benefits on the incomes of the elderly and on the significance of these results for future modifications in Social Security policy.

INCOMES OF THE ELDERLY

This study uses data from the Retirement History Survey (RHS) conducted by the Social Security Administration during the 1970s. The survey is based on a nationally representative sample of Americans aged 60–65 years in 1971. For purposes of this study only respondents who remained in the survey through 1977 and who received Old Age and Survivor benefits from Social Security between 1970 and 1976 were included, yielding a sample of nearly 8000 persons.[1] As shown in Table 6.1, married men constituted the largest portion of the sample, 53 per cent in 1976.[2] Predictably, the proportions of the sample describing themselves as retired increased over time, from 24 per cent in 1970 to 60 per cent in 1976.

Median household income (in current dollars) was $8002 in 1970. It increased by 5 per cent to $8410 in 1976. Thus, household incomes of the respondents were low, representing approximately 91 per cent of median household income of the general population in 1970 and falling to 66 per cent by 1976.[3] The decrease in real income as the respondents aged and retired is evident when respondents' incomes are deflated by the CPI during that period. In real terms, median income decreased by 44 per cent. Of the three demographic groups, married men, unmarried men, and unmarried women, households headed by married men enjoyed the largest incomes. Their median income was approximately double that of unmarried men and two and a half times that of unmarried women (see Table 6.2).

Throughout the survey, the most important sources of income for RHS respondents were earnings, private and government pensions, and Old Age and Survivors benefits from Social Security (see Appendix Table 6.A1 for details on sources of respondents' income). Income from rent, interest and dividends, from public assistance (including Supplemental Security Income after 1974), Social Security Disability benefits, and from other sources (such as annuities) was not large for most respondents.

Predictably, as the cohort aged and retired, earnings became a much less important source of income; the proportion of the sample who had earnings dropped from 80 per cent in 1970 to 39 per cent in 1976. Median earnings also dropped, from $6500 to $2954 in current dollars, (see Table 6.A1) indicating either that those who continued to work did so on a substantially reduced scale or that it was primarily those with lower earnings who continued to work. Earnings of men, both married and unmarried, dropped by about half, but earnings of unmarried women who continued to work fell only 9 per cent. This is compatible with the fact that a substantially larger proportion of men were better able to maintain their incomes as they aged without working because they received various forms of pension income and received it in much larger amounts than did the women.

Old Age and Survivors benefits from Social Security became a much more important source of income for the entire group as they aged and retired. The proportion of respondents receiving Social Security benefits[4] rose from 28 per cent in 1970 to 86 per cent in 1976.

Table 6.1 Respondent characteristics

	1970					*1972*					*1974*					*1976*				
	Total	*MM*	*UM*	*MW*	*UW*	*Total*	*MM*	*UM*	*MW*	*UW*	*Total*	*MM*	*UM*	*MW*	*UW*	*Total*	*MM*	*UM*	*MW*	*UW*
Sample size[5]	7 992	5 103	789	67	2 025	7 992	[4]	[4]	[4]	[4]	7 992	4 529	718	99	2 634	7 992	4 193	804	100	2 895
% of total	100	64	10	1	25	100					100	57	9	1	33	100	53	10	1	36
% men	74					69					66					63				
% women	26					31					34					37				
Ages	60–65					62–7					64–9					66–71				
Work Status[1]																				
% working[2]	75	73	74	84	80	58	53	58	68	72	47	36	27	58	66	38	24	20	51	55
% not working[3]	24	27	26	16	20	41	47	42	32	28	52	64	73	42	34	60	76	80	49	45

Home-ownership	*Year*	*Owns*	*Rents/Other*
	1970	71%	29%
	1972	71%	29%
	1974	72%	28%
	1976	72%	28%

Key: MM – Households headed by married men
UM – Households headed by unmarried men
MW – Households headed by married women
UW – Households headed by unmarried women

Notes:
1. Totals may be less than 100 per cent because 'other' is excluded.
2. Totals include 'keeping house'.
3. Includes 'disabled'.
4. 1972 uses marital status from 1971 since 1972 marital status is not available.
5. Total numbers of respondents for 1970 and 1974 do not add to 7992 because 8 and 12 respondents did not report marital status in 1970 and 1974, respectively.

Table 6.2 Respondent incomes

	1970				*1972*				*1974*				*1976*			
	T	MM	UM	UW	T	MM	UM	UW	T	MM	UM	UW	T	MM	UM	UW
No. of recipients	7639	4974	746	1919	7572	4869	592	2111	7542	4326	693	2523	7660	4086	786	2788
Total income																
Mean ($)	8002	9967	5475	3892	8091	10104	6380	4009	8049	10502	5816	4454	8410	11212	6323	4892
Median ($)	6300	8113	4000	2815	6051	8000	4465	2900	5892	8101	4344	3233	6114	8564	4601	3540
Mean (1970 $)[a]	7478	9315	5117	3637	7036	8786	5548	3564	5791	7555	4184	3204	5357	7141	4027	3116
Median (1970 $)[a]	5888	7582	3738	2631	5262	6957	3883	2522	4239	5828	3125	2326	3913	5458	2931	2255

[a] Adjusted to constant 1970 dollars using Consumer Price Index

The fraction of total income represented by Social Security benefits was 46 per cent for married men, 59 per cent for unmarried men, and 69 per cent for unmarried women in 1976 (see Appendix Table 6.A2). For the entire sample, Social Security accounted for 50 per cent of median income by 1976, highlighting the importance of Social Security as a source of income for older Americans.

The increases in the amounts of Social Security benefits received by the RHS respondents over the course of the survey reflect several factors. As more people waited until older ages to start collecting benefits, the average benefit level increased. More significantly, all benefit levels increased substantially over the period of the survey. In January 1971, September 1972 and June 1974, increases of 10 per cent, 20 per cent, and 11 per cent, respectively, were legislated. Beginning in 1975, benefit levels were tied to the CPI and rose by 7.4 per cent in 1975 and 5.1 per cent in 1976. The distribution of income within the sample was characterized by considerable concentration at the upper end of the scale. Only 3.4 per cent of total income accrued to the lowest 20 per cent of the population, while the highest quintile received 48 per cent.[5] Over the period of the survey the share of income accruing to the lowest quintile rose relative to the third and fourth quintiles. The share of the top 20 per cent remained nearly constant. That is, as a greater proportion of the respondents retired, the gap between middle and low income respondents narrowed, while the more wealthy, many of whom were still working, were better able to maintain their relative incomes (see Appendix Table 6.A3).

These figures (and the difference between mean and median incomes) indicate that a large proportion of respondents had relatively low incomes, while a small number had incomes substantially above the national median. This distributional pattern is generally consistent among all of the demographic groups studied. As the respondents aged and retired, and as their real incomes decreased, the distribution of income among the sample became more even. This can be partially explained by the fact that inflation during the 1970s eroded the real incomes of elderly persons who receive interest, private pension and property income. Those at the bottom of the distribution, for whom indexed Social Security benefits are the main source of income, maintained real income levels. The decline in inequality is particularly evident from changes in the Atkinson Index[6] of inequality, which fell over 25 per cent for households with unmarried heads, and about 10 per cent for the entire sample (see Appendix Table 6.A3).

The incidence of poverty among the RHS cohort was slightly less than national poverty levels for the elderly in 1970.[7] Approximately one-third of unmarried women in the sample were below the poverty threshold. The incidence of poverty among unmarried men was also high, about 20 per cent. Households headed by married men were substantially better off by this measure, with a poverty rate of about 10 per cent (see Appendix Table 6.A3).

As the respondents aged the incidence of poverty decreased in each demographic group, especially among the unmarried, whose incomes were lowest. However, the poverty rate for the group as a whole increased from 16.8 per cent in 1970 to 19.4 per cent in 1976. This was a function, in part, of the changing demographics of the cohort; unmarried women with their lower incomes increased as a proportion of the cohort, while married men decreased.

In sum, the elderly Americans studied here had relatively low incomes, many of which were near the poverty threshold. The incidence of poverty was substantial. This was particularly true for unmarried women. Income distribution was unequal, reflecting the fact that a small proportion of the respondents were well off, but that most had very limited incomes. As the sample aged and retired, their real incomes decreased and they became more dependent on Social Security benefits as a source of income.

ALTERNATIVE INDEXING SCHEMES FOR SOCIAL SECURITY BENEFITS

A number of indexes have been suggested as alternatives to the CPI, which is currently used to adjust Social Security benefit levels. The intent of most proposals is to slow the increase in benefit levels, thereby slowing increases in the Social Security system's costs. The use of price indexes more appropriate to the elderly has been suggested, as has the linking of benefits to a wage-based index. Other proposals include indexing with some fraction of the CPI or the minimum of a price index and a wage index. For this study, seven alternative indexing schemes are tested. These indexes are discussed below.

Actual Social Security benefits increased more rapidly than did the CPI over the period of the RHS survey. CPI-based indexing was not instituted until 1975, and the legislated increases in Social Security benefits between 1970 and 1974 were greater than the CPI. We begin by estimating the effect that using only the CPI-U would have had on benefits had it been in effect between 1970 and 1976.

The CPI-U replaced the CPI-W in 1978 as the most widely used price index.[8] It measures changes in the price of a fixed basket of goods and services representing the consumption patterns of urban wage-earners and clerical workers, as well as salaried, unemployed, self-employed, and retired persons. The effect of this indexing scheme on Social Security benefits is compared to actual increases in benefits, to benefits had no indexing occurred, and to the effects of other indexes.

In addition to the CPI-U, two modified consumer price indexes are also tested . The first, CPI X-I, includes a housing component which reflects rental rather than purchasing costs. This index may be more appropriate for the elderly because few elderly persons buy and sell homes. This is corroborated by the fact that homeownership rates for RHS respondents were extremely stable, ranging between 70.6 per cent and 71.8 per cent over the 1970–76 period.

The second consumer price-based index, CPI-E, is one developed specifically for the elderly by Boskin and Hurd (1982). It is based on a market basket of goods and services purchased by elderly persons. All of the consumer price indexes are fixed-weight (Laspeyres) indexes.

The third price index tested is the Personal Consumption Expenditures index (PCE). It is based on national income accounts, measures the cost-of-living for all consumers, and includes some goods not covered by the CPI-U. Like the CPI X-1, the PCE uses a rental equivalent for housing costs. Unlike the other price indexes used here, the PCE is a deflator (Paasche) index, not a fixed-weight index.

The use of wage indexes instead of price indexes has been advocated on the grounds that changes in real Social Security benefits should reflect changes in the real incomes of the working population. Two wage-based indexes are tested here. The Average Hourly Earnings index (AHE) is the most commonly used wage-based index. It is based on the dollar value of wages and salaries of production and non-supervisory workers. The second wage-based index, Compensation Per Hour (CPH), is similar to the AHE but also includes the value of certain non-wage benefits.

Proposals to reduce the rate of increase of Social Security benefits through partial compensation for price increases are tested in the form of an index based on three-quarters of the change in the CPI-U (3/4 CPI).

Table 6.3 Alternative indexes

Actual increases in social security benefits (%)

January	1970	15.0
January	1971	10.0
September	1972	20.0
June	1974	11.0
June	1975	8.0
June	1976	6.4

Source: *Social Security Bulletin*, Annual Statistical Supplement, 1977–9, p. 18.

Annual percentage change of indexes

	CPI-U	*CPI-X*	*CPI-E*	*PCE*	*AHE*	*CPH*	*3/4CPI*
1970	4.8	4.5	4.9	4.4	6.6	6.7	3.6
1971	3.5	3.7	4.6	3.9	6.9	5.7	2.6
1972	3.4	3.3	3.1	3.6	7.7	7.4	2.6
1973	8.3	8.0	6.2	7.3	6.6	8.1	6.2
1974	12.2	11.1	10.2	11.0	8.3	11.0	9.2
1975	7.4	6.8	8.4	6.1	6.2	7.7	5.6
1976	5.1	5.2	6.2	4.9	7.7	8.5	3.8

Alternative social security income as a percentage of actual social security income

	CPI-U	*CPI-X*	*CPI-E*	*PCE*	*AHE*	*CPH*	*3/4CPI*	*Unindexed*
1972	0.924	0.923	0.934	0.924	0.971	0.961	0.920	0.852
1974	0.892	0.869	0.863	0.867	0.940	0.941	0.845	0.791
1976	0.934	0.896	0.896	0.886	0.939	0.977	0.846	0.624

Alternative social security income as a percentage of social security income under CPI-U indexing

	CPI-U	*CPI-X*	*CPI-E*	*PCE*	*AHE*	*CPH*	*3/4CPI*	*Unindexed*
1972	1.000	0.999	1.011	1.000	1.051	1.040	0.996	0.922
1974	1.000	0.974	0.967	0.972	1.054	1.055	0.947	0.887
1976	1.000	0.959	0.959	0.949	1.017	1.046	0.906	0.668

Note: Although Social Security cost of living adjustments are based on first quarter changes in the CPI, the figures shown here are fourth to fourth quarter changes and are based on those in the CBO report cited below to insure comparability among the different indexes.
Source: Congressional Budget Office (1981); Boskin and Hurd (1982).

Table 6.3 shows the actual benefit increases and values for all the indexes tested. The implied differences between actual benefits and payments under each alternative indexing scheme, including entirely unindexed benefits, are indicated. In addition, alternatively indexed benefits are shown as a proportion of benefits indexed to the CPI-U over the entire period.

Actual benefit increases rose most quickly, followed by wage-based, consumer price-based, and other indexing schemes. Specifically, because wages rose more rapidly than prices during most of the period of the survey, benefits would have been 2 to 6 per cent higher under wage-based indexing than under the CPI-U, while they would have been to 2 to 6 per cent lower than actual benefits. The full spread between actual benefits and the alternative indexing scheme is 8 to 11 per cent, an indication of the magnitude of savings the system might realize if it changed to a different indexing scheme.

ESTIMATES OF THE EFFECTS OF ALTERNATIVE INDEXING SCHEMES

We estimated the effects of alternative indexing schemes in several stages. These include estimates of Social Security benefits, total incomes, income distribution among the cohort, and poverty rates under the various schemes[9] (see Appendix Tables 6.A4 and 6.A5).

Mean Social Security income for respondents was $3280 in 1976; median benefits were $3072. Had benefits been linked to the CPI-U from 1970 to 1976, the mean amount in 1976 would have been $3063, and the median $2869. The impact on total income would have been to reduce the 1976 mean from $8410 to $8195, and the median from $6114 to $5908. The decline in total income would have been more marked for households headed by unmarried women: this mean 1976 income of $4892 would have been $4634 under CPI-U indexing. Median income for the group would have been $2275 instead of $2436. Linking Social Security benefits to three-quarters of the CPI would have a correspondingly greater impact on incomes.

Had CPI-U indexing been in effect over the entire period, the size distribution of income would have been only slightly more unequal than it actually was (see Appendix Table 6.A6). The same is true for all of the other indexing schemes tested, although the increase in inequality is more marked when the slowest indexing scheme, 3/4CPI, is used. Had a 3/4CPI indexing scheme begun in 1970, by 1976 the lowest quintile would have received 4.8 per cent total income, instead of the

5.1 per cent they actually received. 50.6 per cent of total income, instead of 49.1 per cent, would have accrued to the top quintile of the sample population. The results for each of the demographic groups are similar. This suggests that the redistributive impact of Social Security benefits among recipients is small relative to the existing inequalities from other income sources.

This conclusion is modified, however, by the changes in over-all inequality, as measured by the Atkinson Index (see Appendix Table 6.A7.) These results indicate more strongly that the more rapid the increase in Social Security benefits is, the more equal the distribution of income among the elderly. Had benefits been increased by three-quarters of the increase of the CPI from 1970 to 1976, the Atkinson Index of Inequality for the total elderly population would have fallen 3 per cent to 8 per cent (depending on the weight placed on inequality in the social welfare function) instead of the 9 to 12 per cent it actually fell. In other words, a decline in the rate of increase of benefits would increase income inequality among the elderly. Minor modifications of the indexing scheme, such as use of an alternative wage or price index, would have an insignificant effect, but any major reduction in real benefits would measurably reduce income equality among Social Security recipients.

The different indexing schemes would have substantial effects on the incidence of poverty among the elderly, as indicated in Table 6.4. Poverty rates among RHS respondents in 1976, when the effects of alternative indexing schemes were most evident, ranged from 19.6 per cent (AHE) to 24.1 per cent (3/4CPI) for the group as a whole, a difference of 23 per cent. The variation in poverty rates under the different schemes was highest for unmarried women, and lowest for married men, reflecting their relative dependence on Social Security benefits as a source of income. By 1976, 40.5 per cent of unmarried women would have been below the poverty level had benefits been linked to 3/4CPI since 1970. Poverty among all groups would have continued to increase as real benefit levels declined over time. The extreme effect of declining real benefits can be seen in the 51.3 per cent of unmarried women who would have fallen below the poverty level in 1976 had Social Security benefits been entirely unindexed since 1970. In sum, these estimates indicate that any indexing scheme which significantly slows the rate of increase in Social Security benefits would greatly exacerbate the incidence of poverty among the elderly.

Table 6.4 Rates of poverty for alternative social security indexing schemes (%)

Year	*Actual*	*CPI-U*	*CPI X-1*	*CPI-E*	*PCE*	*AHE*	*CPE*	*3/4CPI*	*Unindexed*
				Total population					
1970	16.8	–	–	–	–	–	–	–	–
1972	17.0	18.3	18.3	18.0	18.3	17.5	17.6	18.3	19.2
1974	18.5	21.3	21.9	22.0	21.9	20.1	20.1	22.0	25.8
1976	19.4	21.2	22.5	22.5	22.8	21.0	19.6	24.1	32.2
				Married men					
1970	8.5	–	–	–	–	–	–	–	–
1972	10.0	10.7	10.7	10.6	10.7	10.3	10.3	10.7	11.2
1974	9.2	10.7	11.1	11.2	11.2	10.0	10.0	10.7	13.7
1976	9.9	10.9	11.5	11.5	11.7	10.8	9.8	12.3	18.1
				Unmarried men					
1970	25.7	–	–	–	–	–	–	–	–
1972	19.6	20.3	20.3	20.2	20.3	19.8	19.8	20.3	20.9
1974	21.9	25.9	26.1	26.9	26.8	25.0	25.0	28.1	32.0
1976	22.8	24.3	25.1	25.1	25.6	23.9	22.8	27.6	37.9
				Unmarried women					
1970	34.8	–	–	–	–	–	–	–	–
1972	30.8	33.7	33.7	33.1	33.7	32.0	32.2	33.7	35.7
1974	33.0	37.9	38.8	38.9	38.9	35.8	35.8	39.7	44.8
1976	32.5	35.5	37.8	37.8	38.4	35.3	33.1	40.5	51.3

Notes: 1. Poverty rates are estimated according to the proportion of respondents whose simulated incomes fell below the official federal poverty income level for comparable demographic groups in a given year. It should be noted that the standard federal definition of poverty income used here is adjusted according to annual changes in the CPI.
2. Under current policy, some respondents would have become eligible for SSI had their Social Security benefits increased more slowly than the CPI. However, because SSI benefits are not large enough to raise recipients' incomes above poverty levels, the impact of SSI on these estimates is negligible.

CONCLUSIONS

Attempting to alleviate the Social Security system's difficulties by slowing the rate at which nominal benefits are adjusted for inflation has a potentially large cost in terms of the economic well-being of many elderly recipients. Social Security benefits are an important source of income to the elderly. Many older Americans receive only limited income from other sources, so the Social Security benefits they receive keep them marginally above the poverty level. The major impact of altering the current benefit indexing scheme would be to substantially increase poverty among the elderly. In addition, income inequality among the elderly would be increased. Decreasing cost-of-living increases in Social Security benefits would have an especially significant impact on the incidence of poverty among widows and other unmarried women, a demographic group whose proportionate size increases as the population ages.

The cohort studied represents 'young' older Americans. As this group ages, we can anticipate that their incomes will continue to decrease and that they will become increasingly dependent on Social Security benefits as a source of income. Thus, for the truly elderly, we can expect that decreases in real Social Security benefits will result in greater increases in poverty rates than those estimated here.

In sum, this evidence provides a strong indication that poverty among the elderly could be a significantly worsened if Social Security benefits increased more slowly than consumer prices. Increased poverty among the elderly would create greater need and eligibility for other forms of social services. In particular, it would result in greater demands on the Supplemental Security Income (SSI) program. In its current form SSI would not solve the potential poverty problem because it guarantees older Americans a minimum income which is considerably below the official poverty line. The cost of Medicaid and some other publicly supported programs would also increase.

Thus, choosing to improve the Social Security system's financial status by reducing expenditures for cost-of-living benefit increases is potentially very costly in terms of increased expenditures for other programs. It would also mean a real and significant decrease in the economic and social well-being of many older Americans.

Notes

1. This study is based on a series of four cross-sections. We used this data arrangement in order to have a sample whose demographic characteristics reflect those of the national population at comparable ages, a particularly important consideration for income distribution analysis.
2. Respondents were characterized by sex and marital status. Households headed by married women are not included in subsequent tables because they represent less that 2 per cent of the sample.
3. Median household income in the US was \$8754 in 1970 and \$12 686 in 1976 (*U.S. Statistical Abstract*, 1978, Table No. 747).

Appendix

Table 6.A1 Sources of respondents' incomes

Year	*1970*				*1972*				*1974*				*1976*			
	T	*MM*	*UM*	*UW*	*T*	*MM*	*UM*	*UW*	*T*	*MM*	*UM*	*UW*	*T*	*MM*	*UM*	*UW*
Earnings																
No. of recipients	6107	4394	526	1187	4952	3575	343	1034	3887	2677	275	935	2967	1981	237	749
% Receiving	80	88	77	62	67	73	58	49	52	62	40	37	39	48	30	27
Mean ($)	7871	9137	5647	4171	7722	8885	6526	4099	6963	8147	5454	4018	6172	7220	4939	3789
Median ($)	6500	8000	5000	3400	6000	7200	5000	3101	4400	5355	3000	2400	2954	3500	2400	2438
Private pensions (non-gov't)																
No. of recipients	767	578	76	113	1371	1025	126	220	1923	1389	182	352	2171	1503	245	423
% Receiving	28	12	10	6	19	21	21	10	25	32	26	14	28	37	31	15
Mean ($)	2107	2522	2484	1429	2210	2399	2215	1320	2355	2543	2334	1623	2623	2920	2369	1714
Median ($)	1404	1440	1662	1169	1589	1752	1741	936	1776	1812	1800	1101	1873	2100	1800	1200
Government pensions																
No. of recipients	653	407	75	171	862	555	67	240	1171	732	98	341	1272	761	113	348
% Receiving	36	8	10	9	12	11	11	11	16	17	14	14	17	19	14	14
Mean ($)	2787	3191	2484	1959	3440	3840	3443	2514	4172	4737	3825	3058	4893	5512	4986	3683
Median ($)	1950	2340	1662	1692	2577	3000	2102	2213	3048	3600	2881	2400	3673	4091	3972	3000
Public assistance																
No. of recipients	775	477	77	221	831	469	69	293	1008	463	103	442	1107	415	130	562
% Receiving	10	10	10	12	11	10	12	14	13	11	15	18	14	10	16	20
Mean ($)	852	836	988	836	1005	1084	1003	879	1304	1441	1156	1196	1465	1847	1220	1239
Median ($)	654	599	864	698	720	720	884	710	988	996	932	975	1032	1200	877	1000

Social security																
No. of recipients	2118	1124	204	790	3849	2285	298	1266	5718	3335	500	1883	6616	3641	662	2313
% Receiving	28	23	27	41	52	47	50	60	76	77	72	75	86	89	84	83
Mean ($)	1234	1364	1066	1101	1947	2199	1747	1339	2527	2939	2134	1901	3280	3940	2664	2418
Median ($)	1140	1236	929	1104	1814	2148	1729	1551	2400	2880	2156	1950	3072	3961	2713	2436
Social security disability																
No. of recipients	537	401	49	87	528	396	38	94	392	263	38	91	220	147	17	56
% Receiving	7	8	6	5	7	8	8	4	5	6	5	4	3	4	2	2
Mean ($)	1564	1677	1506	1076	1907	2029	1716	1469	2080	2201	2024	1755	2339	2502	2273	1931
Median ($)	1560	1753	1500	1033	1897	2017	1657	1622	2000	2118	1970	1788	2317	2448	2160	2053
Rent, interest, dividends																
No. of recipients	4009	2770	344	895	3981	2730	248	1003	4198	2660	322	1216	4240	2529	356	1355
% Receiving	52	56	46	47	54	49	42	48	56	61	46	48	55	62	45	49
Mean ($)	1331	1501	1170	865	1670	1890	1571	1095	1949	2327	1487	1244	2363	2870	1890	1542
Median ($)	440	473	400	337	575	600	500	420	600	720	500	422	800	1000	600	550
Other income																
No. of recipients	192	66	16	110	226	68	7	151	239	80	15	144	249	90	18	141
% Receiving	3	1	2	6	3	1	1	7	3	2	2	6	3	2	2	5
Mean ($)	1005	1191	567	958	1275	2439	241	799	1296	1957	672	994	1741	3072	1423	933
Median ($)	351	301	103	417	421	565	103	385	600	1000	479	500	500	721	305	450

Table 6.A2 Social security as percentage of total income

Year	*1970*				*1972*				*1974*				*1976*			
	T	*MM*	*UM*	*UW*	*T*	*MM*	*UM*	*UW*	*T*	*MM*	*UM*	*UW*	*T*	*MM*	*UM*	*UW*
Median benefits	18	15	23	39	30	27	39	50	40	35	48	59	50	46	59	69
Mean benefits	15	14	19	28	24	22	27	33	31	28	36	42	39	35	42	49

Table 6.A3 Income shares by quantities, poverty incidence, and Atkinson inequality index

Year	Total (%)	Married men (%)	Unmarried men (%)	Unmarried women (%)
1970				
Q1	3.4	5.0	3.3	4.1
Q2	9.1	11.2	8.4	8.5
Q3	15.8	16.5	15.2	14.5
Q4	23.7	22.9	25.0	24.7
Q5	48.0	44.5	48.0	48.1
1972				
Q1	3.8	5.0	3.9	5.0
Q2	8.9	10.7	8.8	9.7
Q3	15.1	15.9	14.0	14.3
Q4	23.2	22.7	21.8	23.3
Q5	49.1	45.7	51.5	47.7
1974				
Q1	4.5	5.8	5.4	5.8
Q2	9.1	10.8	9.9	10.2
Q3	14.7	15.5	14.9	14.6
Q4	22.5	21.9	21.6	22.4
Q5	49.2	46.0	48.2	46.9
1976				
Q1	5.1	6.2	6.3	6.8
Q2	9.2	11.2	10.2	10.9
Q3	14.6	15.4	14.6	14.6
Q4	22.0	21.1	21.3	21.7
Q5	49.1	46.1	47.7	46.1
% Under poverty line				
1970	16.8	8.5	25.7	34.8
1972	17.0	10.0	19.6	30.8
1974	18.5	9.2	21.9	33.0
1976	19.4	9.9	22.8	32.5

Atkinson inequality index

	Total		*Married men*		*Unmarried men*		*Unmarried women*	
Parameter:	e=0.5	e=0.9	e=0.5	e=0.9	e=0.5	e=0.9	e=0.5	e=0.9
1970	0.1971	0.3881	0.1520	0.3051	0.2156	0.4317	0.2045	0.4073
1972	0.1964	0.3746	0.1568	0.3071	0.2072	0.3846	0.1776	0.3491
1974	0.1850	0.3510	0.1501	0.2924	0.1675	0.3202	0.1635	0.3261
1976	0.1799	0.3418	0.1479	0.2880	0.1552	0.2903	0.1536	0.3111

Note: Higher values indicate increased inequality.

Table 6.A4 Social security income – alternative indexing ($)

	Actual	*CPI-U*	*CPI X-1*	*CPI-E*	*PCE*	*AHE*	*CPH*	*3/4 CPI*	*Unindexed*
Total population									
1972									
Mean	1947	1798	1797	1818	1798	1889	1870	1790	1657
Median	1814	1673	1673	1693	1675	1760	1741	1667	1544
1974									
Mean	2527	2254	2196	2182	2191	2376	2378	2071	1816
Median	2400	2141	2086	2072	2081	2257	2259	1967	1725
1976									
Mean	3280	3063	2938	2940	2907	3081	3204	2776	2047
Median	3072	2869	2752	2754	2723	2886	3001	2600	1918
Married men									
1972									
Mean	2199	2033	2031	2055	2033	2136	2113	2023	1873
Median	2148	1985	1983	2007	1985	2086	2064	1976	1830
1974									
Mean	2939	2622	2554	2537	2548	2763	2765	2408	2113
Median	2880	2649	2503	2486	2497	2708	2710	2360	2070
1976									
Mean	3940	3679	3529	3532	3492	3701	3849	3335	2459
Median	3961	3699	3548	3551	3511	3721	3870	3353	2473

Unmarried men									
1972									
Mean	1747	1615	1613	1633	1615	1697	1679	1607	1488
Median	1729	1597	1596	1015	1597	1678	1631	1590	1472
1974									
Mean	2134	1904	1854	1842	1850	2006	2008	1749	1534
Median	2156	1923	1873	1861	1869	2027	2028	1767	1550
1976									
Mean	2664	2487	2386	2388	2361	2502	2602	2255	1663
Median	2713	2533	2430	2431	2404	2548	2650	2296	1693
Unmarried women									
1972									
Mean	1539	1422	1421	1438	1422	1494	1478	1415	1311
Median	1551	1433	1432	1449	1433	1506	1490	1426	1321
1974									
Mean	1901	1696	1653	1642	1649	1788	1790	1558	1337
Median	1950	1739	1695	1683	1690	1833	1835	1598	1402
1976									
Mean	2418	2258	2166	2167	2143	2271	2362	2047	1509
Median	2436	2275	2182	2184	2159	2289	2380	2062	1521

Table 6.A5 Total household income – alternative indexing for social security ($)

	Actual	*CPI-U*	*CPI X-1*	*CPI-E*	*PCE*	*AHE*	*CPH*	*3/4 CPI*
Total population								
1972								
Mean	8091	8015	8014	8025	8015	8062	8052	8011
Median	6051	5980	5977	6000	5980	6000	6000	5976
1974								
Mean	8049	7845	7802	7791	7798	7936	7938	7757
Median	5892	5621	5568	5553	5563	5742	5743	5513
1976								
Mean	8410	8195	8086	8088	8059	8211	8319	7944
Median	6114	5908	5772	5776	5736	5928	6040	5620
Married men								
1972								
Mean	10104	10024	10023	10035	10024	10074	10063	10020
Median	8000	7947	7945	7971	7947	8000	8000	7940
1974								
Mean	10502	10263	10212	10199	10207	10370	10372	10160
Median	8101	7810	7742	7726	7736	7978	7982	7697
1976								
Mean	11212	10793	10927	10795	10760	10947	11097	10619
Median	8569	8047	8192	8051	8010	8213	8367	7852

Unmarried men								
1972								
Mean	6380	6313	6314	6323	6314	6355	6346	6310
Median	4465	4369	4370	4384	4370	4422	4409	4368
1974								
Mean	5816	5652	5616	5608	5335	5454	5455	5580
Median	4344	4174	4135	4134	3963	4116	4117	4089
1977								
Mean	6353	6032	6119	6034	5988	6111	6197	5920
Median	4601	4336	4414	4337	4465	4581	4686	4209
Unmarried women								
1972								
Mean	4099	4029	4030	4037	4030	4073	4063	4026
Median	2900	2800	2800	2809	2800	2856	2842	2796
1974								
Mean	4454	4302	4270	4266	4266	4370	4371	4286
Median	3233	3070	3018	3012	3013	3140	3141	3016
1976								
Mean	4892	4634	4712	4635	4591	4701	4770	4502
Median	3540	3248	3343	3249	3205	3330	3432	3102

continued on page 108

Table 6.A5 *continued*

Lowest and highest adjusted median incomes as a percent of CPI-U adjusted median incomes:

Total	*Lowest*	*Highest*
1972	100.0	101.2
1974	98.1	102.2
1976	95.1	102.2
Married men		
1972	100.0	100.7
1974	98.9	102.2
1976	97.5	104.0
Unmarried men		
1972	100.0	101.2
1974	97.9	99.9
1976	97.0	91.9
Unmarried women		
1972	99.8	101.6
1974	98.1	101.9
1976	95.5	105.7

Table 6.A6 Income shares by quintiles – alternative indexing schemes (%)

	Actual	*CPI-U*	*CPI X-1*	*CPI-E*	*PCE*	*AHE*	*CPI*	*3/4 CPI*
Total population								
1972								
Q1	3.8	3.7	3.7	3.7	3.7	3.7	3.7	3.7
Q2	8.9	8.7	8.7	8.9	8.7	8.8	8.8	8.7
Q3	15.1	15.0	15.0	15.0	15.0	15.0	15.0	15.0
Q4	23.2	23.2	23.2	23.2	23.2	23.2	23.2	23.2
Q5	49.1	49.5	49.5	49.4	49.5	49.2	49.3	49.5
1974								
Q1	4.5	4.3	4.3	4.2	4.3	4.4	4.4	4.2
Q2	9.1	8.8	8.7	8.7	8.7	8.9	8.9	8.6
Q3	14.7	14.4	14.3	14.3	14.3	14.5	14.5	14.3
Q4	22.5	22.5	22.5	22.5	22.5	22.5	22.5	22.5
Q5	49.2	50.1	50.2	50.3	50.3	49.7	49.7	50.4
1976								
Q1	5.1	5.0	4.9	4.9	4.9	5.0	5.0	4.8
Q2	9.2	9.0	8.8	8.8	8.8	9.0	9.1	8.7
Q3	14.6	14.5	14.3	14.3	14.3	14.5	14.6	14.2
Q4	22.0	21.9	21.8	21.8	21.8	21.9	22.0	21.8
Q5	49.1	49.7	50.1	50.1	50.2	49.7	49.3	50.6
Married men								
1972								
Q1	5.0	4.9	4.9	4.9	4.9	4.9	4.9	4.9
Q2	10.7	10.6	10.6	10.6	10.6	10.7	10.7	10.6

continued on page 110

Table 6.A6 *continued*

	Actual	*CPI-U*	*CPI X-1*	*CPI-E*	*PCE*	*AHE*	*CPI*	*3/4 CPI*
Q3	15.9	15.8	15.9	15.9	15.9	15.9	15.9	15.8
Q4	22.7	22.7	22.7	22.7	22.7	22.7	22.7	22.7
Q5	45.7	46.0	46.0	46.0	46.0	45.8	45.9	46.0
1974								
Q1	5.8	5.5	5.5	5.5	5.5	5.7	5.7	5.4
Q2	10.8	10.5	10.4	10.4	10.4	10.7	10.7	10.4
Q3	15.5	15.2	15.2	15.2	15.2	15.3	15.3	15.2
Q4	21.9	21.9	21.9	21.9	21.9	21.9	21.9	21.9
Q5	46.0	46.8	46.9	47.0	47.0	46.4	46.4	47.1
1976								
Q1	6.2	6.0	5.9	5.9	5.9	6.0	6.1	5.8
Q2	11.2	11.0	10.8	10.8	10.8	11.0	11.1	10.6
Q3	15.4	15.2	15.1	15.1	15.1	15.2	15.3	14.9
Q4	21.1	21.1	21.1	21.1	21.1	21.1	21.1	21.1
Q5	46.1	46.7	47.1	47.1	47.2	46.7	46.3	47.6
Unmarried men								
1972								
Q1	3.9	3.8	3.8	3.8	3.8	3.9	3.9	3.8
Q2	8.8	8.6	8.6	8.6	8.6	8.7	8.7	8.6
Q3	14.0	13.9	13.9	13.9	13.9	14.0	14.0	13.9
Q4	21.8	21.8	21.8	21.8	21.8	21.8	21.8	21.8
Q5	51.5	51.9	51.9	51.8	51.9	51.6	51.7	51.9
1974								
Q1	5.4	5.2	5.2	5.1	5.1	5.3	5.3	5.1
Q2	9.9	9.5	9.4	9.4	9.4	9.7	9.7	9.3

Q3	14.9	14.7	14.6	14.6	14.6	14.8	14.8	14.5
Q4	21.6	21.4	21.4	21.4	21.4	21.6	21.6	21.5
Q5	48.2	49.1	49.3	49.4	49.4	48.7	48.7	50.0
1976								
Q1	6.3	6.1	6.0	6.0	6.0	6.1	6.2	5.9
Q2	10.2	10.0	9.8	9.8	9.8	10.0	10.1	9.6
Q3	14.6	14.4	14.3	14.3	14.2	14.4	14.5	14.1
Q4	21.3	21.2	21.2	21.2	21.2	21.2	21.3	21.1
Q5	47.7	48.3	48.7	48.7	48.8	48.3	47.9	49.3
Unmarried women								
1972								
Q1	5.0	4.9	4.9	4.9	4.9	5.0	5.0	4.9
Q2	9.7	9.4	9.4	9.4	9.4	9.5	9.5	9.4
Q3	14.3	14.1	14.1	14.2	14.1	14.3	14.2	14.1
Q4	23.3	23.3	23.3	23.3	23.3	23.3	23.3	23.3
Q5	47.7	48.3	48.3	48.2	48.3	47.9	48.0	48.3
1974								
Q1	5.8	5.6	5.5	5.5	5.5	5.7	5.7	5.5
Q2	10.2	9.8	9.7	9.7	9.7	10.0	10.0	9.6
Q3	14.6	14.3	14.2	14.2	14.2	14.5	14.5	14.2
Q4	22.4	22.3	22.3	22.3	22.3	22.4	22.4	22.3
Q5	46.9	48.0	48.2	48.3	48.2	47.5	47.5	48.5
1976								
Q1	6.8	6.7	6.6	6.6	6.6	6.7	6.8	6.5
Q2	10.8	10.6	10.4	10.4	10.4	10.6	10.7	10.2
Q3	14.6	14.3	14.2	14.2	14.2	14.4	14.5	14.0
Q4	21.7	21.7	21.6	21.6	21.6	21.6	21.7	21.6
Q5	46.1	47.8	47.2	47.2	47.3	46.7	46.3	47.7

Table 6.A7 Atkinson index of inequality under alternative indexing schemes

	Actual	*CPI-U*	*CPI X-1*	*CPI-E*	*PCE*	*AHE*	*CPH*	*3/4 CPI*	*Unindexed*
1970									
ε = .5	.1971	–	–	–	–	–	–	–	–
ε = .9	.3881	–	–	–	–	–	–	–	–
1972									
ε = .5	.1964	.1998	.1998	.1993	.1998	.1977	.1981	.1999	.2032
ε = .9	.3746	.3796	.3796	.3789	.3796	.3764	.3771	.3799	.3848
1974									
ε = .5	.1850	.1902	.1913	.1916	.1914	.1878	.1878	.1926	.1997
ε = .9	.3510	.3589	.3607	.3611	.3608	.3552	.3552	.3626	.3737
1976									
ε = .5	.1799	.1846	.1875	.1874	.1882	.1842	.1815	.1914	.2131
ε = .9	.3418	.3480	.3519	.3518	.3528	.3475	.3439	.3572	.3867
Married men									
1970									
ε = .5	.1520	–	–	–	–	–	–	–	–
ε = .9	.3051	–	–	–	–	–	–	–	–
1972									
ε = .5	.1568	.1590	.1591	.1587	.1590	.1576	.1579	.1592	.1614
ε = .9	.3071	.3107	.3107	.3102	.3107	.3084	.3089	.3109	.3144
1974									
ε = .5	.1501	.1513	.1516	.1516	.1516	.1508	.1508	.1518	.1535
ε = .9	.2924	.2948	.2953	.2955	.2954	.2937	.2936	.2959	.2993
1976									
ε = .5	.1479	.1514	.1536	.1535	.1541	.1511	.1491	.1565	.1714
ε = .9	.2880	.2930	.2960	.2960	.2968	.2926	.2897	.3002	.3219

Unmarried men									
1970									
ε = .5	.2156	–	–	–	–	–	–	–	–
ε = .9	.4317	–	–	–	–	–	–	–	–
1972									
ε = .5	.2072	.2109	.2110	.2104	.2109	.2086	.2091	.2112	.2148
ε = .9	.3846	.3897	.3897	.3890	.3897	.3865	.3871	.3900	.3950
1974									
ε = .5	.1675	.1686	.1688	.1689	.1689	.1681	.1681	.1691	.1706
ε = .9	.3202	.3224	.3230	.3231	.3230	.3214	.3214	.3235	.3268
1976									
ε = .5	.1552	.1604	.1636	.1636	.1644	.1599	.1570	.1681	.1924
ε = .9	.2903	.2975	.3019	.3018	.3030	.2968	.2927	.3080	.3423
Unmarried women									
1970									
ε = .5	.2045	–	–	–	–	–	–	–	–
ε = .9	.4073	–	–	–	–	–	–	–	–
1972									
ε = .5	.1776	.1818	.1818	.1812	.1818	.1791	.1797	.1820	.1862
ε = .9	.3491	.3548	.3549	.3540	.3548	.3512	.3520	.3552	.3609
1974									
ε = .5	.1635	.1642	.1643	.1644	.1643	.1639	.1639	.1645	.1654
ε = .9	.3261	.3279	.3283	.3284	.3284	.3271	.3271	.3288	.3314
1976									
ε = .5	.1536	.1576	.1601	.1601	.1608	.1573	.1550	.1636	.1838
ε = .9	.3111	.3161	.3913	.3192	.3201	.3157	.3128	.3238	.3505

Note: 1. Higher values represent greater insecurity. 2. ε = measure of inequality.

4. Hereinafter, Social Security benefits refers only to Old Age and Survivor's benefits. Disability benefits are a separate category of income.
5. We have chosen to focus on inequality of income distribution among older Americans rather than on their incomes relative to the general population for two reasons. First, an inter-generational comparison obscures the impacts of life-cycle changes on income distribution (Paglin, 1975). Secondly, relative income positions are an important indicator of well-being within the elderly cohort.
6. For a complete discussion of the Atkinson Index of Inequality see Atkinson (1970). The measure can be computed with different parameters to represent different social welfare functions. Higher values of ε suggest greater weight on inequality at the bottom of the distribution. The two values of ε used here, ε × 0.5 and ε × 0.9, generate results comparable to other commonly used measures of inequality.
7. Poverty income levels for the elderly during the period of the survey were:

	Two-person Household	*One-person Household*	
	Male head ($)	*Male head ($)*	*Female head ($)*
1970	2349	1879	1855
1972	2734	2025	2000
1974	2984	2387	2357
1976	3447	2758	2722

During this period, national poverty rates among the elderly were:

Year	*Age 60 +*	*Age 65 +*
1970	21.3%	24.6%
1976	12.9%	14.1%

Sources: US Department of Commerce Statistical Abstract (1974) Table No. 632; (1977) Table No. 733; (1978) Table No. 767; (1980) Table No. 770; (1981) Table No. 744;
Note: RHS respondents were younger than the general elderly population.

8. Social Security benefits continue to be linked to the CPI-W. The movement of the two indexes has been very similar.
9. In computing alternative benefits, benefits received were deflated by actual increases and recalculated from a 1970 base using the alternative indexing schemes.

References

ATKINSON, A. B. (1970) 'On the Measurement of Inequality', *Journal of Economic Theory*, 2: 244–63.
BOSKIN, M. and HURD, M. D. (1982) 'Are Inflation Rates Different for the Elderly?' Working Paper, National Bureau for Economic Research (Stanford, Ca.).
CONGRESSIONAL BUDGET OFFICE, (1981) *Indexing with the Consumer Price Index: Problems and Alternatives* (Washington, D.C.: Government Printing Office)
PAGLIN, M. (1975) 'The Measurement and Trend of Inequality: A Basic Revision'. *American Economic Review*, 65: 548–609.
US DEPARTMENT OF COMMERCE (1974, 1977, 1978, 1980, 1981) *Statistical Abstract of the U.S.*

7 Distributional Analyses of Three Deficit Reduction Options Affecting Social Security Cash Benefits

Frank J. Sammartino and
Richard A. Kasten*

INTRODUCTION

Prompted by concerns with projected large and rising federal budget deficits, in the spring of 1985 Congress considered a number of options for either reducing or taxing back a portion of cash benefit payments to the elderly and disabled. Although the budget resolution passed by Congress at the end of those deliberations included none of those options, they may be reconsidered in the future if the budget deficit remains high.

While discussing potential changes in total federal outlays and revenues, the participants were concerned with possible effects on the distribution of after-tax incomes. In this paper we compare the distributional impacts of three deficit reduction proposals involving Social Security cash benefits: (1) reducing automatic cost-of-living adjustments in benefit payments, (2) eliminating the income thresholds below which benefits are not taxable, and (3) increasing the maximum percentage of benefits includable in taxable income.[1] To focus exclusively on distributional questions, we consider variants of the three proposals that achieve a roughly equal one-year reduction in outlays or increase in revenues.

In addition to presenting these distributional results, in the appendix we discuss at length the methodological problems involved in

* This paper was written prior to passage of the Tax Reform Act of 1986. References to current tax law in the text and the results reported in the tables do not reflect changes made by that act. The views expressed in this paper are those of the authors and do not represent the position of the Congressional Budget Office.

making necessary adjustments to existing data to simulate the proposals. Particularly at issue are the strengths and weaknesses of using data from the annual March income supplement to the Current Population Survey (CPS) to simulate the effects of policy options on the distribution of after-tax incomes. We conclude that despite problems with the data, the CPS can be used effectively for analysis of certain options.

Section 2 presents some background on Social Security cash benefit payments and specifies the three deficit reduction options. Section 3 presents a comparison of the simulated distributional results. The appendix discusses the methodology used to simulate the distributional impacts of these options.

DEFICIT REDUCTION OPTIONS

In the fiscal year 1985 estimated outlays for Social Security cash benefits were $185 billion, 33 per cent of estimated non-defense and non-interest federal outlays in that year. Spending for Social Security is projected to rise by over 37 per cent during the next six years reaching $254 billion by fiscal year 1990. In addition to direct outlays, estimated foregone tax revenue, because of the partial exclusion of Social Security benefits from taxable income, was $18 billion in fiscal year 1985. This tax expenditure, which will grow more slowly than direct spending, is projected to reach $22 billion by fiscal year 1990.[2]

Not only the relative size of Social Security expenditures but their projected growth makes the program a likely candidate for deficit reduction options. Because Social Security is an indexed entitlement program, cash benefits will rise automatically over time. Some growth will occur as more people become entitled to retirement and disability benefits and as the average benefit for new retirees increases, reflecting higher lifetime earnings for each succeeding generation. However, in the short run most of the increase in benefits will come from the annual automatic cost-of-living adjustment (COLA). Thus, one way to achieve immediate and substantial reductions in spending compared with current law is to reduce or eliminate future COLAs.

The first option we consider is completely eliminating the Social Security COLA for one year. This action would not reduce nominal benefits for any recipients but would permanently reduce real benefits for all currently eligible beneficiaries. Unless a corresponding reduction were made to the benefit formula that will determine the benefits for future retirees, future Social Security recipients would not suffer the same reduction in benefits. Without this corresponding reduction, eliminating one COLA would reduce aggregate benefits by about the same amount in each year in the near future. The number of beneficiaries affected would fall over time but the average amount by which their benefits would be reduced would grow at the same rate as future COLAs. Eventually savings would fall to zero when all persons who were eligible for benefits at the time the COLA was eliminated for that single year had died.

As an alternative to eliminating the COLA for one year, an equivalent deficit reduction could be achieved by reducing the tax expenditure from the partial exclusion of Social Security benefits from adjusted gross income (AGI). Under current law taxpayers must include in AGI up to one-half of their benefits if the sum of their adjusted gross income, non-taxable interest income, and one-half of benefits exceeds a threshold level of \$25 000 for single taxpayers, \$32 000 for married taxpayers filing joint returns, and \$0 for married taxpayers filing separate returns. Because these thresholds are not adjusted for increases in the level of consumer prices, more benefits will become subject to taxation over time. However, in the near term most benefits will remain tax exempt. The amount of benefits subject to taxation can be increased, and hence the tax expenditures reduced, by either lowering the thresholds above which Social Security benefits must be included in gross income, or increasing the maximum percentage of benefits subject to tax.

The two tax options we consider are to (1) eliminate the taxing thresholds and (2) tax up to a maximum of 85 per cent of benefits. To make the second tax option have about the same one-year effect on the federal deficit as the COLA freeze and the first tax option, the second tax option reduces the taxing thresholds to \$12 000 and \$18 000 – the levels now used to determine the taxable part of unemployment insurance compensation – in addition to increasing the maximum taxable percentage of benefits. The first tax option would reduce tax expenditures by a declining amount in each year compared to current law, because current law taxing thresholds will decline in real dollars over time, increasing the portion of total Social Security benefits subject to income taxation. In the long run the first tax option and current law tax treatment of benefits would have similar revenue effects. It is not possible, *a priori*, to say whether the reduction in tax expenditures from the second tax option would increase or decrease in future years. The proposed thresholds under option two also would decline in real dollars over time. The change in tax revenues would depend on the distribution of Social Security benefits in the income range between current law and the proposed taxing thresholds as both thresholds fell in real terms. A brief discussion of these proposals, as well as of eliminating one year's COLA, follows.

Reducing automatic cost-of-living adjustments

Automatic cost-of-living adjustments were first paid in July 1975. The legislation authorizing these adjustments was passed as part of the 1972 Social Security Amendments. Two primary considerations motivated the decision to provide automatic increases. The first was an intent to maintain the real level of benefit payments. Up until the late 1960s statutory increases in benefits roughly kept pace with increases in consumer prices. However, there were substantial lags in the adjustment of benefits to changes in prices. Between 1940 and 1950 consumer prices grew by 72 per cent, yet benefit levels remained unchanged until September 1950 when they were increased by approximately 77 per cent. Similarly, after two real increases in benefits during the early 1950s, benefits rose by 29 per cent while consumer prices rose by 27 per cent between 1954 and February 1968. Yet the benefit increases came in three steps in 1959, 1965 and 1968, lagging behind the increase in prices.

Secondly, automatic increases were also a way to limit large *ad hoc* benefit increases. Between 1968 and 1972 Social Security benefits grew by 52 per cent, compared to a 23 per cent increase in consumer prices over the same period. A good part of the benefit increase came from a 20 per cent increase in September 1972 that was passed as part of the 1972 Amendments.

The way in which benefits were indexed by the 1972 Amendments and the way in which *ad hoc* increases had been provided in the 1950s and 1960s resulted in rising real benefit levels over time. Both benefits for current recipients and the benefit formula that determined initial benefit levels for new retirees were increased by the same factor. Absent any increases in the benefit formula, benefits for new retirees would have grown over time reflecting the higher earnings of each succeeding generation. During the highly inflationary period of the mid 1970s, indexing the benefit formula compounded the effect of higher earnings levels causing initial benefits to grow much faster than anticipated. Between 1972 and 1978 the real dollar value of the maximum retirement benefit payable to men retiring at age 65 grew by 40 per cent. The Social Security Amendments of 1977 separated the way in which the benefit formula and benefits for currently entitled beneficiaries were indexed.

The Social Security Amendments of 1983 made further changes in the cost-of-living adjustment, postponing the July 1983 increase until January 1984, and changing the effective date for all future increases from July to January.

Eliminating automatic cost-of-living adjustments in benefits for one year would substantially reduce federal spending while spreading the burden of the benefit reduction over many people. Over the period 1985 to 1990 CBO projects the annual cost-of-living increase to average 4.6 per cent. In January 1985 average monthly benefits were $450 for a retired worker and $780 for a retired couple. Missing a 4.6 per cent increase in benefits would cost the average retired worker $21 per month and the average retired couple $36 per month.

Those who favor a COLA freeze note that many of the retirees who would suffer these losses currently receive relatively high benefits as a result of the compounded indexing of initial benefits during the mid-1970s. Moreover, these same retirees continued to receive full cost-of-living increases during the late 1970s and early 1980s during a period when average real wages were falling. A COLA freeze would thus more equally distribute some of the economic burden that so far has fallen primarily on current workers. Finally, it is argued that the Supplemental Security Income (SSI) program, a means-tested income support program for the elderly and disabled, would protect low income Social Security recipients from undue hardships due to a COLA freeze.

Opponents of a COLA freeze argue that the youngest and oldest of current recipients did not benefit from the compounded indexing of benefits during the mid 1970s. In addition, they contend that many recipients of Social Security are wholly or primarily dependent on their benefits and would have to reduce their standard of living if no COLA were paid. They argue further that it is not reasonable to expect SSI to protect many low income recipients. SSI does not now protect many poor or near poor beneficiaries because program income eligibility levels are below the poverty line in most states, asset eligibility limits are relatively low, and many eligible persons decline to participate.

Changing the income tax treatment of social security benefits[3]

Benefits from the Old Age, Survivors, and Disability Insurance (OASDI) program first became taxable in 1984. The income tax status of Social Security benefits was not addressed in the law that created the OASI program in 1935. Benefits derived their tax exempt status from administrative rulings by the Internal Revenue Service in 1938 and 1941.[4] The IRS held that benefits were a form of public assistance in the nature of gratuities or gifts, and thus exempt from taxation. There was little interest in changing the tax exempt status of benefits as long as income tax rates and benefits remained low.

In the 1960s both the Kennedy and Johnson administrations advanced proposals that would have subjected some portion of Social Security benefits to taxation. Congress did not act on either proposal. In the late 1970s and early 1980s, three of the four major commissions reporting on the Social Security program recommended some limited taxation of Social Security benefits, culminating with the recommendations of the National Commission on Social Security Reform in 1983, which became the basis for the 1983 Social Security Amendments.

Congress made two choices in adopting the recommendations of the National Commission for taxing Social Security benefits. The first was to limit the maximum percentage of benefits taxable to 50 per cent, while the second was to tax the benefits only of recipients with incomes above certain threshold levels.

Maximum taxable percentage of benefits

Taxing less than 100 per cent of Social Security benefits is consistent with the current tax treatment of public and private pension plans. Current tax law requires pensioners to include all pension benefits in taxable income except for an amount equal to the employee's direct contribution. If the employee's contribution can be recouped within three years after the beginning of benefit receipt, the three-year rule must be used which defers taxes until the contribution is recovered. Otherwise the general rule applies under which a percentage of each year's benefit, equal to the ratio of the employee's total contributions to total expected benefits, is excluded from taxable income.

In choosing to tax only a maximum of one-half of Social Security benefits, Congress acceded to the commonly-held notion that employees pay for one-half of benefits. However, because both for current and future retirees employee contributions actually account for a much smaller percentage of benefits, many analysts argue that more than 50 per cent of benefits should be taxable.

For current Social Security retirees, lifetime employee payroll taxes are estimated to be less than ten per cent of expected lifetime benefits. This is true even for retirees who earned the maximum amount of covered earnings in every year of employment and hence have paid the maximum amount of payroll taxes. The low ratio of lifetime employee payroll taxes to lifetime expected benefits is reflected in the short payback period necessary to recoup past employee contributions. For a beneficiary retiring at age 65, lifetime employee payroll taxes are recouped in much less than the maximum years allowed under the three-year rule (Congressional Research Service, 1982). Considering only the portion of taxes used to finance retirement and survivor benefits, workers who earned the maximum covered earnings in every year of employment can recover their payroll taxes in 17 months or 11 months if a dependent benefit is also received by their non-working spouse.[5] The payback period is even shorter for workers with less than maximum lifetime covered earnings. Workers who earned the average of covered wages in every year of employment would need only 13 months to recover all their contributions, while workers who always earned the federal minimum wage would recover all employee payroll taxes in 10 months.

The ratio of contributions to benefits and corresponding payback periods will increase for future retirees. By the year 2000, the payback period for a maximum earner should rise to approximately 5 years, while the ratio of lifetime employee payroll tax contributions to lifetime benefits is projected to be almost 12 per cent. Yet even when this ratio rises to its maximum level, which should occur around the year 2030, it still will not surpass 15 per cent. After 2030 the ratio of contributions to benefits is projected to decline as continuing improvements in mortality extend the expected number of retirement years.

The differences in payback periods and the ratio of lifetime payroll taxes to expected lifetime benefits for workers with different lifetime covered earnings reflect the redistributive nature of Social Security benefits. Within any particular cohort, the ratio of benefits to taxes is always lower for workers with higher lifetime earnings. If Social Security benefits were treated exactly as private pension benefits for purposes of taxation, beneficiaries with higher benefits would exclude a higher percentage of their lifetime benefits from taxation. This would offset some of the redistributive effects of taxing benefits, which can be viewed as appropriate or inappropriate tax policy depending upon whether one believes that there is excessive or insufficient redistribution through the tilt in the benefit formula.

An alternative that would maintain the redistributive effect of the benefit structure is to set the same payback period (or under the general rule, the same exclusion percentage) for all beneficiaries. Choosing the maximum period, corresponding to the number of months needed for recoupment by lifetime maximum earners, would insure that no retiree would pay taxes on benefits directly attributable to past employee payroll tax contributions.

Current projections suggest that 15 per cent would be an appropriate upper bound to the percentage of benefits excluded from taxable income. Including 85 per cent of benefits in taxable income would be more generous than the tax treatment of contributory pensions for all current Social Security recipients and would assure that even the highest earners among retirees in the twenty-first century would not pay income taxes on the part of their benefits equal to their past contributions.

However, supporters of the current tax treatment of benefits argue that a 50 per cent exclusion is necessary to achieve an analogous outcome to the way most pension benefits actually are treated. Private pensions with employee contributions are rare. Most plans are non-contributory or, in the case of 401-K pension plans to which both employers and employees contribute, employee contributions are tax exempt. While benefits from these plans are fully taxable, participants enjoy the benefit of collecting tax-deferred compound interest on these contributions. Achieving a similar outcome in the tax treatment of Social Security would require that not only the percentage of benefits equal to direct employee payroll tax contributions, but also the percentage attributable to the implicit interest on these contributions be tax exempt. While there is no direct interest component to Social Security benefits, the excess of expected lifetime benefits over the sum of actual employer and employee payroll tax contributions can be thought of in this way. Because lifetime employee and employer contributions essentially are equal, excluding 50 per cent of benefits from taxation would exempt the employee share of contributions and the interest attributable to those contributions from taxation.

Tax-exempt income thresholds

In choosing to tax the benefits only of recipients with incomes above certain threshold levels, Congress followed the model established by the tax treatment of unemployment insurance benefits. While unemployment compensation was the only transfer payment included in taxable income prior to the 1983 Amendments, tax theorists have argued that this treatment should be extended to other wage replacement transfer payments as well.

The case for taxing transfer payments rests on both horizontal and vertical equity criteria. Excluding transfers from taxable income causes identical families with equal incomes to pay unequal taxes if one family receives more income in the form of tax exempt transfer payments. On vertical grounds, families with unequal incomes but with equal amounts of tax exempt transfer income receive unequal advantages from the tax exclusion which is worth more to the family in the higher marginal tax bracket.

These arguments suggest that wage replacement transfer payments of all recipients should be taxable. Proponents of eliminating the income thresholds below which Social Security benefits are tax-exempt contend that there are sufficient other protections in the tax system for low-income recipients. First, the tax system itself is progressive and thus the redistributive character of benefits would be increased if benefits were subject to taxation. Secondly, the combined effect of the extra personal exemption for the elderly and the zero bracket amount, both of which are indexed to changes in consumer prices beginning with the 1985 tax year, and the tax credit for the elderly or disabled would keep most low-income recipients from paying income taxes even if the tax-exempt income thresholds were eliminated.[6]

For example, in 1985 single persons age 65 or older could have adjusted gross income (AGI) up to $4470 before any of their income was taxable, while a couple could have AGI up to $7700 before any of their income exceeded the tax-entry level. If half of all Social Security benefits were included in adjusted gross income, elderly single persons with no other gross income would not pay income taxes for 1985 unless they had total benefits in excess of $9552. Elderly couples with no other gross income would not pay income taxes unless their total benefits exceeded $15 400.[7] These benefit levels are well above the average Social Security benefits for 1985 which were about $5400 for a single retiree and $9400 for a retired couple. An elderly individual with average benefits could have $4629 of non-Social Security gross income without paying any taxes, while an elderly couple with average benefits could have $6150 in other gross income and owe no taxes.

Proponents of maintaining income thresholds argue that Social Security benefits should retain their tax-exempt status for moderate-, as well as for low-income, families. Even fully tax-exempt benefits replace less than 100 per cent of post-tax pre-retirement earnings. They argue that reducing replacement rates by taxing benefits is acceptable only for recipients with sufficient other income.

Proponents of thresholds argue further that families already retired or just about to retire have planned for their retirement under the assumption that benefits would not be taxable. Retirees have limited opportunity to supplement existing sources of retirement income and thus would find it difficult to adjust if their disposable income were reduced.

RESULTS OF THE SIMULATIONS

The simulations of the three options were performed using data from the March 1985 (calendar year 1984 incomes) Current Population Survey. These data were adjusted for underreporting of income and income and expenditure items necessary for tax simulations, but not available from the CPS, were imputed from tax return data. A complete description of the adjustment and imputation methods is presented in the appendix. To simulate a one-year elimination of the cost-of-living increase in Social Security benefits, benefits for 1984 were reduced to 96.6 per cent of the reported amount, reflecting the absence of the 3.5 per cent COLA paid to beneficiaries in January 1984.[8] The two tax simulations, reducing the Social Security tax thresholds to zero and increasing the maximum taxable percentage of benefits from 50 to 85 per cent, while reducing the thresholds to the levels used for unemployment insurance, were also simulated for 1984 and thus reflect changes in tax liabilities for that year.

The analysis partially reflected the effects that the COLA option would have had in expanding eligibility under means-tested cash transfer programs, primarily SSI, assuming that the scheduled COLA for SSI was maintained. Benefit increases were simulated for current recipients of these programs to make up for reduced Social Security benefits, but changes in the number of SSI participants were not. The results also reflect lower tax payments for some families whose benefits were reduced.

Tables 7.1 to 7.3 show the distributional consequences of the three policy changes. The tables show the number of families and individuals with Social Security benefits who would have had a loss in disposable income relative to actual law and the size of the losses for those who would have lost. The effects are shown for families by their level of disposable income under actual 1984 policy. Disposable income is total cash income, including transfer payments and capital gains, minus Social Security payroll taxes and federal individual income taxes, including income taxes paid on Social Security benefits and Unemployment Insurance benefits. Separate panels are shown for couples living apart from their relatives in which at least one spouse received benefits and for unmarried recipients not living with relatives. Together these two groups account for nearly 60 per cent of recipient units and about the same percentage of benefits.

Table 7.1 shows the effect of skipping the 3.5 per cent COLA paid in January 1984. All recipient families, except the 8 per cent who received SSI, would have been affected. SSI families were assumed to have received their normal cost-of-living increase. SSI would have protected nearly 30 per cent of families and individuals with after-tax incomes of less than $5000. Nearly all recipients in families with incomes of at least $15 000 or more would have been affected; most of the exceptions would have been SSI recipients living with relatives with higher incomes. The mean loss for all families with a decrease in disposable income would have been about $210. The mean loss rises with level of income, but there is little difference among the four highest categories. The percentage decrease in disposable income falls as income rises, because families with high incomes are less dependent on social security than families with lower incomes.

The final column of the table shows the mean loss as a percentage of disposable Social Security benefits, where disposable benefits are benefits minus the income taxes paid on benefits under current law. The loss of a 3.5 per cent COLA would have made average disposable Social Security benefits 3.4 per cent lower than they would have been for all families not protected by SSI.[9]

Table 7.2 shows the effect of including 50 per cent of Social Security benefits in taxable income regardless of income level. The total reduction in disposable income from this option would have been approximately the same as eliminating the COLA for 1984, nearly $5 billion. However, the fraction of families who would have

Table 7.1 Effect of eliminating 3.5 per cent COLA on families with social security, 1984

Level of disposable income	*All families with social security*	*Families with decrease in disposable income*		*Decrease in disposable income for families with a loss*		
		Number	*Percentage*	*Mean loss*	*As % of mean disp. inc.*	*As % of mean soc. sec. after tax*
		All families and individuals				
All units ($)	30 560	28 183	92.2	211	1.0	3.4
5 000 or less	3 047	2 165	71.1	114	3.4	3.4
5 000–10 000	7 035	6 178	87.8	179	2.4	3.3
10 000–15 000	5 139	4 843	94.2	221	1.8	3.3
15 000–20 000	4 008	3 887	97.0	236	1.4	3.4
20 000–30 000	5 445	5 295	97.3	242	1.0	3.4
30 000–40 000	2 827	2 788	98.6	236	0.7	3.4
40 000 or above	3 058	3 025	98.9	223	0.4	3.4
		Married couples, living alone				
All units ($)	8 062	7 856	97.4	269	1.2	3.4
5 000 or less	187	175	93.5	121	4.9	3.4
5 000–10 000	1 253	1 119	89.3	221	2.8	3.4
10 000–15 000	1 652	1 615	97.7	269	2.1	3.4
15 000–20 000	1 541	1 529	99.2	281	1.6	3.4
20 000–30 000	1 848	1 838	99.5	290	1.2	3.4
30 000–40 000	797	797	100.0	293	0.9	3.4
40 000 or above	783	783	100.0	272	0.4	3.4

continued on page 128

Table 7.1 *continued*

Level of disposable income	*All families with social security*	*Families with decrease in disposable income*		*Decrease in disposable income for families with a loss*		
		Number	*Percentage*	*Mean loss*	*As % of mean disp. inc.*	*As % of mean soc. sec. after tax*
		Single individuals, living alone				
All units ($)	9 566	8 544	89.3	170	1.5	3.4
5 000 or less	2 338	1 604	68.6	116	3.1	3.4
5 000–10 000	3 889	3 620	93.1	175	2.5	3.4
10 000–15 000	1 539	1 529	99.3	187	1.5	3.3
15 000–20 000	793	789	99.5	197	1.2	3.4
20 000–30 000	668	666	99.7	204	0.8	3.4
30 000–40 000	179	179	100.0	189	0.6	3.4
40 000 or above	159	158	99.1	160	0.2	3.4

lost would have been less than half as large, and the average loss for families affected would have been more than twice as big, about $450. Most low-income families and many high-income families would have been unaffected by this option. Low-income families would have continued to have taxable incomes below the level at which income taxes must be paid; high-income families already would have had to include 50 per cent of their benefits in taxable income when the current law taxing thresholds were in effect.

The reduction in incomes as a fraction of disposable benefits rises with income except at the bottom of the distribution, where few families are affected, and at the top, where most families would be paying income taxes on some part of their benefit under current law. The reduction as a fraction of disposable income rises more slowly because the declining fraction of incomes contributed by Social Security offsets increasing marginal tax rates as income rises.

The effect of increasing the maximum fraction of Social Security benefits included in taxable income from 50 to 85 per cent while lowering the taxing thresholds to the levels used for unemployment insurance is shown in Table 7.3. Less than one-third of families with Social Security would have been affected by this option, but the average loss for those families would have been nearly $700. This option would not have affected families with less than $10 000 of income and would have affected nearly all individuals and couples with at least $20 000 of income. The reduction in disposable income as a fraction of disposable Social Security benefits grows with income, reflecting the progressive nature of federal income taxes.

Table 7.4 shows the distribution of the reduction in disposable income across income levels. The first column shows the distribution of 1984 Social Security benefits reported on the March 1985 CPS. The second column shows the distribution of benefits after subtracting the extra income taxes paid because of current law taxation of benefits. The share of the highest two income categories is lower after taxation of benefits is taken into account.

The third column of Table 7.4 shows the distribution of the reduction in disposable income if the 1984 COLA had not been paid. The distribution is approximately the same as the after-tax distribution of benefits except for the lowest income categories. The fourth column shows the effect of making half of all benefits taxable. The share of the reduction in income from this option for those between $20 000 and $40 000 is about twice as large as their share of benefits. The last column shows that well over half of the reduction in

Table 7.2 Effect of including 50 per cent of social security benefits in taxable income, 1984

Level of disposable income	*All families with social security*	*Families with decrease in disposable income*		*Decrease in disposable income for families with a loss*		
		Number	*Percentage*	*Mean loss*	*As % of mean disp. inc.*	*As % of mean soc. sec. after tax*
		All families and individuals				
All units ($)	30560	13127	43.0	451	1.9	6.2
5 000 or less	3047	25	0.8	100	4.6	3.4
5 000–10 000	7035	642	9.1	130	1.6	3.0
10 000–15 000	5139	2389	46.5	244	1.9	4.2
15 000–20 000	4008	3015	75.2	375	2.1	5.2
20 000–30 000	5445	4164	76.5	560	2.3	7.2
30 000–40 000	2827	1737	61.4	676	2.0	7.9
40 000 or above	3058	1156	37.8	531	1.0	6.5
		Married couples, living alone				
All units ($)	8062	4534	56.2	571	2.5	6.7
5 000 or less	187	4	1.9	233	5.1	8.4
5 000–10 000	1253	42	3.3	127	1.5	3.4
10 000–15 000	1652	463	28.0	223	1.7	3.3
15 000–20 000	1541	1428	92.7	374	2.1	4.5
20 000–30 000	1848	1830	99.0	676	2.8	7.9
30 000–40 000	797	638	80.1	951	2.8	9.5
40 000 or above	783	129	16.5	793	1.8	6.6

		Single individuals, living alone				
All units ($)	9566	3329	34.8	374	2.5	6.5
5 000 or less	2338	15	0.6	72	1.7	6.1
5 000–10 000	3889	464	11.9	137	1.7	2.9
10 000–15 000	1539	1407	91.4	256	2.1	4.5
15 000–20 000	793	775	97.8	491	2.9	8.4
20 000–30 000	668	609	91.2	671	2.8	10.7
30 000–40 000	179	54	30.2	569	1.7	6.8
40 000 or above	159	4	2.3	403	0.8	5.9

Table 7.3 Effect of using 85 per cent of benefits and lowering thresholds for taxing social security, 1984

Level of disposable income	*All families with social security*	*Families with decrease in disposable income*		*Decrease in disposable income for families with a loss*		
		Number	*Percentage*	*Mean loss*	*As % of mean disp. inc.*	*As % of mean soc. sec. after tax*
		All families and individuals				
All units ($)	30560	9291	30.4	687	2.1	9.7
5 000 or less	3047	0	0.0	0	0.0	0.0
5 000–10 000	7035	0	0.0	0	0.0	0.0
10 000–15 000	5139	598	11.6	101	0.7	2.0
15 000–20 000	4008	1294	32.3	324	1.8	5.5
20 000–30 000	5445	3443	63.2	581	2.4	7.7
30 000–40 000	2827	1830	64.7	948	2.7	12.3
40 000 or above	3058	2126	69.5	1021	1.7	14.1
		Married couples, living alone				
All units ($)	8062	3587	44.5	828	2.4	10.1
5 000 or less	187	0	0.0	0	0.0	0.0
5 000–10 000	1253	0	0.0	0	0.0	0.0
10 000–15 000	1652	0	0.0	0	0.0	0.0
15 000–20 000	1541	292	19.0	93	0.5	1.5
20 000–30 000	1848	1728	93.5	501	2.0	6.0
30 000–40 000	797	790	99.2	1289	3.8	14.8
40 000 or above	783	776	99.1	1361	2.1	16.9

		Single individuals, living alone				
All units ($)	9566	2276	23.8	612	2.6	10.8
5 000 or less	2338	0	0.0	0	0.0	0.0
5 000–10 000	3889	0	0.0	0	0.0	0.0
10 000–15 000	1539	539	35.0	102	0.7	1.9
15 000–20 000	793	745	94.0	440	2.6	7.5
20 000–30 000	668	654	97.9	1070	4.4	17.8
30 000–40 000	179	179	100.0	923	2.7	16.5
40 000 or above	159	159	100.0	917	1.3	19.4

Table 7.4 Distribution of current law benefits and of changes in disposable income

	Total benefits	*Benefits after current law taxation*	*Loss in disposable income*		
			No COLA	*No thresholds*	*Tax up to 85% UI thresholds*
Total amount (billions of dollars)	150.4	148.1	4.8	4.9	5.4
	Distribution by level of disposable income				
All units ($)	100.0	100.0	100.0	100.0	100.0
5 000 or less	6.0	6.1	4.8	0.0	0.0
5 000–10 000	21.3	21.6	20.9	1.6	0.0
10 000–15 000	18.3	18.6	18.8	10.7	1.1
15 000–20 000	15.1	15.3	15.8	21.0	7.2
20 000–30 000	19.5	19.8	20.5	40.8	33.2
30 000–40 000	9.5	9.4	9.7	18.6	27.2
40 000 or above	10.2	9.2	9.6	7.4	31.4

disposable income under the option to raise the maximum taxable fraction of benefits and lower the taxing thresholds would come from families with at least $30 000 of income.

There were 36.7 million poor persons in 1984 if cash income after federal taxes, adjusted for underreporting of property income, is used to measure poverty. If the 3.5 per cent Social Security COLA had not been paid but the SSI COLA was paid, about 37.0 million persons would have been poor after taxes. In comparison, the number of poor persons would have increased by less than 20 000 if half of all benefits had been taxable. The option to lower the thresholds and tax up to 85 per cent of benefits would have had no effect on poverty.

The after-tax poverty gap was $272.2 billion in 1984.[10] Withholding the COLA would have raised the gap by about $1 billion. Taxing 50 per cent of all Social Security benefits would have raised the gap by less than $50 million. Taxing up to 85 per cent of Social Security benefits with lower taxing thresholds would have left the gap unchanged.

Appendix

SIMULATING CHANGES IN THE SIZE DISTRIBUTION OF AFTER-TAX INCOMES

A complete distributional analysis of the three deficit reduction options requires data on Social Security cash benefit payments, total cash income, and total taxable income for families receiving benefits. To avoid the difficulties of aging the data, it also is desirable to have information from the most recent year possible. Unfortunately, no single source provides such complete information. The three best alternatives each have a number of shortcomings.

Program data from the Social Security Administration is the best source of benefit payment data. However, this data does not include any information about family incomes or sufficient detail about family size and composition. While it is possible to simulate the savings from a COLA freeze using this data, it is not possible to estimate the effects on the distribution of income, nor is it possible to simulate either of the tax proposals.

Annual individual income tax return data collected by the Internal Revenue Service are available on the Statistics of Income (SOI) individual tax model file. The file contains a large sample (approximately 80 000 records) of actual tax returns. It is the best source of information about incomes upon which federal individual income taxes are based. There are a number of serious drawbacks, however. For the years for which these data currently are available, Social Security benefits were completely tax exempt and thus benefit amounts were not reported on tax returns. Data on other tax exempt income is missing as well. The unit of observation is tax returns. These records cannot be converted into families because only limited information about family size and composition is available and income of other family members is not reported. The file does not contain records for most of the low-income population who are not required to file tax returns.

A third data set is the annual March income supplement to the Current Population Survey (CPS) collected by the Bureau of the Census. The CPS is an annual survey with a constant methodology, a substantial sample size (over 60 000 families), and a great deal of economic and family structure information. The data also are current, with complete income information for the year usually available by August of the following year. The CPS has a number of problems. First, the quality of income reporting is not as good as either Social Security program data or SOI tax data. Secondly, the CPS does not contain all the necessary income and expenditure items necessary for computing taxes. Finally, because of top coding of separate types of income and possible undersampling, the CPS does not capture accurately all income at the higher end of the income distribution.

We chose to use CPS data for the simulations because of the broader demographic information, the better sampling of persons at the low end of the income distribution and the availability of Social Security benefit information. The CPS is also much more recent than tax return data. At the time the simulations were performed, the latest CPS was from March 1985, and thus had income information for calendar year 1984. The latest SOI available contained tax return information for 1982. In the section below we discuss some of the problems in using the CPS in more detail as well as the measures taken to remedy these problems.[11]

Creating tax filing units

The CPS provides no information on the federal income tax status of individuals. We assigned a filing status based on individual characteristics. All married people with a spouse in the same household were assumed to file a joint return. All people who were unmarried or married without a spouse currently residing in the same household and whose household included an unmarried child (or another relative with adjusted gross income of less than $1000) were assumed to file as a head of household. All others were assumed to file as unmarried individuals.

Adjusted gross income (AGI) was constructed as the sum of wages and salaries, self-employment income, interest, rents, dividends, and pensions as reported on the CPS. Unemployment Insurance and Social Security, also as reported on the CPS, were added to AGI according to the appropriate tax treatment under current law. For married couples in which both spouses had earnings or self-employment income, an amount equal to the two earner deduction under current law was subtracted from AGI.

Because few low-income units actually file a tax return, the CPS has many more constructed tax filing units than the number of filing units reported on the SOI. Average income and the distribution of types of income received by tax filing units on the CPS will not correspond to actual tax return data because of the number of additional low-income units.

Imputing income not reported on the CPS

Some types of taxable income are not reported on the CPS. The most important of these is capital gains, particularly for units receiving Social Security benefits. SOI data for all tax returns in 1982 show that net capital gains made up 1.9 per cent of total adjusted gross income, but 4.6 per cent of the adjusted gross income of units with at least one member age 65 or over.

Incomes at the upper end of the income distribution are underrepresented on the CPS. This results not only from missing income items such as capital gains, which are more likely to be received by persons at the upper end of the distribution, but also because of top-coding of income amounts. Beginning with the March 1985 CPS, all income items are top-coded at $99 999.[12] Because this limit applies to each source of income, the sum of income from all sources can well exceed this amount. However, in practice, no person on the 1985 CPS has reported total income in excess of $260 000.

To account for missing income, two corrections were made to the CPS data. First, 1982 SOI data were used to compute the average amount of income received from a particular source for units receiving an amount greater than or equal to the CPS top-coding amount from that source. These averages were then assigned to persons on the CPS with top-coded income from that source. Assigning averages suppresses variation in incomes for high income units. Because averages are assigned for separate income items, some variation is introduced when incomes are summed to construct adjusted gross income.

Secondly, after incomes were adjusted for top-coding, capital gains and losses were assigned based on a probability of capital gains receipt, and a proportion of AGI received as capital gains calculated from SOI data. Separate probabilities and proportions were calculated for each of 1080 different cells based on classification by AGI, filing status, family size, number of age exemptions, and whether or not the unit received dividend or interest income.

Imputing statutory and itemized deductions

The CPS has no information about how the income received by each unit is spent. Thus it is not possible to determine from the data the amount of tax deductible expenses of producing income, the amount of tax favored expenditures such as interest payments and medical expenditures or the amount distributed to tax favored retirement savings.

Statutory deductions for employee business expenses, and for contributions to an individual retirement account, and a total for itemized deductions, were imputed to the CPS file based on probabilities of taking those deductions and a deduction amount as a percentage of AGI calculated from 1982 SOI data.

Adjusting for underreported income

There are three types of underreporting of income on the CPS: (1) respondents fail to report that they receive a particular type of income or report the income as some other type, for example, reporting Supplemental Security Income payments as Social Security; (2) respondents report that they receive a particular type of income but fail to report the amount; (3) respondents report that they receive a particular type of income but report less than the full amount received.

The Bureau of the Census attempts to correct the second type of underreporting before the CPS file is made available for public use. About 30 per cent of persons report incomplete income information. Missing income items are imputed to these persons based on the reported values for persons on the survey with similar economic and demographic characteristics. Overall, about 20 per cent of the income reported on the CPS is derived by this allocation method. The proportion of income allocated varies significantly from item to item. For example, while about one-fifth of wages and salaries on most CPS files are allocated amounts, closer to one-third of interest and dividends are allocated.[13]

The first and third type of underreporting are not corrected before the files are released. Each year the Bureau of the Census compares income amounts reported on the CPS to independently derived control totals. Even after allocations, total income is underreported by about 10 per cent. The degree of underreporting varies greatly for different types of income. While wages and salaries are usually within a few percentage points of independent totals, interest and dividend income are only about 45 per cent of the independent totals.

CPS data compared with social security program data

For the current simulations the most important source of income is Social Security benefits. According to the March 1985 CPS, Social Security provided 40 per cent of the income of unmarried individuals and couples receiving benefits. Other major sources of income for recipients were interest, wages and salaries, and pensions which provided 19, 16 and 14 per cent of income, respectively. Table 7.A1 shows Social Security benefits and the number of beneficiaries for 1984 from the March 1985 CPS and actual data from administrative records of the Social Security Administration. Statistics are shown for all beneficiaries and for aged beneficiaries.

Most of the discrepancy in the number of beneficiaries can be accounted for by the nature of the CPS sample and questionnaire. Children under the age of 15 are not asked about their sources of income in the CPS. Five per cent of the caseload in 1982, the most recent year for which detailed administrative data have been published, were under 15. If beneficiaries under 15 are excluded from the actual total, the CPS samples about 93 per cent of recipients.

Most of the remaining discrepancy for total beneficiaries and almost all of the discrepancy for beneficiaries age 65 or older can be accounted for by the number of elderly persons missing from the survey. Institutionalized persons

Table 7.A1 Comparison of 1984 social security program data with data from the March 1985 Current Population Survey

	Number of beneficiaries (millions)		*Total benefits (billions of dollars)*	
	Total	*Age 65 or older*	*Total*	*Age 65 or older*
CPS data	32.2	24.3	148.4	117.5
Program data	36.4	26.0	175.7	134.2
CPS data as a percentage of program data	88.5	93.5	84.5	87.6

are not sampled on the CPS. According to the 1980 Census, 5.3 per cent of elderly persons live in institutions. Others are absent from the survey because of deaths between the end of 1984, when recipients were counted by the Social Security administration, and March of 1985, when the CPS interviews were conducted. About 4 per cent of Social Security recipients die each year, so about 1 per cent of December 1984 beneficiaries would be expected to die before they could be interviewed.

The entire difference between benefits reported on the CPS and actual benefits paid during 1984 cannot be accounted for by CPS sampling methods. If the average benefit paid to the institutionalized elderly is the same as the average benefit paid to all elderly, total benefits for the elderly on the CPS should be about 5 per cent too low. Approximately 5 per cent of elderly persons who received benefits sometime during 1984 would have died before March 1985, but, because most of them would have received benefits for only part of 1984, they would have received only about 3 per cent of the benefits. Together these two factors account for a discrepancy of about 8 per cent in total benefits. In fact, only about 88 per cent of the benefits are reported on the CPS, so the average benefit reported on the CPS for the elderly is about 4.5 per cent less than actually paid.

CPS data compared with SOI tax return data

After Social Security benefits, the primary income sources of Social Security recipients are interest, wages and salaries, pensions and dividends. The SOI provides the most reliable data on these sources of income but there are two major problems with comparing the CPS with the SOI. First, it is not possible to identify Social Security recipients from currently available tax return data. Secondly, many recipients do not file tax returns because they do not have gross income in excess of the required amounts. The most useful comparison is between tax return data on the income received by units paying income taxes and claiming at least one additional exemption for some member age 65 or older and simulated tax paying units with at least one member age 65 or older from the CPS.

Table 7.A2 Comparison of simulated 1982 taxes from the CPS with reported taxes from the 1982 SOI

Source	*All taxpayers* *Number (millions)*	*Average AGI*	*Average Taxes*	*Elderly taxpayers* *Number (millions)*	*Average AGI*	*Average Taxes*
SOI	76.4	23 463	3 598	8.7	23 272	4 065
CPS simulation (no adjustments)	76.9	23 003	3 391	7.6	20 666	3 143
CPS simulation (adjusted only for top-coding)	76.9	23 709	3 666	7.6	21 904	3 320

The following tables compare income reported on the SOI for total and aged taxpaying units with income reported on the CPS for similar units.

Table 7.A2 compares data on taxpayers from the SOI for 1982 with data on taxpayers simulated with the CPS for 1982. The first simulation was done using CPS values for all income items as they are reported on the CPS after amounts of capital gains, statutory and itemized deductions had been imputed.[14] The simulated number of taxpayers is approximately 0.5 million too high. Average AGI is about 2 per cent too low, and average taxes are about 6 per cent too low. For the elderly, the discrepancies are larger. There are over a million too few simulated taxpayers, while average AGI is 11 per cent below the SOI value and average taxes are 23 per cent below the SOI average.

Part of the reason that incomes and taxes are too low in the simulation is the result of top-coded income. The maximum income from any source reported on the public use CPS for 1982 was $75 000. The third row of Table 7.A2 shows the result of adjusting top-coded incomes. Amounts of income that were top-coded at $75 000 were replaced with the average amount reported on the SOI for filers who had at least $75 000 from that source. Capital gains, statutory and itemized deductions were reassigned to units that had had top-coded incomes. After adjusting for top-coding, average AGI for simulated taxpaying units rises to about 1 per cent above the SOI value, and average taxes are about 2 per cent too high. The discrepancies between SOI data and simulated data for units with an elderly person are reduced by the top-coding adjustment but remain high. The average simulated AGI is 6 per cent too low and average taxes are 18 per cent too low.

Table 7.A3 shows income by source from the SOI and from the CPS simulation that includes adjustments for top-coding. For most sources of income, the percentage of all taxpayers with that type of income is approximately the same for the SOI and the CPS. The largest differences are that about one-third too few persons report dividends and nonfarm self-employment income on the CPS. Most of the discrepancy for self-employment is in the number of units that have a loss from self-employment. About 10 per cent more units report interest income on the CPS.

Table 7.A3 Comparison of income by source from the 1983 CPS, after adjustments, with reported income from the 1982 SOI

	SOI		*CPS (adjusted for top-coding)*	
	% with income type	*Average amount*	*% with income type*	*Average amount*
		All taxpayers		
Wages and salaries	88	22 019	88	22 058
Self-employment, non-farm	14	5 858	10	14 518
(positive)	9	13 046	9	15 886
(negative)	5	−6 295	1	−2 654
Self-employment, farm	2	−921	2	6 980
(positive)	1	9 511	2	9 651
(negative)	1	−6 382	0	−3 930
Interest	61	3 221	66	2 209
Dividends	16	4 101	10	2 890
Rents, other prop. inc.	11	958	10	3 374
(positive)	5	5 917	8	4 500
(negative)	5	−4 237	2	−2 263
Pensions	11	7 863	10	8 163
		Elderly taxpayers		
Wages and salaries	36	14 547	35	15 818
Self-employment, nonfarm	12	5 983	8	14 139
(positive)	9	11 649	7	14 900
(negative)	4	−8 117	0	−2 169
Self-employment, farm	3	−49	2	5 201
(positive)	1	8 664	2	6 987
(negative)	2	−6 584	0	−2 388
Interest	95	9 324	92	7 852
Dividends	41	6 842	28	4 498
Rents, other prop. inc.	22	5 303	19	5 549
(positive)	18	7 535	18	5 954
(negative)	5	−2 640	1	−1 708
Pensions	52	7 434	53	7 757

The differences in average amounts received by all taxpayers are fairly large for all sources except wage and salary and pension income. Average wage and salary income on the CPS is within 0.2 per cent of the average from the SOI. Average income from pensions was about 4 per cent too high in the CPS simulation. However, 12 per cent of pension income reported on the SOI by tax paying units was non-taxable. Because it was not possible to identify non-taxable pensions on the CPS, all pension income was treated as taxable income. Each of the three sources of income that can have both positive and negative income have too few units reporting losses and average losses that are too small. Thus, the average amounts received from these

Table 7.A4 Comparison of reported interest income from the 1983 CPS, after adjustments, with reported amounts from the 1982 SOI

AGI Category	*SOI* % with interest	*SOI* Average amount	*CPS (adjusted for top-coding)* % with interest	*CPS (adjusted for top-coding)* Average amount	*CPS (after all adjustments)* % with interest	*CPS (after all adjustments)* Average amount
		All taxpayers				
Less than $10 000	44	1 893	48	1 342	47	1 417
$10 000–$15 000	47	2 594	54	1 651	54	1 825
$15 000–$25 000	58	2 596	65	1 537	66	1 844
$25 000–$40 000	74	2 459	78	1 827	78	2 275
$40 000 or more	89	6 542	90	5 158	90	6 883
Total	60	3 133	66	2 209	66	2 766
		Elderly taxpayers				
Less than $10 000	91	4 163	88	3 422	88	3 597
$10 000–$15 000	94	5 931	91	5 105	91	5 602
$15 000–$25 000	96	8 813	92	7 463	93	8 284
$25 000–$40 000	97	11 602	96	10 902	96	12 935
$40 000 or more	100	24 211	96	22 488	97	27 352
Total	94	9 178	92	7 852	92	9 550

sources is much higher on the CPS than on the SOI. In the case of farm income, there is a net loss on the SOI but a net gain on the CPS. Average income from interest and from dividends was about 30 per cent lower on the CPS than on the SOI, although the discrepancy in interest income for the elderly was only about half as large.

Adjustments were made to CPS incomes to correct for some of these discrepancies. Sources from which negative amounts are possible are difficult to reconcile between the CPS and the SOI. Many of the losses reported on tax returns are not captured by the questions asked on the CPS. Negative incomes were doubled to try to lower average income from sources for which losses are possible, but no attempt was made to add losses or to switch units from gainers to losers.

For the elderly, however, the sum of all income from these sources is not an important fraction of total income. According to 1982 SOI, data, interest, wages and salaries, pensions and dividends make up 88 per cent of total income before deductions for taxpayers age 65 and older, 90 per cent of total income excluding capital gains. Because average wages and salaries and pensions from the CPS are reasonably close to the SOI averages, we confined our adjustments to interest and dividends.

Table 7.A4 shows the discrepancies in reported interest for elderly taxpayers between the SOI and the CPS at different income levels.[15] Because the percentage difference in interest income does not vary systematically by AGI, a constant adjustment factor of 1.25 was used to adjust interest income. The fifth and sixth columns of the table show the effect of the

Table 7.A5 Comparison of reported dividend income from the 1983 CPS, after adjustments, with reported amounts from the 1982 SOI

AGI Category	*SOI* % with dividends	*SOI* Average amount	*CPS (adjusted for top-coding)* % with dividends	*CPS (adjusted for top-coding)* Average amount	*CPS (after all adjustments)* % with dividends	*CPS (after all adjustments)* Average amount
		All taxpayers				
Less than $10 000	9	1 283	5	1 321	5	1 359
$10 000–$15 000	9	1 803	5	1 801	6	1 906
$15 000–$25 000	12	2 119	7	2 158	7	1 986
$25 000–$40 000	18	2 321	11	2 425	12	2 868
$40 000 or more	40	8 929	28	4 380	32	7 905
Total	16	4 101	10	2 890	11	4 391
		Elderly taxpayers				
Less than $10 000	28	1 399	17	1 569	16	1 642
$10 000–$15 000	33	2 389	23	2 228	23	2 357
$15 000–$25 000	42	3 424	27	3 533	27	3 377
$25 000–$40 000	52	5 341	40	5 423	40	6 133
$40 000 or more	76	20 548	56	9 561	59	19 147
Total	41	6 842	28	4 498	29	7 273

adjustment. Elderly taxpaying units simulated from the CPS have average interest income that is about 2 per cent too high. The fraction of units receiving interest is 3 percentage points too low. Average interest rose by little in the lower income categories, even falling for units with AGI of less than $5000, because the adjustment pushed some units into higher categories and caused the income of some units that previously were not simulated to pay taxes to cross the tax entry thresholds.

Data on dividends for elderly taxpayers from the SOI and the CPS is shown in Table 7.A5.[16] The difference between average dividends from the SOI and the CPS after adjustment for top-coding increases with the level of AGI. Because the differences in dividend income depends on the level of AGI, a three-step factor was used to adjust dividends. For those with incomes below $35 000, dividends were increased by 25 per cent; for those with incomes between $35 000 and $75 000, dividends were increased by 50 per cent; and for those with AGI of $75 000 or more, dividends were tripled. The fifth and sixth columns of Table 7.A5 show the results of adjusting dividends. Average dividends are 6 per cent too high for elderly taxpaying units simulated from the CPS despite averages that are close to, or below, the reported average from the SOI for most AGI classes, indicating that units with low dividends amounts are missing. Overall, the number of elderly units with dividend income is 12 percentage points too low.

The pattern of underreporting of interest may actually vary with level of income as we found for dividends. Interest on the CPS includes interest that is exempt from federal taxation. The SOI data on interest include only

Table 7.A6 Comparison of income by source from the 1983 CPS, after all adjustments, with reported income from the 1982 SOI

	SOI		*CPS (after all adjustments)*	
	% with income type	*Average amount*	*% with income type*	*Average amount*
		All taxpayers		
Wages and salaries	88	22 019	88	22 026
Self-employment, non-farm	14	5 858	10	14 461
(positive)	9	13 046	9	15 867
(negative)	5	−6 295	1	−4 546
Self-employment, farm	2	−921	2	6 592
(positive)	1	9 511	2	9 613
(negative)	1	−6 382	0	−6 966
Interest	61	3 221	66	2 766
Dividends	16	4 101	11	4 391
Rents, other prop. inc.	11	958	10	2 833
(positive)	5	5 917	8	4 341
(negative)	5	−4 237	2	−4 957
Pensions	11	7 863	10	8 053
		Elderly taxpayers		
Wages and salaries	36	14 547	34	15 650
Self-employment, nonfarm	12	5 983	7	14 273
(positive)	9	11 649	7	14 900
(negative)	4	−8 117	0	−2 361
Self-employment, farm	3	−49	2	4 797
(positive)	1	8 664	2	6 930
(negative)	2	−6 584	0	−4 404
Interest	95	9 324	92	9 550
Dividends	41	6 842	29	7 273
Rents, other prop. inc.	22	5 303	19	5 342
(positive)	18	7 535	18	5 848
(negative)	5	−2 640	1	−3 268
Pensions	52	7 434	52	7 566

interest income that must be reported to the IRS, and thus excludes tax-exempt interest from sources such as municipal bonds. If we could exclude tax-exempt interest from the CPS simulation, the interest of those with low AGI and low marginal tax rates would be little different from the values shown in Table 7.A4. Interest for those in high brackets would be considerably lower and we would see the gap between the CPS and the SOI rising with level of income.

Table 7.A6 shows the differences between income from various sources after all taxpaying units simulated from the CPS had been adjusted for underreporting of interest, dividends, and losses. The same factors for

Table 7.A7 Comparison of simulated 1982 taxes from the CPS, after all adjustments, with reported taxes from the 1982 SOI

	SOI			*CPS (after all adjustments)*		
Source	*Number (millions)*	*Average AGI*	*Average taxes*	*Number (millions)*	*Average AGI*	*Average taxes*
			All taxpayers			
Less than $10 000	17.4	6 703	391	15.5	6 790	382
$10 000–$15 000	13.6	12 422	1 091	14.1	12 235	1 071
$15 000–$25 000	19.0	19 682	2 288	20.5	19 613	2 287
$25 000–$40 000	17.3	31 427	4 472	17.5	31 335	4 501
$40 000 or more	9.1	64 663	14 524	9.7	65 222	15 093
Total	76.4	23 463	3 598	77.3	24 090	3 795
			Elderly taxpayers			
Less than $10 000	2.4	7 471	313	2.1	7 357	274
$10 000–$15 000	2.0	12 372	892	1.8	12 311	837
$15 000–$25 000	2.1	19 114	2 079	1.9	19 100	2 067
$25 000–$40 000	1.2	31 034	4 720	1.2	31 247	4 709
$40 000 or more	1.0	82 465	22 708	0.9	78 608	21 796
Total	8.7	23 272	4 065	7.9	23 161	4 004

adjusting interest and dividend income of elderly taxpaying units were used to adjust the interest and dividend income of non-elderly taxpaying units with the exception that dividends of units in the highest income category were adjusted by a smaller factor. Average interest income rose considerably, but the simulated average for all taxpayers with interest income was still about 14 per cent too low. Interest averaged over all taxpayers, including units with interest income, was much closer because the number of units reporting interest in the CPS was about 8 per cent too large. The average dividend level is 7 per cent higher in the CPS after all adjustments have been made than in the SOI. For elderly taxpaying units large differences remain for the sources of income for which losses are possible but average incomes from wages and salaries, interest, dividends and pensions all are within about 7.5 per cent of SOI averages.

Table 7.A7 compares incomes and tax payments on the SOI with those simulated on the CPS after all adjustments have been made. The CPS simulation shows about 1 per cent more taxpayers, 3 per cent higher incomes, and 5 per cent higher taxes. Most of the excess income results from the smaller number of units with losses in the CPS.

The number of filing units with an elderly taxpayer simulated with the CPS is nearly 10 per cent lower than the number from the SOI. Much of this discrepancy can be attributed to the fact that the CPS sample includes only persons who are alive and not institutionalized at the time of the survey. About 5 per cent of the elderly are institutionalized at any point in time and about 5 per cent die each year. The average amounts of income and taxes are very close for units with an elderly person. Average AGI is 0.5 per cent lower in the CPS simulation and average taxes are 2 per cent too low.

Adjusting 1984 CPS data

The imputation probabilities and factors derived from 1982 tax return data were applied to 1984 CPS data. This implicitly assumed that average capital gains, statutory deductions and itemized deductions grew at the same rate as nominal incomes between 1982 and 1984.[17] Top-coding factors based on the higher maximum of $99 999 for the 1984 CPS data were used to adjust the reported incomes of persons with top-coded income of a particular type. Underreporting adjustment factors for interest and dividend income derived for 1982 were used to adjust the 1984 data. This assumed that the percentage by which these types of income were underreported remained constant between 1982 and 1984.

Notes

1. For a study of 16 different options, including three similar to those analyzed here, see Congressional Budget Office, 1985.
2. Outlay estimates are Congressional Budget Office (CBO) baseline projections prepared in February 1985. The tax expenditure estimate for 1985 is from the Joint Committee on Taxation. The estimate for 1990 is from the CBO.
3. A complete discussion of the issues concerning the tax treatment of Social Security benefits is presented by Sunley, 1977, and Munnell, 1982.
4. The origin and history of the tax exemption is reviewed in Koitz, 1979.
5. Even when contributions for disability and hospital insurance are excluded, the payback period is still slightly overstated because some portion of OASI payroll taxes pay for pre-retirement survivors insurance protection.
6. Persons age 65 and older and certain disabled persons are eligible to receive the tax credit for the elderly or disabled on their federal income taxes. This non-refundable credit is equal to a maximum of 15 per cent of a base amount. For 1985 the base amounts are $5 000 for single persons and $7 500 for elderly couples. The base amount is reduced by the sum of non-taxable Social Security and non-taxable pensions benefits plus one-half of AGI above a threshold amount.
7. The amount of benefits that single persons can receive without paying taxes is more than twice the tax-entry point for elderly single tax filers because of the tax credit for the elderly. The tax credit is zero for couples with benefits equal to twice the tax-entry point for elderly married tax filers.

8. A beneficiary who had been receiving $100 in monthly benefits in 1983 would have received $103.50 once the 1984 COLA was paid. Eliminating the COLA would keep the benefit at $100, which is 96.6 per cent of $103.50. That percentage was applied to reported 1984 benefits.
9. Some families lose less than 3.4 per cent of disposable income. These families receive the tax credit for the elderly or disabled on their federal income taxes. The dollar amount of this credit will increase by 15 per cent of any reduction in non-taxable Social Security benefits.
10. The poverty gap is the number of dollars required to lift the income of all poor families up to the poverty thresholds.
11. Others facing this choice have opted to match the CPS with tax return data. This can be done either through an exact or statistical match. The last publicly available exact match was done in 1973, and contains limited tax return information. Statistical matches have been done at the Brookings Institution (the MERGE files), the Office of Tax Analysis at the Department of the Treasury, and more recently at ICF, Inc. While statistical matching of files has its weaknesses, it can greatly enhance data files while preserving the statistical integrity of the original files. However, statistical matching is time consuming and expensive. Existing matched files must be aged to some more recent year to make the result relevant. Aging these files creates its own problems, and can undo some of the desirable statistical properties of the file.
12. Income reported on the March CPS for 1981 to 1984 was top-coded at $75 000. Prior to 1981, income was top-coded at $50 000. The Bureau of the Census received information on incomes up to $99 999 in all years, but did not release that data in order to preserve the confidentiality of the file.
13. Beginning with the March 1985 CPS, the Census began using a new allocation method for interest income. This new allocation raised overall interest by about 25 per cent, raising total income by 1 per cent but income of the elderly by 4 per cent.
14. Interest on the CPS for 1982 was adjusted using the new allocation method that the Bureau of the Census began to use in 1985 for assigning interest to persons who failed to report an amount.
15. Interest from the SOI is all interest income reported for 1982 including non-taxable interest from all-savers certificates.
16. For 1982, taxpayers could exclude up to $100 ($200 on a joint return) of eligible dividends from adjusted gross income. Average dividends in the tables for both the SOI and the CPS are total dividends less the dividend exclusion.
17. Deductions for IRA contributions were limited to the amount allowed by law. Because many units already were contributing the maximum amount in 1982, average IRA deductions grew only marginally by 1984.

References

CONGRESSIONAL BUDGET OFFICE (1985) *An Analysis of Selected Deficit Reduction Options Affecting the Elderly and Disabled*, Congressional Budget Office Staff Working Paper, Washington, D.C.

CONGRESSIONAL RESEARCH SERVICE (1982) *How Long Does It Take For Current Retirees To Recover the Value of Their Social Security Contributions?* Report No, 82–76 EPW, US Library of Congress, Congressional Research Service, Washington, D.C.

KOITZ, D. (1979) *Social Security: The Tax-Free Status of Benefits*, Report No. 79–247 EPW, US Library of Congress, Congressional Research Service, Washington, D.C.

MUNNELL, A. H. (1982) 'Is it Time to Start Taxing Social Security Benefits?' *New England Economic Review*, May/June: 18–27.

SUNLEY, E. M. (1977) 'Employee Benefits and Transfer Payments,' In J. A. PECHMAN (ed.) *Comprehensive Income Taxation* (Washington, D.C.: Brookings Institution) 75–114.

8 The Effects of Taxing Unemployment Insurance Benefits Accounting For Induced Labor Supply Responses

David M. Betson, Jennifer L. Warlick and Timothy M. Smeeding*

INTRODUCTION

Taxation of Unemployment Insurance (UI) benefits has been a topic of debate for more than a decade. Arguments for and against taxation revolve around issues of equity, efficiency, and redistributive objectives. The debate bore fruit in 1979 with the passage of legislation which provides for partial taxation of UI benefits. Because the legislation falls short of total taxation and leaves unsettled most of the analytic issues, this paper adds to this debate by presenting new estimates of tax induced changes in total revenues which account for the potential labor force responses to taxation of UI. Estimates of the impact of full taxation are compared to similar estimates for a world in which UI benefits are totally excluded from the tax base (the recent past), and also to the situation which prevails under current law. New information regarding the income replacement function and work disincentive effects of UI under alternative tax schemes is also presented. All of the estimates are based on data from the Survey of Income and Education (SIE). The method of analysis is microsimulation.

The primary finding of the study is that potential revenues from taxing all UI are significantly greater when the induced labor supply

* This research was supported in part by funds granted to the Institute for Research on Poverty at the University of Wisconsin-Madison by the Department of Health, Education and Welfare pursuant to the provisions of the Economic Opportunity Act of 1964. The authors are grateful to Daniel Hamermesh and Olivia Mitchell for helpful comments.

response to the tax change is accounted for than when it is not. This result is explained partially by the fact that UI recipients return to work sooner than in the absence of taxation, because including UI benefits in the income tax base effectively lowers the marginal tax rate on the next dollar which can be obtained by returning to work.[1] Revenues rise to the extent that the gross wages to former recipients exceed their UI benefits, and also because total UI benefits disbursed decline.

The remainder of this paper is organized as follows: Section 2 reviews basic features of the UI system and summarizes arguments for and against taxation of UI. Section 3 outlines the anticipated labor supply response and its effect on tax revenues and total budgetary impacts via algebraic model. In the fourth section, we discuss the important assumptions underlying the simulation methodology. The simulation results are presented and discussed in Section 5, followed by concluding remarks in Section 6.

THE RATIONALE BEHIND TAXATION

Although mandated by the Social Security Act of 1935, the Unemployment Insurance system is a collection of state programs, diverse in all aspects yet linked together by coverage rules and by certain minimum provisions in the federal law (Hamermesh, 1977). Subject to these requirements, individual states raise most of the taxes to finance the system and determine benefit levels, duration, and rules surrounding the receipt of benefits. Eligibility is defined in terms of prior work attachment and reason for separation (quit or laid off for cause), and benefits are based on the unemployed worker's past wages during a legally specified base period. This mode of determining benefits reflects the system's intention of treating recipients with identical work experiences as equals. The maximum benefit is defined either in dollar amounts, or as a percentage of a state's average weekly wage in covered employment (32 states). In no case is the maximum to a worker with no dependents higher than two-thirds of the state average weekly wage. In most states the ratio of UI benefits to average weekly wages is 0.50 (Hamermesh, 1977). Benefits are reduced if the claimant is partially unemployed, but are not affected by the amount of non-employment income received by the claimant, nor by any income received by the claimant's spouse regardless of its source. Under present law, some proportion of benefits are taxable if a worker filing a single return has adjusted gross income (AGI), including unemployment insurance in excess of $20 000 ($25 000 for joint returns). When this condition is met, 50 cents of every dollar of UI benefits is included in taxable income for each dollar of total income above the specified limit (US Congress, 1978). For example, a single taxpayer with AGI equal to $21 000, including $4 000 in UI benefits, would pay taxes on a base of $17 500.[2] Prior to 1979, UI benefits were not taxable.

Any exclusion of UI benefits from the definition of taxable income raises issues of equity and efficiency. Prior to and under current law, a family which receives part of its annual income in UI benefits will pay a lower tax than an identical family which receives the same gross income in earnings. Consequently the family which receives UI benefits has a higher net income than the family which receives only earnings (Hutchens, 1979). An additional inequity is illustrated by two eligible claimants who have identical work experiences but who received different wages while employed. Assuming that both claimants are eligible for benefits less than the maximum, the claimant with the higher wage will have proportionately more of his net income lost due to unemployment replaced than his lower wage counterpart. If the system is to be consistent with its objective of treating recipients with identical employment experiences equally, the net wage loss of beneficiaries at different wage levels (tax brackets) should be proportional. Total taxation would insure this proportionality as well as righting the horizontal inequity between families with equal gross incomes but different employment experiences (Hamermesh, 1977).

Other proponents of taxation argue that inclusion of UI benefits in the taxable base will reduce disincentives to work associated with receiving UI (Feldstein, 1974; Hamermesh, 1977). An unemployed financial worker's disincentive to seek work while receiving UI benefits can be measured by the ratio of unemployment compensation to the net earnings that the worker would receive if she or he were employed. Feldstein refers to this ratio as the net tax rate and presents calculations which show that this rate varies from 0.31 for a married man earning 130 per cent of the state median wage to 1.19 for an unemployed wife of a working couple who earns 70 per cent of her state median wage to her husband's 100 per cent (Feldstein, 1974). Evidently, in some cases it is possible for a family to receive higher net income when one of its members is a UI recipient, than if all members were employed! The mean marginal net tax rate for single males receiving the median wage is 0.63; that for a married man in a one-earner couple earnings 70 per cent of the median is 0.69. These numbers contrast sharply against the average gross replacement rates of 0.50 or less which are prescribed by state regulations.

Taxation of UI benefits would increase the financial incentive to return to work by reducing the net tax rate associated with doing so. Feldstein estimates that including all of UI benefits in taxable income would lower net tax rates by one-fifth to one-fourth of their values when UI benefits are not taxed. For example, the effective tax rate for the unemployed wife described above would fall from 1.19 to 0.93. The mean marginal tax rate for a single man receiving the median wage would fall from 0.63 to 0.46 (Feldstein, 1974).

Including some portion or all of UI benefits in the definitions of taxable income produces the controversial result that a greater percentage of all UI flows to lower income groups. Hutchens estimated that the tax provisions obtained by the Carter Administration would decrease the sum of UI benefits flowing to upper income groups (annual income greater than $20 000) by about a quarter, but would not affect middle ($5000 to $20 000) and lower (less than $5000) income groups. Additional estimates show that upper income groups would be similarly effected by taxation of all UI benefits. Unlike the current provisions, however, total taxation would also be felt by the middle income groups, and to a lesser extent by lower income groups, reducing total benefits 18 and 4 per cent respectively (Hutchens, 1979).

In a recent paper Hamermesh (1982) has argued that an appropriate benefit level for the unemployed is one which prevents drops in consumption during the spell of unemployment. He finds that about half of all UI benefits accrue to households who spend them as if they exceed the level of benefits which would prevent a drop in consumption. Further, it is, as one might expect, low (high)-income households who are likely to have benefits which are too low (high). Thus any policy which targets greater amounts of payments toward low-income eligible households, such as full taxation of UI benefits, will improve the aggregate welfare of UI recipients.

These results are controversial in the context of the debate of whether UI is to be a pure tax-transfer or a needs-based transfer program. Persons disturbed by provisions with needs-based redistributive objectives may oppose total taxation, all else being equal, on these grounds.

Finally, in arguing for taxation some proponents may point to the revenues which are lost by excluding UI benefits from the taxable base. Feldstein estimates the value of these to be nearly $1 billion in 1970 (Feldstein, 1974).

LABOR SUPPLY RESPONSE TO THE TAXATION OF UI

Official Treasury estimates of tax revenues and budget impacts which would result from taxation of UI, do not account for any individual behavioral response to the change in the tax code. Consequently, the change in revenues associated with the inclusion of q per cent of UI benefits in the tax base can be estimated for a hypothetical individual as

$$\Delta TR = t\,q\,B \tag{1}$$

where

ΔTR = change in tax revenues,
B = UI benefits,
t = marginal federal income tax rate faced by individuals.
q = the proportion of UI benefits subject to taxation.

Since the Treasury does not impute any response to individuals, the total budgetary impact of the inclusion of UI in the tax base would just be equal to the change in tax revenues as expressed in equation 1. But if individuals do respond to the changes in the tax treatment of UI, then these responses would manifest themselves in terms of increases in earnings and reductions in UI payments which would have budgetary impacts. In this case, the additional tax revenues from inclusion of UI in the income tax base would equal the marginal tax rate times the sum of UI benefits adjusted for the induced change in work behavior and the induced change in earnings:

$$\Delta TR^* = t\,q\,(B+\Delta B) + t\,\Delta E \tag{2}$$

where

ΔTR^* = change in total revenues taking into account behavioral response,
ΔB = induced change in UI benefits,
ΔE = induced change in earnings.

To derive estimates of ΔTR^* it is necessary to have estimates of ΔB and ΔE. We turn our attention first to ΔB.

We begin by noting that B is simply the product of the numbers of weeks a worker is unemployed and receiving UI benefits and the worker's weekly UI benefits prior to taxation:

$$B = K \cdot U$$

where

K = number of weeks unemployed and receiving UI prior to taxation.
U = gross weekly UI benefits.

It follows that the induced changes in benefits (ΔB) is equal to weekly benefits times the induced changes in weeks of unemployment:

$$\Delta B = U \Delta K \tag{3}$$

where

ΔK = the induced change in the number of weeks of unemployment.

An expression of ΔK may be found by noting that the elasticity of weeks of unemployment with respect to UI (ε) is defined by

$$\varepsilon = \frac{\Delta K / K}{\Delta U / U}$$

Now the change in the effective (net) weekly UI benefit due the taxation of the payment is

$$\Delta U = -t\, q\, U.$$

Thus the change in the number of weeks unemployed can be rewritten as

$$\Delta K = \frac{\varepsilon\, K\, \Delta U}{U}$$

or

$$\Delta K = -\varepsilon\, K\, t\, q \tag{4}$$

Substituting this expression into equation 3, we find that the induced change in UI benefits is equal to the negative of the product of the elasticity of the duration of unemployment with respect to UI benefits, taxable UI benefits, and the marginal tax rate:

$$\Delta B = -\varepsilon\ U\ K\ q\ t = -\varepsilon\ B\ t\ q.$$

The tax induced change in earnings ($\varepsilon\Delta E$) is equal to the weekly wage when employed times the additional number of weeks employed. The latter term, the change in the number of weeks employed, is equal to minus the change in the number of weeks of unemployment, or

$$\Delta E = W(\Delta K), \tag{5}$$

where

W = weekly wage if employed.

Substituting equation 4 into this expression we see that

$$\Delta E = \varepsilon\ K\ W\ t\ q.$$

Having solved for the induced changes in both UI benefits and earnings, we can substitute equations 4 and 5 into equation 2 to solve for the change in total tax revenues taking into account changes in individual labor response:

$$\Delta TR^{*} = t\ q\ B\ (1-\varepsilon\ t\ q) + \varepsilon\ t^{2}\ q\ K\ W$$

The relationship of this estimate to the traditional Treasury estimates is illustrated by the ratio:

$$\frac{\Delta TR^{*} - \Delta TR}{\Delta TR} = \varepsilon\ t \left[\frac{W - qU}{U} \right].$$

Thus given full taxation of UI benefits ($q = 1$), the percentage difference in the two estimates for a given individual is equal to the percentage change in net income resulting from returning to work times the elasticity of the duration unemployment with respect to UI benefits. This expression clearly indicates that estimates of the change in total revenues which account for the tax-induced labor supply response of individuals will be greater than (less than) those omitting behavioral response if recipients return to work at a weekly wage which is greater than (less) his or her weekly UI benefits.

The above discussion noted that responses of individuals to the taxation of UI would tend to make the actual tax revenues larger than Treasury estimates. These responses would also have budgetary consequences for other government programs. In particular, the reductions in the duration of unemployment would imply direct savings in the UI program. Thus a more comprehensive estimate of the budgetary impacts should include not only the tax revenues collected, but also the savings in other government programs, namely UI.[3] Employing this more comprehensive definition, the budgetary impact of taxing UI for the individual would be

$$TBI^* = \Delta TR^* - \Delta B$$

where

TBI^* = Total Budgetary impact of taxing UI given that individuals respond,
$-\Delta B$ = savings in UI.

Since the Treasury does not impute a response to individuals, the total budgetary impact of taxation of UI as estimated by the Treasury would be equal to just the tax revenues collected (that is, $TBI = \Delta TR$). The percentage differences between these two estimates is

$$\frac{TBI^* - TBI}{TBI} = \varepsilon(1 - t\,q + t\,W/U).$$

The above discussion has been made in terms of an hypothetical individual, but it has been helpful in highlighting the important parameters that are involved in the imputation of labor supply responses and the consequences of these responses for estimates of the effects of taxing UI on revenues and the federal budget. Clearly, the effect of ignoring these responses will depend on how t, U, W, and ε are distributed throughout the unemployed population. In the next section, we will describe how we computed these variables within our simulation population.

THE SIMULATION METHODOLOGY

Estimates of ΔTR^* and TBI^* are produced by a microsimulation model adapted from the KGB model (Betson, Greenberg and Kasten, 1980) using data from the Survey of Income and Education. To obtain reliable estimates of both ΔTR^* and TBI^*, precise data must be available on an individual basis for the following variables: U, the weekly UI benefit received; W, the weekly wage received upon return to work; ε, the elasticity of the duration of unemployment with respect to UI benefits; and t, the marginal tax rate on each additional dollar of taxable income. The SIE data do not satisfy these needs, and thus it is necessary to estimate these values with procedures which employ other SIE data on non-transfer income, family size and structure, and demographic characteristics, our knowledge of the state's UI statutory provisions, and several predictive regression equations. In particular, unemployment insurance benefits, U, are derived from three regression equations estimated at the Urban Institute for specific use in KGB microsimulation model. These regressions predict the probability for various workers of receiving payments when unemployed, their length of eligibility, and their weekly payment. Individuals are chosen randomly to receive payments on the basis of the probability estimates.

The value assigned to W, the weekly wage received upon returning to work, is the market wage earned prior to unemployment computed directly from the data times the number of hours worked per week. Job search theorists espouse the proposition that higher UI benefits foster higher subsequent earnings by enabling the recipient to invest more resources in his or her job search (as compared to unemployed non-UI recipients). A growing body of literature investigating empirically the effects of UI benefits on subsequent wages has failed to provide consistent evidence in support of this proposition, however (see Welch, 1977, for a review and evaluation of a number of these studies; see also Kiefer and Neuman, 1979; Sandell, 1980). In the absence of more convincing evidence to the contrary, we assume that UI recipients receive market wages equivalent to their previous employment when they return to work.

Another issue in this area which has been the subject of much study is the effect of UI benefits on the duration of unemployment. The results of empirical studies are quite diverse with estimates of the elasticity of the duration of unemployment with respect to UI benefits $\left(\varepsilon = \dfrac{\Delta K/K}{\Delta U/U}\right)$ ranging from less than zero (a positive increment in benefits decreases duration) to 1.6 (a 10 percentage-point benefit increment increases duration by 1.6 weeks). The reliability of the estimates is thrown into deeper doubt by numerous problems involving sample bias, information errors, and questionable estimation procedures (Welch, 1977). However, based on those studies which he reviews (Welch, 1977: 460) does hazard to present a 'guesstimate' that, on average, a $10 increase in benefits in 1970 leads to an increase in unemployment duration of 1.5 weeks. Given an average duration of 12 weeks of unemployment (Hamermesh, 1977: 32) and an average weekly UI benefit of about $50 in 1970 (Munts, 1976: Table 3) Welch's guess translates into an elasticity of about 0.63. Such is the state of the art that Hamermesh is tempted into suggesting that a quick perusal of the assembled results 'could lead to the conclusion that the studies tell us nothing' (1977: 36). Despite this seemingly disparaging observation, Hamermesh hazards to guess that a reasonable point estimate is an elasticity equal to 0.25: a 10 percentage-point increase in the gross replacement rate (the ratio of UI benefits to gross wages) leads to an increase in the duration of insured unemployment of about half a week when labor markets are tight (1977: 37). A more recent study by Kiefer and Neuman (1978) finds an elasticity of about 0.5, though their study concentrates on a particular sample of workers, that is, those laid-off due to plant closings.

While there is some variability of the estimate of the average value of ε, there is little conclusive evidence that this value varies for persons of different socioeconomic groups. Two studies (Burgess and Kingston, 1976; Ehrenberg and Oaxaca, 1976) have attempted estimates of ε for persons of different ages and/or sex. But because the samples employed in these studies cannot be generalized to the national population (Burgess and Kingston), or are not inclusive of all relevant age-sex categories (Ehrenberg and Oaxaca), the results are not useful to this study. Based on these less than adequate results, we assume that ε is constant for all individuals in our sample, and in order to bracket the results we chose two values for ε at 0.25 and 0.5.[4]

Table 8.1 Characteristics of the simulation population, 1975

	Less than $5 000	*$5 000 to $15 000*	*$15 000 to $25 000*	*Greater than $25 000*	*All units total*
Number of units (millions)	31.3	38.1	18.1	7.3	94.8
Number of units who have tax liability (millions)	3.8	29.8	18.0	7.3	58.9
Number of units who received UI (millions)	5.6	7.1	2.7	0.6	16.0
Number of units who received UI and had tax liability (millions)	0.8	5.3	2.7	0.6	9.4
Number of unemployed individuals (millions)	6.1	7.8	2.9	0.6	17.4
Average duration of unemployment (weeks)	21.0	19.0	15.4	17.7	19.0[a]
Federal income tax liability ($billions)	0.2	26.2	44.6	56.5	127.5
UI payments ($billions)	4.0	9.5	3.5	0.8	17.8

[a] Weighted average for all units.

The marginal tax rate t faced by the unemployed worker is determined by calculating his taxable income for federal purposes including the amount of UI benefits consistent with the proposal to tax UI in question.[5] Each individual is then assigned the value of t appropriate for the tax bracket and the type of filing unit of which he or she is a member at the calculated level of taxable income.

RESULTS

Descriptive data for the simulation population are presented in Table 8.1. The data refers to calendar year 1975 at which time UI benefits were totally excluded from the definition of taxable income. Almost $18 billion in UI benefits was distributed to 16 million federal income tax filing units or 17 per cent of all tax filing units in 1975. Nearly 59 per cent of the units receiving UI had federal tax liability on their non-UI income, a percentage almost identical to the 62 per cent of all tax filing units with tax liability. Total tax liability equalled approximately $128 billion dollars.

How well did UI compensate the unemployed for lost income due

Table 8.2 Mean replacement ratios and tax rates for unemployed individuals, 1975

	Less than $5 000	*$5 000 to $15 000*	*$15 000 to $25 000*	*Greater than $25 000*	*All units*[a]
Without taxation of UI					
(1) Gross replacement rate	.51	.51	.46	.40	.50
(2) Net replacement rate	.65	.85	.92	.93	.80
(3) Net UI tax rate	.53	.56	.53	.52	.54
'Current' law provisions					
(4) Net replacement rate	.65	.85	.92	.92	.80
(5) Net UI tax rate	.53	.56	.50	.43	.53
Full taxation of UI					
(6) Net replacement rate	.65	.83	.90	.91	.78
(7) Net UI tax rate	.51	.46	.40	.33	.46

[a] Weighted average for all units.

to unemployment in 1975? An answer to this question is provided by the data in Table 8.2 which presents estimates of mean gross and net replacement rates (rows 1 and 2) for the total sample of unemployed individuals by income class. In this table, gross replacement rate is defined as the ratio of weekly UI Benefits to weekly gross wages. The net replacement rate is the ratio of annual income actually received to that annual income which would have been received if the worker had not experienced unemployment. Annual income actually received is the sum of UI benefits plus all other income net of taxes. That income which would have been received is computed by annualizing reported non-UI income.

The average estimated gross replacement rate is equal to 0.50; that is, UI replaces a half of each dollar of gross wage loss. This average is a better estimate of the gross replacement rate to recipients with annual incomes less than $15 000 (including UI) than for those above this level, however. For UI recipients with annual incomes between $15 000 and $25 000, this rate is only 0.46, and for recipients with incomes above $25 000 the mean falls to 0.40.

The decline in gross replacement rates at successively higher income levels would seem to suggest that the UI system is more valuable for lower than for upper income classes. This conclusion is misleading for two reasons, however. First, estimates of the gross replacement rate vary substantially within each income category.

Secondly, and more importantly, the gross replacement rate is not a true measure of how well the UI system protects purchasing power because it is based on pre-tax rather than post-tax earnings and thus does not consider the disposable income available to the consumer. Further, the gross replacement rate refers only to the benefits and wages of the unemployed individual, while it is the total earnings of the tax filing unit of which the individual is a member which is relevant to the determination of marginal and average tax rates and hence to the individual's post-tax income (Hamermesh, 1977). Because the net replacement rate (row 2) remedies both these deficiencies it is a truer measure of the recipient value of the UI system. Examining row 2 we see that the net replacement rate is significantly higher than the gross replacement rate for every income class, and in contrast to the gross replacement rate, it increases dramatically through successively higher income classes. For recipients in tax filing units with annual incomes over $25 000, on average annual income actually received (net earnings plus UI benefits) is 93 per cent of that income which would have been received had there not been unemployment.

To determine the financial incentive to seek work faced by an unemployed worker, a measure is needed of the proportion of the next dollar of earnings the worker will receive as disposable income should he or she return to work. The net tax rates presented in rows 3, 5, and 7 of Table 8.2 provide such a measure. They are defined as the ratio of UI benefits net of taxes to net wages. The financial incentive to seek work is one minus the net tax rate.

When UI benefits are excluded from the income tax base, the net tax rate is uniformly greater than the gross replacement rate for every income class. For the total population the difference is not great at 4 percentage points. Incorrectly employing the gross replacement rate as a measure of incentive effects, a common mistake, would not appear too misleading in this case. But to assume that this relationship holds for different income classes introduces serious error. Because the net tax rate is fairly constant across income classes while the gross replacement rate declines with progressively higher income, the differential between these rates increases with income. For unemployed individuals with annual income greater than $25 000, the gross replacement rate overstates the financial incentive to return to work by almost a quarter relative to the net tax rate.

A favorite strategy of the opponents of taxing UI benefits is to argue that taxation necessarily implies a tradeoff between the efficiency and benefit adequacy effects of the UI system: taxation will increase financial incentives to seek work, but only at the cost of significantly decreased adequacy. Comparison of rows 3, 5, and 7 confirms the first half of this tradeoff. Net tax rates do fall, thereby increasing incentives to work under both the current tax treatment of UI and the scheme which would implement full taxation . Consistent with earlier findings by Hutchens, these effects are targeted exclusively on units with income less than $15 000. All income classes would experience a reduction in mean tax rates if there were no exclusion of UI benefits, the greatest reduction experienced once again by units with the greatest income. Comparison of net replacement rates under the alternate tax schemes (rows 2, 4, and 6) do not substantiate the assertion that taxation comes at the cost of significantly decreased benefit adequacy. The net replacement rates are remarkably stable across the alternate schemes, with the greatest decline equaling merely 2 percentage points. The net replacement rate for the lowest income groups is completely unaffected. Surely the tradeoff between incentive effects and adequacy, should it exist at all, has been greatly exaggerated.

The budgetary impact of taxation and labor supply response

If taxation of UI benefits has only minimal adverse effect on the income protection provided average recipients, can it simultaneously increase federal tax revenues to the Treasury or reduce total program costs to a significant degree? The results presented in Tables 8.3 and 8.4 clearly indicate that such may be the case. Even when not accounting for potential labor supply responses, taxation of UI under current law yields an estimated additional $.4 billion in the tax revenues, while full taxation would yield six times this amount. We argued earlier, however, that the search decisions of unemployed workers are influenced by the size of their UI benefits and that taxing these benefits will encourage an earlier return to work than otherwise. The results of the simulations indicate that the tax provisions under current law lead to a marginal reduction in the duration of unemployment (–0.05 to –0.1 weeks), resulting in an increase in total earnings of $0.5 to $1 billion. In contrast, full taxation of UI benefits would cut the average duration of unemployment by more than a week with a concomitant increase in total earnings of $2.7 to $5.1 billion. Accounting for these behavioral changes increases the additional tax revenues yielded by the two tax schemes by 150 per cent:

Table 8.3 Measures of the impact of labor supply response on tax revenue, budgets and output (ε = 0.25)

	Less than $5 000	*$5 000 to $15 000*	*$15 000 to $25 000*	*Greater than $25 000*	*All units*
'Current' law tax provisions					
Change in federal taxes – no imputed response ($billions)	0.0	0.0	.2	.2	.4
Change in federal taxes – imputed response ($billion)	0.0	0.0	.25	.3	.6
Savings in UI program ($billions)	0.0	0.0	.05	.05	.1
Total budget impact ($billions)	0.0	0.0	.3	.3	.6
Change in earnings ($billions)	0.0	0.0	.2	.3	.5
Change in average duration of unemployment (weeks)	0.0	0.0	–.1	–.9	–.05[a]
Full taxation of UI					
Change in federal taxes – no imputed response ($billions)	.1	1.4	.8	.2	2.5
Change in federal taxes – imputed response ($billions)	.17	1.7	.9	.5	3.3
Savings in UI program ($billions)	.06	.4	.2	.1	.8
Total budget impact ($billions)	.2	2.1	1.1	.6	4.0
Change in earnings ($billions)	.15	1.1	.7	.6	2.6
Change in average duration of unemployment (weeks)	–.2	–.8	–1.0	–1.7	–.7[a]

[a] Weighted average for all units.

full taxation could potentially increase federal tax revenues by $3.8 billion dollars.

Accounting for changes in labor supply has the additional implication of decreasing UI expenditures. UI savings under current law are estimated to $0.1 billion to $0.2 billion. UI expenditures would be cut by an estimated $0.8 to $1.5 billion if benefits were fully taxed, putting the total budgetary impact of full taxation (increased tax revenues plus UI savings) from $4.0 to $5.3 billion. Estimates which do not acknowledge behavioral changes place this figure at $4.0 billion thereby underestimating the potential effect by roughly 19 to 33 per cent depending upon the value of ε chosen. Traditional projections of the total impact of current law appear similarly to

Table 8.4 Measures of the impact of labor supply response on tax revenue, budgets and output ($\varepsilon = 0.5$)

	Less than $5 000	*$5 000 to $15 000*	*$15 000 to $25 000*	*Greater than $25 000*	*All units*
'Current' law tax provisions					
Change in federal taxes – no imputed response ($billions)	0.0	0.0	0.2	0.2	0.4
Change in federal taxes – imputed response ($billions)	0.0	0.0	0.3	0.4	0.7
Savings in UI program ($billions)	0.0	0.0	0.1	0.1	0.2
Total budget impact ($billions)	0.0	0.0	0.4	0.5	0.9
Change in earnings ($billions)	0.0	0.0	0.4	0.6	1.0
Change in average duration of unemployment (weeks)	0.0	0.0	–0.3	–1.6	–0.1[a]
Full taxation of UI					
Change in federal taxes – no imputed response ($billions)	0.1	1.4	0.8	0.2	2.5
Change in federal taxes – imputed response ($billions)	0.2	1.8	1.0	0.8	3.8
Savings in UI program ($billions)	0.1	0.8	0.4	0.2	1.5
Total budget impact ($billions)	0.3	2.6	1.4	1.0	5.3
Change in earnings ($billions)	0.3	2.3	1.3	1.2	5.1
Change in average duration of unemployment (weeks)	–0.4	–1.5	–1.8	–3.2	–1.2[a]

[a] Weighted average for all units.

understate the potential effects of those provisions by approximately the same percentage.

Because our study concentrates on only labor supply side response to taxing UI, we may also be underestimating the total budgetary effects of taxing UI benefits by ignoring two potentially important demand side effects. Because of induced reduction in unemployment duration, UI benefits will decrease. This implies that future UI taxes paid by employers will also decrease. Given that the UI tax is only partly experience rated, recent evidence (Halpin, 1979) suggests that if decreased UI tax rates reduce experience rating imperfections the number of spells of unemployment would also decrease, thus further increasing employment and income tax revenues.[6]

Moreover, because the incidence of the UI tax is generally assumed to be borne by workers (Musgrave and Musgrave, 1980), any decrease in employer taxes should, *ceteris paribus*, lead to increased wages and again then, larger income tax revenues. However, an estimate of increased government revenues due to these demand factors is beyond the scope of this paper.

CONCLUDING REMARKS

In the previous section, we presented results from simulations in order to analyze the effect of the inclusion of UI in the tax base. Our findings can be summarized by the following observations:

1. Even when compared to the current tax provisions, full taxation of UI would drastically reduce adverse incentives created by high rates of UI compensation.
2. Full taxation of UI would not seriously affect the income replacement role of the UI program.
3. Full taxation of UI when compared to no taxation of UI represents a tax loss of 21 per cent of UI benefits paid. This figure compares favorably with the estimate of the tax loss by Feldstein which was computed at 23 per cent of UI benefits.
4. Current methods employed by the Treasury to estimate tax revenues and budget impacts drastically underestimate the potential impacts by factors of two to one.
5. Moving from the partial taxation of UI as implied in current law to full taxation of UI would not only have favorable budget impacts, but would serve to increase output by as much as a half per cent.

In these days of supply-side economics it seems counter to popular notions that further taxation would lead to greater output. But given these results, it seems that the full taxation of UI would be the prudent course to follow, for it would go a long way in addressing the adverse disincentive created by UI and the problems of both tax and transfer equity without seriously affecting the income maintenance role of UI.

Notes

1. One study (Sandell, 1980) indicates that recipiency of UI has a strong positive effect on both the asking (or reservation) wage and the duration of unemployment for unemployed workers. Another study, (Warner,

Poindexter, and Fearn, 1980) found that unemployed workers receiving UI were *ceteris paribus* 51 per cent less likely to leave unemployment in any given week as compared to unemployed non-UI recipients. While neither of these studies directly address the relationship between unemployment duration and the level of UI benefits, their findings indicate that UI recipients are likely to have longer spells of unemployment thus indirectly supporting this hypothesis.

2. That is, because AGI exceeds the $20 000 minimum by $1000, $500 of UI benefits are subject to tax. Thus, in our example, only one-eighth ($500/$4000) of total benefits are taxable. If AGI were $20 000 before counting UI, half of all UI benefits would be subject to tax. Thus the percentage of UI subject to tax under the current law is 50 per cent at most. For a large number of workers the current law taxes less than 50 per cent of benefits.
3. Other government programs that would be directly affected would be the food stamps and Aid to Families with Dependent Children (AFDC-UP) programs.
4. Two recent independent studies of the British UI system estimate values of the elasticity of duration with respect to the gross replacement rate ranging from 0.6 to 0.8, somewhat above the magnitude of Hamermesh's 'best point estimate' (see Lancaster, 1979; Nickell, 1979).
5. We do not consider the possibility that states with income taxes would follow a federal precedent to include all UI benefits in their tax base. Were states to follow such a procedure, however, the aggregate budgetary impact of taxing UI benefits would be somewhat greater than the estimates presented below.
6. We are grateful to Dan Hamermesh for pointing out this potential effect.

References

BETSON, D., GREENBERG, D. and KASTEN, R. (1980) 'A Micro-Simulation Model for Analyzing Alternative Welfare Reform Proposals: An Application to the Program for Better Jobs and Income', in R. HAVEMAN and K. HOLLENBECK (eds) (1980) *Microeconomic Simulation Models for Public Policy Analysis* (New York: Academic Press).

BURGESS, P. L. and KINGSTON, J. L. (1976) 'The Impact of Unemployment Insurance Benefits on Reemployment Success', *Industrial and Labor Relations Review*, 30(1): 25–31.

EHRENBERG, R. G. and OAXACA, R. L. (1976) 'Unemployment Insurance, Duration of Unemployment, and Subsequent Wage Gain', *American Economic Review* 66(5): 754–66.

FELDSTEIN, M. (1974) 'Unemployment Compensation: Adverse Incentives and Distributional Anomalies', *National Tax Journal*, 27(2): 231–44.

HALPIN, T. C. (1979) 'The Effects of Unemployment Insurance on Seasonal Fluctuations in Employment', *Industrial and Labor Relations Review*, 32(3): 353–62.

HAMERMESH, D. (1977) *Jobless Pay and the Economy* (Baltimore: Johns Hopkins Press).

HAMERMESH, D. (1982) 'What is an Appropriate Benefit Level for the Unemployed?', in P. M. SOMMERS (ed.) (1982) *Welfare Reform in America* (Boston: Kluwer-Nijhoff).

HUTCHENS, R. (1979) 'The Effect of Policy Parameters Changes and the Distribution of Unemployment Insurance Benefits', *National Tax Journal*, 32(4): 513–25.

KIEFER, N. and NEUMAN, G. R. (1978) 'Structural and Reduced Form Analyses of the Duration of Unemployment', NBER Conference on Low Income Labor Markets. 9 June.

KIEFER, N. and NEUMAN, G. R. (1979) 'An Empirical Job Search Model, with a Test of the Constant Reservation Wage Hypothesis', *Journal of Political Economy*, 87(1): 89–107.

LANCASTER, T. (1979) 'Econometric Methods for the Duration of Unemployment', *Econometrica*, 47(4): 939–56.

MUNTS, R. (1976) 'Policy Developments in Unemployment Insurance', Institute for Research on Poverty Discussion Paper, No. 361–76.

MUSGRAVE, R. and MUSGRAVE, P. (1980) *Public Finance in Theory and Practice*, 3rd ed. (New York: McGraw-Hill).

NICKELL, S. (1979) 'Estimating the Probability of Leaving Unemployment', *Econometrica*, 47(5): 1249–66.

SANDELL, S. (1980) 'Job Search by Unemployed Women: Determinants by Asking Wages', *Industrial and Labor Relations Review*, 33(3): 368–78.

SUNLEY, E. (1977) 'Employee Benefits and Transfer Payments', In J. A. PECHMAN (ed.) *Comprehensive Income Taxation* (Washington, D. C.: Brookings Institution) 75–114.

US CONGRESS 1978 House. *A Bill to Amend the Internal Revenue Code of 1954* (95th Congress, 2nd Session, HR12078: 129–31).

WARNER, J., POINDEXTER, J. and FEARN, R. (1980) 'Employer-Employee Interaction and the Duration of Unemployment', *Quarterly Journal of Economics*, 94(2): 213–33.

WELCH, F. (1977) 'What Have We Learned from Empirical Studies of Unemployment Insurance?' *Industrial and Labor Relations Review*, 36(4): 451–61.

Part III
Distributional Impacts of Tax Policies

9 The Growth and Distribution of Tax Expenditures*

John F. Witte

INTRODUCTION

Tax expenditures are officially defined in the Congressional Budget and Impoundment Act of 1974 as 'those revenue losses attributable to provisions of the Federal tax laws which allow a special exclusion, exemption, or deduction from gross income or which provide a special credit, a preferential rate of tax, or a deferral of tax liability . . .' (US Government, 1974). The 'expenditure' notion, popularized by Stanley Surrey, implies that tax reduction provisions can be viewed as the equivalent of direct budget outlays. Considerable controversy surrounds the concept. Even the term is controversial, with critics arguing that to consider reductions from a hypothetical tax base as 'expenditures' implies that by fiat government has some claim on all private income. This semantic controversy has become somewhat pedantic in recent years as the term has increased in popular use and as the policy implications of tax expenditures have received increasing attention. Since 1974 an official tax expenditure 'budget', listing individual provisions and estimates of lost revenue, has been published as an appendix to the federal budget.

Older controversial debates, predating the term 'tax expenditure', encompass both the growth and distribution of benefits from tax reduction provisions. The expansion of tax expenditures in comparison with a theoretically broad and comprehensive tax base has been the subject of periodic analysis for over three decades. Liberals tend to view this expansion with alarm under the generic heading 'erosion of the tax base' (Pechman and Okner, 1972). Conservatives often join in the call for base-broadening, but also emphasize the impact of high marginal tax rates on investment and thus link base broadening to lower rates and may also justify at least part of the tax expenditure system (Freeman, 1973; Ture, 1978).

* The research reported in this paper was supported by National Science Foundation Grant No. DAR-8011902 and a fellowship from The Russell Sage Foundation.

Attitudes probably vary more on the distributional effects of tax expenditures. Many liberal critics view such tax reduction devices as 'loopholes' or 'tax shelters', which imply narrowly drawn provisions that benefit small groups of wealthy taxpayers – examples are drawn from a large set of such provisions, and estimated benefits are presented in terms of absolute dollar amounts for different income levels. Whether the dollar amounts are based on analysis of actual return data or on hypothetical cases the disproportionate dollar amount going to higher income groups is emphasized (Stern, 1964; Surrey, 1970, 1972, 1973). On the other hand, Conservatives stress that: tax reduction provisions are based on reasonable treatments of income and expenses; the middle classes benefit as well as the rich; the upper-income groups still pay most of the income taxes; and tax expenditures should be calculated as a percentage of taxes paid (Freeman, 1973). Usually both sides in this debate support their claims by the use of selective examples rather than a more comprehensive analysis of the tax expenditure system.

This chapter provides an analysis of the growth of tax expenditures, and presents a broad view of their distribution based on estimates of benefits generated by the Department of Treasury for 67 tax expenditures for the year 1977.[1] A distribution coefficient similar to Suit's *S* (Suits, 1977) is used to analyze the distribution of individual provisions, the aggregate totals for all provisions, and the distribution of benefits for classes of tax expenditures which are categorized on the basis of the primary rationale for the provisions. A taxonomy of tax expenditures is necessary to make sense of the variations in distributions across a large number of tax reduction provisions. Section 1 briefly describes that taxonomy. Section 2 analyzes the scope and growth of revenue losses due to the tax expenditure system. Section 3 explains the calculation of distribution coefficients based on different equity standards. Section 4 describes aggregate distributions of benefits and variations between individual provisions and classes of tax expenditures. Section 5 is a discussion of the policy implications and the prospects for tax reform.

A TAXONOMY OF TAX EXPENDITURES

Although an official definition of tax expenditures exists, a definitive listing of tax expenditures does not. Since 1976, when the first full list of tax expenditures was published, there have been slight variations in the official lists because different political regimes include some provisions and exclude others. However, a common core has existed over these years and is the basis of a larger study of the development and legislative history of tax expenditures (Witte, 1982, 1985). The list employed in that study includes, with slight exceptions, the common elements from official tax expenditure lists from 1976 to 1982. Those provisions are listed by category in Table 9.1. The full list of tax expenditures is included for reference because distribution estimates are not available for some of the tax expenditures. Notably, estimates are not available for provisions which exclusively aid corporations. This is because the estimates are derived from information directly available on individual tax returns (for example, itemized deductions) and estimates obtained from a merge program that adds data not available directly on the returns (for example, income excluded from taxes that need not be reported). Estimating the distribution of benefits from provisions that lower corporate income taxes requires a complex set of assumptions which were not calculated for this data set (see Pechman and Okner, 1974). However, distribution data exists for 67 of 90 provisions, and those 67 account for 78 per cent of the estimated revenue lost through tax expenditures.

Since it is difficult to summarize the growth and distribution of 67 different tax provisions, they have been categorized on the basis of what appears to be the primary rationale or purpose behind the provision. The categorial divisions are functionally relevant in terms of policy ends but also are theoretically relevant in terms of the frequently referenced tradeoff between equity and economic efficiency. Two types of equity and efficiency are imbedded in this taxonomy. Equity provisions address either conditions of *economic need*, or provisions designed to produce *tax equity* by eliminating double taxation. Efficiency provisions are divided into *general economic incentive* provisions, which are intended to induce general investment that is not exclusive to a particular industry or sector, and *specific economic incentives* which are designed to encourage specific forms of desired economic behavior. The latter are more narrowly focused and may be targeted on specific industries. A fifth category, which creates the most difficulty, is labelled *special group benefits*. This category accounts for provisions that provide an exclusive benefit for a clearly defined group or organization. Because this taxonomy is the basis for the estimates that follow, the methodology needs to be explained in detail.

Placing provisions in appropriate categories depends on the most basic logical rationale for a provision. Historical arguments are considered in this process, but often are inconclusive in that a string of rationalizations are often presented in political arguments for a particular benefit. Although in most cases using the definitions and explanations below leads to a relatively obvious category for a provision, there are some provisions that can be reasonably classified into two categories. Nearly all of those cases come down to a determination of whether a provision should be primarily considered a special group provision. It is interesting to note that the pivotal group is the elderly, and whether provisions affecting the elderly should be considered as 'need-based' provisions or benefits going to a special group. Since I believe that the primary rationalization for expenditures targeted on the elderly is economic need, and the distribution of benefits from these provisions clearly indicates that they primarily affect the poor, I have placed these provisions in the need category. The following definitions apply. The reader may wish to refer to Table 9.1 which lists individual tax expenditures by category.

Category I – Need-based provisions

This category is meant to identify provisions designed to take into account presumed economic need. Only provisions affecting current conditions of need will be included. Those designed to induce behavior that may insure against future hardships (for example, employer contributions to pensions, health care, life insurance, and so on) will be considered incentive provisions (Category V). Need includes: conditions imposing restraints in income-earning potential; extraordinary expenses; conditions of economic hardship; and provisions affecting the elderly.

Category II – Tax equity

Provisions in this category are designed to either:

1. eliminate taxes on taxes; *or*
2. take into consideration expenses accrued in earning income.

Category III – Special group benefits

The critical conditions in determining if provisions fall into this category are:

1. that the provision affects a reasonably permanent and identifiable demographic or occupational group; *and*
2. that the economic conditions addressed by the provision cannot be assumed to be exclusive to the group; *and*
3. that there is *no* overriding presumption that the benefit is being granted primarily on other grounds.

The first condition applies a restrictive definition to the concept of a group. The reason for this is that without this restriction every tax provision could be classified as a special group benefit, in that at any point in time they affect identifiable categories of individuals. Also, one of the major concerns of this paper is the political implications of tax expenditures, thus I am particularly (although not exclusively) interested in groups that might conceivably become organized political interest groups. Three tests apply to this condition: (1) whether the 'group' has formal organizations or associations, (2) whether membership in the group is likely to be accompanied by common identifications, and (3) whether membership reflects a relatively permanent condition and not just a temporary economic circumstance.

The second condition is designed to give concrete meaning to the term 'special'. An example of this is the inclusion in this category of the income exclusion for armed forces' benefits or veterans' pensions on the grounds that there are other occupational groups with similar pension and payment plans which do not receive the tax benefits.

The final condition is admittedly something of a judgment call. In some cases the choice between fundamental purposes seems clear (for example, the exemption for the blind or exclusion of unemployment benefits); however, it is much more difficult for some other provisions. Since in some cases a provision fulfills conditions one and two but also has an equally plausible rationale based on need or economic incentives, presuming that these rationales take precedence has the effect of reserving this category for the relatively blatant cases of narrow special interest.

Category IV – General economic incentives

The provisions in this category are:

1. designed to induce investment and, at least theoretically, to lead to economic growth; *and*,

2. are not exclusive to a particular industry or class of economic producers.

Category V – Specific economic incentives

The provisions in this category include an assortment of provisions designed to create economic incentives meant to encourage specific forms of desirable behavior other than general economic investment. The distinction between Category V and Category III entails the nature of organized interests and whether the provision is primarily designed to simply aid a group or to induce a specific activity.

THE GROWTH OF TAX EXPENDITURES

Growth in numbers of tax expenditures

One simple method of understanding the growth of tax expenditures is to study the origin of the 'current' set of tax expenditures. This is not a totally accurate measure of change because it does not include provisions that have been repealed in years prior to 1974, which is the starting point for the set of tax expenditures on which this study is based. For example, in the early years of the income tax exclusions existed, but were latter repealed, for income of the President, US Judges, federal, state and local government employees, and certain income in the form of gifts and inheritance. Deductions at one time were granted for interest on federal bonds and federal income taxes paid in the prior year. Further, if the many exceptions, exclusions and special provisions that affected wartime excess profits taxes were included as tax expenditures, this list would grow significantly.

Since the Second World War several provisions that would be classified as tax expenditures, but do not appear in the set in Table 9.1 have also been repealed. These include exclusion of taxation of building and loans and co-operative banks in 1951 (leaving only credit unions); repeal of deductions for customs, excise, and miscellaneous state and local taxes and fees in 1964; eliminating the five-year amortization for child care facilities; and keeping temporary the one-year tax credit for the purchase of a new home enacted in 1977. In the current list, the deduction of state gasoline taxes was repealed during the energy crisis in 1977, and the differentials between the

Table 9.1 The tax expenditure system

Tax expenditure	*(1) Year of origin*	*(2) 1975 $ amount (millions)*	*(3) 1982 $ amount (millions)*	*(4) Distribution coefficient*[1]
Category I – Need-based provisions		13 460	30 489	+.308
Exclusion of social security – OASI	1941	2 740	9 980	+.535
Deduction of medical expenses	1942	2 315	3 924	−.140
Exclusion of workmen's compensation	1918	505	3 100	+.536
Additional exemption for the elderly	1948	1 100	2 355	+.196
Exclusion of unemployment benefits	1938	2 300	2 060	+.409
Exclusion of social security – survivors	1941	450	1 915	+.535
Exclusion of veterans' disability	1917	540	1 360	+.184
Earned income credit	1975	0	1 255	+.955
Exemption of students over 18	1918	670	995	+.162
Exclusion of social security-disability	1941	275	915	+.540
Deduction of casualty loss	1913	280	800	−.260
Exclusion of public assistance	1913	105	445	+.808
Exclusion of capital gains on home sales of the elderly	1964	40	415	−.493
Exclusion of railroad retirement	1935	170	380	+.537
Exclusion of military disability	1942	70	165	+.559
Exclusion of disability (sick) pay	1954	315	155	+.244
Retirement tax credit	1954	130	135	+.739
Exclusion of coal miners' disability	1972	50	95	+.575
Additional exemption for the blind	1943	20	30	+.140

continued on page 178

Table 9.1 *continued*

Tax expenditure	*(1) Year of origin*	*(2) 1975 $ amount (millions)*	*(3) 1982 $ amount (millions)*	*(4) Distribution coefficient*[1]
Deduction of adoption expenses	1981	0	10	NA
Excess of percentage over minimum standard deduction	1964	1 385	repeal	+.007
Category II – Tax equity provisions		18 230	40 105	−.417
Deduction of state and local taxes	1913	8 490	20 395	−.457
Deduction of real estate taxes	1913	4 510	10 065	−.329
Exclusion state and local bond interest	1913	3 805	6 645	−.818
Child care credit	1954	295	1 120	+.161
Deduction for two-earner couples	1981	0	705	NA
Exclusion of employer-furnished meals and lodging	1918	265	655	+.078
Deferral of taxes on foreign corporate income	1913	NA	520	NA
Deduction of state gasoline tax	1913	865	repeal	−.131
Category III – Special group benefits		3 345	4 930	+.201
Exclusion of military benefits	1918	650	1 885	+.606
Capital gains for timber income	1943	205	600	−.690
Deduction of noncash agricultural co-op dividends	1913	NA	545	NA
Expensing of farm capital outlays	1916	610	545	−.371
Capital gains for certain farm income	1921	485	460	−.686
Excess bad debt for financial institutions	1947	880	250	NA

Exclusion of GI bill benefits	1917	255	175	+.710
Exclusion of reinvested utility dividends	1981	0	130	NA
Capital gains on coal royalties	1951	40	105	−.674
Exclusion of veterans' pensions	1917	25	85	+.898
Deferral of tax on shipping companies	1970	70	65	NA
Exclusion of certain agricultural cost sharing	1954	NA	60	NA
Capital gains on iron ore royalties	1964	10	20	−.847
Exemption of credit union income	1909	115	5	NA
Category IV – General economic incentives		14 770	58 205	−.622
Investment credit	1962	5 810	20 035	−.266
Capital gains	1921	5 785	18 315	−.683
Asset depreciation range	1971	NA	7 300	−.622
Capital gains at death	1921	NA	5 245	−.683
Research and development benefits	1954	635	2 390	−.798
Dividend exclusion	1916	315	2 185	−.188
Expensing construction period interest and taxes	1913	1 510	745	−.756
Excess first-year depreciation	1958	275	205	−.753
All savers' certificates	1981	0	515	NA
Depreciation of buildings in excess of straight line	1954	440	285	−.753
Category V – Specific economic incentives		28 475	101 905	−.240

continued on page 180

Table 9.1 *continued*

Tax expenditure	*(1) Year of origin*	*(2) 1975 $ amount (millions)*	*(3) 1982 $ amount (millions)*	*(4) Distribution coefficient*[1]
Exclusion of employer contributions to pensions	1926	5 225	25 765	−.169
Deduction for mortgage interest	1913	5 405	23 030	−.209
Exclusion of employer contributions to health plans	1954	3 275	15 330	−.065
Deduction of charitable contributions	1917	4 770	8 345	−.466
Exclusion of interest on life insurance	1913	1 545	4 535	−.204
Expensing exploration and development costs	1917	620	4 145	−.744
Excess of percentage over cost depletion	1913	2 475	2 750	−.750
Exclusion of self-employed contributions to pensions	1962	390	2 560	−.442
Exclusion of employer contributions to life insurance	1920	740	1 900	−.066
Exclusion of interest on industrial development bonds	1938	175	1 650	−.627
Domestic international sales corp. (DISC)	1971	1 130	1 465	NA
Deduction of charitable contributions to health organizations	1917	NA	1 360	−.634
Tax credit for corporations in US possessions	1921	245	1 200	NA
Deferral of capital gains on homes	1951	255	1 070	−.017

Investment credit for employee stock ownership plans (ESOPs)	1975	0	1 005	NA
Exclusion of interest on housing bonds	1968	0	920	+.574
Deduction of charitable contributions for education	1917	645	895	−.774
Exclusion of interest on pollution control bonds	1969	140	835	−.835
Credit for residential energy expenses	1978	0	670	NA
Credit for new energy technology and alternative fuels	1978	0	595	NA
Exclusion of scholarship and fellowship income	1954	200	465	+.602*
Depreciation of rental housing in excess of straight-line	1954	520	430	−.753
General and targeted jobs credit	1977	0	300	−.264
Investment credit for housing rehabilitation	1978	0	255	NA
Exclusion of employer contributions to accident insurance	1951	50	100	−.064
Exclusion of interest on student loan bonds	1976	0	100	NA
Credit for political contributions	1971	40	80	−.049*
Benefits for preserving historic structures	1976	0	80	NA
Five-year amortization for housing rehabilitation	1969	105	45	−.815
Credit for employing WIN recipients	1971	10	45	NA
Exclusion of employer educational assistance	1978	0	40	NA

continued on page 182

Table 9.1 *continued*

Tax expenditure	(1) *Year of origin*	(2) *1975 $ amount (millions)*	(3) *1982 $ amount (millions)*	(4) *Distribution coefficient*[1]
Exclusion of prepaid legal services	1976	0	20	+.161
Deferral of interest on savings bonds	1951	525	−80	−.709
Exclusion of employer child care benefits	1981	0	0	NA
Category VI – Miscellaneous provisions		1 475	13 720	−.379
Deduction of interest on consumer credit	1913	1 185	9 285	−.210
Safe harbors leasing	1981	0	3 450	NA
Exclusions and deductions for income earned abroad	1926	130	985	−.369
Maximum tax on personal services 'earned' income	1969	160	repeal	−.935
Total expenditures		80 270	248 470	−.231

Source: US Budgets, Special Analyses for Tax Expenditures. Estimated amounts include both individual and corporate revenue losses.

Note: 1. This coefficient is explained in the text. It ranges from +1 to −1, with +1 representing maximum distribution of the tax expenditure to low-income tax payers. It is based on 1977 distributions of individual income tax returns only. Distributions designated by a * are based on 1974 distributions.

minimum standard and percentage deductions and the earned and unearned rates were technically repealed, although in each case the repeal had the effect of adding to revenue losses.[2]

Thus, while the assumption which is sometimes made that tax benefits once conferred are never repealed is incorrect, the numbers are not substantial relative to new provisions that have been enacted. Further, some provisions that are repealed are technical in that the benefit is broadened to the point that it goes away by definition, or the benefit is traded for a parallel provision that means less revenue loss.[3] In any event, new provisions passed are for the most part cumulative, and thus by analyzing the dates of origin of the current list, we have an adequate, if not perfect measure of the expansion of the number of major tax-reduction provisions available in the income tax codes.

Table 9.2 depicts the dates of origin of tax expenditures broken down by the categories previously defined. The totals confirm what is already well known, that significant expansion in provisions has taken place over the 70 years of the income tax. However, perhaps less well understood, and clearly at odds with some official statements, the growth seems to be relatively steady, with almost exactly half of the current list originating prior to or during The Second World War.[4] Eleven of these provisions were part of the initial income tax deliberations in either 1909 or 1913. Although the pace of growth may have increased slightly in the last two decades, the increase is modest. If there has been a significant change in the pace of tax legislation, it has occurred very recently. Since 1976, 13 new provisions have been created. A careful examination of Table 9.1 indicates that many of these have been in Category V – evidence that in recent years the tax code is being viewed as a multifaceted policy tool. Both the Carter and Reagan Administrations, while sometimes stating the opposite philosophy, backed numerous tax initiatives in the areas of energy, housing, education and job creation (Witte, 1985).

Growth in revenue loss of tax expenditures

The revenue loss of the tax expenditure system can be partly understood by reviewing the totals for the years 1975 and 1982 depicted in Table 9.1.[5] However, the numbers are more meaningful when compared to total tax receipts, as is done in column 3 of Table 9.3. By whatever standard the growth has been enormous. As a percentage of federal outlays total tax expenditures have grown from 18 per cent

Table 9.2 Year of origin of tax expenditures

Category	*1909–19*	*1920–45*	*1946–69*	*1970–82*	*Totals*
I Need-based	5	8	5	3	21
II Tax equity	5	0	1	1	7
III Special group	6	3	3	2	14
IV Economic stimulus	2	2	4	2	10
V Economic incentive	7	4	10	13	34
VI Miscellaneous	1	1	1	1	4
All expenditures	26	18	24	22	90

in 1975 to an estimated 35 per cent in 1982. As a percentage of total income tax receipts (corporate and individual) they have increased from 49 per cent to 72 per cent over the same period.[6] As is apparent in Table 9.1, the growth has not been evenly distributed although all categories of tax expenditures have increased significantly. Excluding Category VI which includes four provisions which could not be classified, the most rapid expansion has been in the two economic efficiency categories. On a yearly basis since 1975 these provisions have grown at an average of approximately 20 per cent per year. The result has been an increase in the percentage of total tax expenditures going to categories IV and V from 54 per cent to 64 per cent (Table 9.3, columns 2 and 3). As shown in column 1 of Table 9.1, this is due partly to the initiation of new provisions in these categories (particularly Category V). However, the increase is also due to legislated expansion of existing provisions and to inflationary effects which disproportionately increase the value of some of these provisions.

MEASURING THE DISTRIBUTION OF TAX EXPENDITURES

As implied by the contradictory views of tax expenditures as either narrow, special interest loopholes, or legitimate adjustments to income tax calculations, how one interprets and measures the distribution of tax expenditures depends on the standard of comparison employed. In discussions of equality of income and wealth, the usual standard is equal division between people. This standard, for example, is assumed in construction of the Gini Index. However, for tax

Table 9.3 Tax expenditure growth by category

Category	(1) % dollar change 1975–82	(2) % of tax expenditures 1975	1982	(3) % of tax receipts 1975	1982	(4) Average annual change 1974–82[2]
I Need-based	126.5	16.8	12.3	8.2	8.8	13.2
II Tax equity	120.8	22.7	16.2	11.1	11.6	12.5
III Special group benefits	47.4	4.2	2.0	2.0	1.4	4.6
IV General economic incentives[1]	287.4	18.4	23.0	9.0	16.6	21.2
V Specific economic incentives	250.8	36.2	41.0	17.7	29.5	19.6
VI Miscellaneous	837.6	1.8	5.6	.9	4.0	30.1
All expenditures	209.5	100.1	100.1	48.9	71.9	16.9

Source: Author's estimates based on tax expenditure list and classification in Table 9.1.

Notes: 1. Unfortunately, published estimates for two of the largest provisions in this category, capital gains at death and asset depreciation ranges, are not available before 1977. Estimating these amounts for 1974 to 1976 by assuming an amount based on their average share of tax expenditures for 1977–82 changes the calculations for Category IV to: *% dollar change, 1975–82* = 185%; *% of tax expenditures, 1975* = 23.5%; *% tax receipts, 1975* = 12.2%. *Average annual change* is unaffected, so the growth rate of Category IV is still substantial.

2. Missing data in any year eliminate a provision from the change calculation for the year.

expenditures this standard cannot be used because relevant data only exist on those filing tax returns. More importantly, however, even the assumption that tax expenditures should be equally distributed among filers is unrealistic. Tax expenditures offset or reduce taxes due. Since low-income taxpayers pay very small amounts in taxes, the assumption that they should get an equal dollar amount of the tax expenditure pie misrepresents the political intent of these provisions, and would mean that many low-income taxpayers would have to receive a lump sum, negative tax rebate of thousands of dollars. However, because the standard of equality between persons is so common in equity discussions, distributional effects relative to filers will be included, though not emphasized.

Two more meaningful standards are to compare tax expenditures to the amount of income earned by different income groups, and to compare it to the amount of taxes ultimately paid. The first allows one to judge the distribution relative to the notion of a proportional or flat tax rate; and the second allows one to estimate how tax expenditures relate to differing final tax burdens. For both of these standards it is relevant to compare distributions for increasing levels of income. Percentage breakdowns by income group of total tax expenditures and the different classes are depicted in Table 9.4. Also shown are the percentages of total returns, adjusted gross income, and income taxes paid.

There are several statistics that can be used to interpret and summarize the basic data presented in Table 9.4. One simple method is to create ratios of percentages of tax expenditure to, respectively, percentages of returns, income and taxes paid for different income classes. Given whichever standard is selected, one can describe ratios of relative advantage for different income levels, with a ratio of one representing a proportionate share. Thus, for example, those with incomes between $5000 and $10 000 received 7.7 per cent of the benefits from tax expenditures, but had 12.3 per cent of aggregate income, thus they received less than a proportionate share based on income with a ratio of 0.63. However, the same calculation based on taxes, of which they pay 5.3 per cent, is 1.4.

Although such ratios are useful in describing the details of distributions, they are not very useful as a summary measure. A summary measure can be created based on cumulative frequencies. Analogous to the GINI Index, a distribution coefficient for tax expenditures can be constructed based on the relationship between the cumulative frequencies of tax expenditures and the cumulative frequencies of whatever standard (income, taxes, or returns) is selected. Figure 9.1 portrays a Lorenz-type curve for selected tax expenditures. As with a standard Lorenz curve, the data is ordered by increasing levels of income. The axes for this figures are the cumulative frequency of adjusted gross income and the cumulative percentage of tax expenditure benefits. A point of the curve indicates the cumulative percentage of a tax expenditure received by those holding a cumulative percentage of income. Thus, for point C, taxpayers who account for 80 per cent of all the adjusted gross income only received 18 per cent of the benefits from capital gains. Since the remaining 20 per cent of income is held by the largest earners, and they received 82 per cent of the benefits of capital gains, it is clear that this provision is highly

Table 9.4 Percentages of returns, income, taxes, and tax expenditures by income class, 1977

	Amount ($ billions)	*Expanded income ($1000s)*[1]								*Distribution coefficients*[2]		
		0–5	*5–10*	*10–15*	*15–20*	*20–30*	*30–50*	*50–100*	*+100*	D_r	D_i	D_t
Returns	86.6	26.9	22.3	16.5	13.2	14.0	5.5	1.3	.6			
Income	1 158.5	4.3	12.3	15.3	17.1	25.2	15.1	6.5	4.2			
Taxes paid	158.5	.4	5.3	10.6	14.5	25.7	19.8	12.0	11.6			
Total tax expenditures	82.3	4.2	7.7	9.1	11.6	19.4	16.7	13.7	17.6	–.59	–.23	.00
Tax expenditure classes												
I Need-Based	15.6	17.3	22.0	14.8	13.1	14.7	9.2	5.9	2.9	–.14	+.31	+.52
II Tax equity	15.1	.1	1.8	5.9	10.7	22.7	21.2	19.2	18.4	–.75	–.42	–.17
III Special group	2.2	10.0	26.2	16.7	9.7	7.7	9.5	8.1	11.9	–.26	+.20	+.39
IV General incentives	17.3	.5	2.2	4.1	5.2	9.7	16.3	20.0	42.0	–.84	–.62	–.44
V Specific incentives	29.3	.8	4.7	10.1	15.0	26.6	19.0	12.3	11.5	–.63	–.24	+.03
VI Miscellaneous	2.9	.4	2.3	5.8	11.7	25.7	21.7	12.2	20.2	–.73	–.38	–.13

Source: Unpublished US Treasury Department estimates.

Note: 1. Expanded income is adjusted gross income plus minimum tax 'preference income', minus investment interest expense to the extent of investment income (See note 9 in text).

2. The coefficients are based on different standards of comparisons as explained in the text. D_r is based on the percentage distribution of *returns*; D_i, the percentage distribution of *income*; and D_t, the percentages of *taxes paid*.

Figure 9.1 Cumulative frequency distributions of selected tax expenditures relative to income

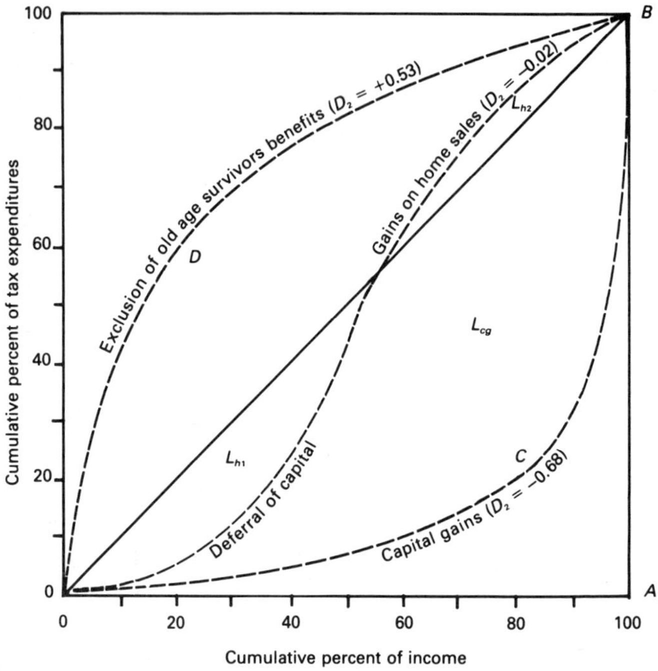

Source of data: Unpublished US Treasury Department estimates for 1977.
Note: Income is adjusted gross income. Units are individual returns ranked from lowest to highest income level.

skewed in favor of the wealthy. On the other hand, the curve depicting the exclusion of Social Security retirement benefits (OASI) represents a distribution skewed in the reverse direction. For this example the 45-degree line represents a distribution of tax expenditures that is proportional to the distribution of income.

An exact set of indices (one for each relevant standard on the horizontal axis) can be computed by calculating the ratio of the area between the curve and the 45-degree line (for example, L_{cg} in Figure 9.1) to the total area of triangle OAB. The latter measures the maximum possible skewness in the respective direction. Unlike the GINI, since tax expenditures may disproportionately aid either low-

or upper-income groups, the curves may fall on either side of the 45-degree line.[7] Therefore, *for this analysis, a negative sign will be used to depict distributions below the 45-degree line and a positive sign for those above.* Thus the distribution index ranges from −1, which represents a distribution of benefits accruing entirely to the highest income group; to +1, which represents a distribution going solely to the poorest. The 0 point indicates an aggregate tax expenditure distribution that is proportional to whatever standard is selected.[8]

WHO GETS WHAT FROM THE TAX EXPENDITURE SYSTEM

Since a principal purpose of this paper is to provide more comprehensive estimates of the distributional effects of tax expenditures than are presently available, it is appropriate to begin by describing the aggregate effects derived from summing the distributional benefits for all 67 tax expenditures. However, the aggregate distribution masks considerable variation between types of tax expenditures. As will become clear below, the final result is a system that disproportionately aids those in upper-income brackets, but also provides some benefits for nearly every income class and population or occupational grouping.

Aggregate effects

The aggregate distribution of tax expenditures is depicted in Table 9.4 and in Figures 9.2 and 9.3. Table 9.4 provides percentage breakdowns by 'expanded income' class. Expanded income, an income concept commonly used by the Department of Treasury, is defined as adjusted gross income, plus minimum tax preference income, less investment interest expense until it exceeds investment income.[9] Figure 9.2 is a cumulative frequency plot of tax expenditures relative to adjusted gross income, and Figure 9.3 is the same plot relative to total taxes paid.

The first obvious and overwhelming conclusion derived from Table 9.4 is that, if the standard of comparison is the total population, the well-off benefit from tax expenditures much more than those in the lower-income brackets. The median or 50th percentile for tax expenditures occurs at approximately $30 000. However, 95 per cent of the tax returns in 1977 were filed by those making $30 000 or less. This

Figure 9.2 Cumulative frequency distributions of tax expenditures relative to income

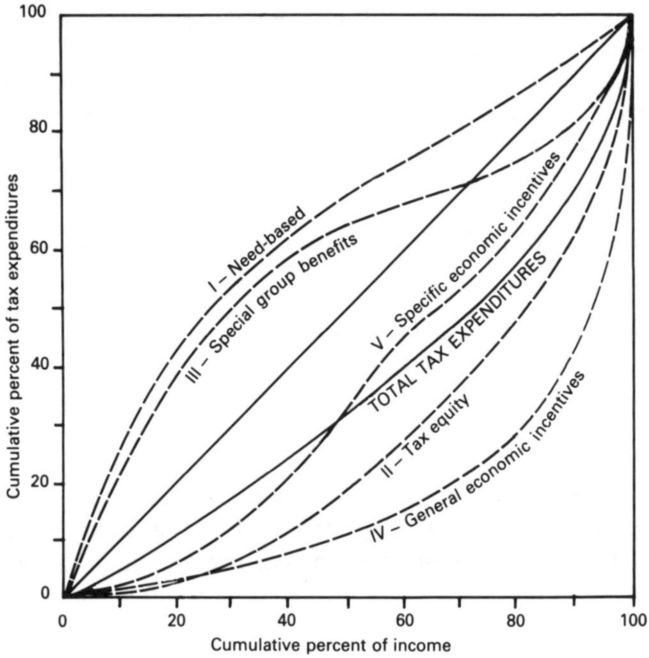

Source of data: Unpublished US Treasury Department estimates for 1977.
Note: Income is adjusted gross income. Units are individual returns ranked from lowest to highest income level.

distribution is reflected in the coefficient D_r, which was calculated based on a standard which assumed that each taxpaying unit would receive an equal proportion of tax expenditures. The −0.59 indicates that the area between the curve of total tax expenditures and the diagonal representing proportionality was 59 per cent of a distribution which would allocate all tax expenditures to the highest income class (that is, 59 per cent of the area of the lower triangle).

However, if the standard of comparison is either income or taxes ultimately paid, tax expenditures are much closer to a proportional distribution. With income as the standard, higher income groups still benefit in a proportion greater than the income they possess, but the distribution coefficient (D_i) decreases to −0.23. The distribution and

Figure 9.3 Cumulative frequency distributions of tax expenditures relative to taxes paid

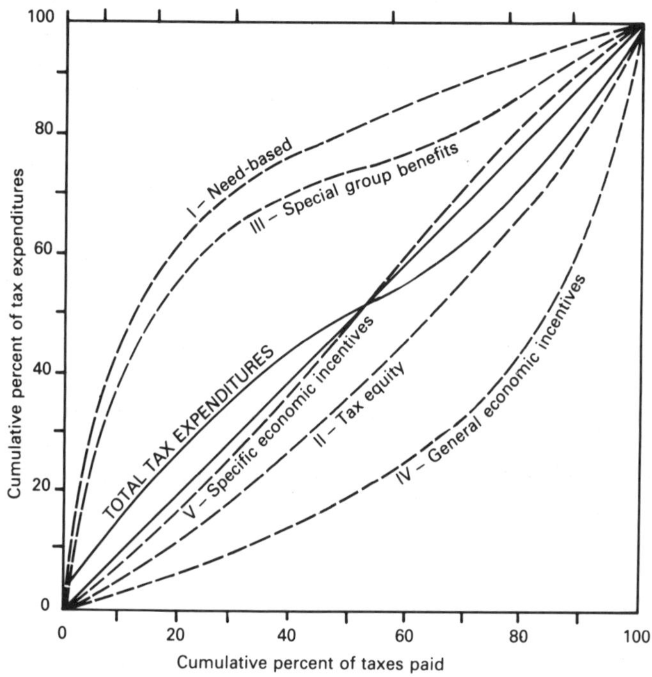

Source of data: Unpublished US Treasury Department estimates for 1977.
Note: Units are individual returns ranked from lowest to highest income level.

the area of deviation from a proportional standard is clearly presented in Figure 9.2. If the standard is taxes, the distributional coefficient (D_t) is exactly zero. This indicates that tax expenditures aggregated across the population are distributed in direct proportion to the amount of taxes paid. However, as can be seen in Figure 9.3, that aggregate masks variation across income classes. More precisely, the figure shows that both lower- and upper-income groups get a higher percentage of tax expenditures than the percentage of taxes they pay.

The distribution of benefits for specific income classes can be analyzed more precisely by calculating 'share' ratios based on different standards. Again, of course, the standard selected makes a great deal of difference. For example, those with incomes below $5000 account for 26.9 per cent of the returns but get only 4.2 per cent of tax expenditures, and thus based on a standard of proportionality between taxpayers, they do very poorly, getting only 15 per cent of what would be expected. On the other hand, if taxes paid is the standard, since they pay very little, they receive 10.5 times their share of tax expenditures. At the other extreme, those making over $50 000 get 19.5 times their share based on returns, but only 1.3 times the proportion of taxes they pay. What is interesting within this wide variation is that, regardless of the standard selected, very-high-income groups ($50 000 or more) never have a ratio below 1.0, and the middle-income groups (from $5000 to $20 000) never have a ratio above 1.0. For the middle-income groups, which accounts for approximately the middle two quartiles of taxpayers, the ratios are 0.55 based on returns, 0.64 based on income, and 0.93 if taxes paid is the benchmark. Thus, a very plausible set of conclusions is that: (1) the highest-income taxpayers get relatively more from tax expenditures, regardless of the equity standard; (2) the poor do very well relative to the taxes they pay; but (3) the middle class is disadvantaged by the aggregate tax expenditure system from any perspective.

Variations between tax expenditures

Although policy analysts in general, and tax experts in particular, are ever conscious of the varying effects of policies on income categories, politicians may be more attentive either to specific policy problems or the effects of policy actions on relevant political groups. A sampling of the distributional variation between types of tax expenditures was depicted in Figure 9.1 for three well-known and frequently-used tax reduction provisions. More complete evidence is available in Table 9.4, Figures 9.2 and 9.3, and in the full list of tax expenditures in Table 9.1. The results portrayed indicate a wide variation in the distribution of tax expenditures, but also a clear differentiation based on the purposes which underlie different categories of provisions.

The range of those who benefit from the tax expenditure 'budget' can be appreciated by glancing through the lengthy list of provisions in Table 9.1. The list confirms how extensive this policy area has become in terms of numbers and assortments of organized and unorganized groups or populations affected, and the range of behaviors supposedly influenced by the tax code. The elderly, blind, military, disabled, militarily disabled, coal-miners, timber owners, farmers, veterans, shipping companies, wage-earners living abroad, wage-earners in two-earner families, parents of students, students, welfare recipients, unemployed and home-owners are only a partial list of people selectively benefiting from one or more provisions. The code provides at least a dozen different mechanisms for encouraging general investment of savings, eight major provisions affecting residential housing, and by my coding, six or more provisions encouraging various forms of energy production, conservation, and use.[10] The tax laws encourage the provision of jobs, job-seeking, making a job comfortable and secure, while also offering a helping hand to those unable to find a job. It encourages health protection, education, life insurance, savings bonds, legal services, and employee ownership of corporations. It supports giving, caring for children, rehabilitating structures, retiring, going on public assistance, and – through the earned income credit – going off public assistance. The lists are so extensive that in an absolute sense the answer to the question of who benefits from tax expenditures is that nearly everyone does.

The various classes of tax expenditures have distinct distributional effects. The differences are graphically portrayed in Figures 9.2 and 9.3. The variation between classes, precisely measured by the distribution coefficients in Table 9.4, is slightly wider when cumulative taxes (Figure 9.3) is the standard. The 20 provisions intended to alleviate problems of economic need or hardship, as one would hope, primarily benefit those with low incomes. However, so do those provisions that are classified as narrow special interest, although these latter provisions are more evenly spread across the higher-income groups, while almost none of the need-based benefits go to those with higher incomes. Those provisions meant to promote specific economic behavior, which is the largest category both in terms of revenue and the number of provisions, 21, occupy a middle-level distribution with large amounts distributed between \$20 000 and \$50 000. The distribution is almost exactly proportional to the amount of taxes paid at every point in the income distribution. Tax expenditures intended to increase tax equity are more favorable to middle- and higher-income groups. By far the most beneficial for the affluent are those designed to promote general economic incentives.

This range can be captured by the striking difference between the two extremes which is revealed in Table 9.4. Of the total tax expenditures classified as need-based, 67.2 per cent go to taxpayers with \$20 000 or less, and only 8.8 per cent go to those with over \$50 000. On the other hand, only 12 per cent of the general economic incentives go to those reporting less than $20 000, while 62 per cent go to those reporting $50 000 or more. This variation is summarized by the spread in distribution coefficients, which for income goes from +0.31 for need-based provisions to −0.62 for those promoting general investment.

The best way to understand how these distributions come about is to relate the aggregates back to the specific provisions which are listed in Table 9.1. The distribution coefficient in column 4 of this table is based on income. The relative position of need-based provisions is evident from the signs of the coefficients of the individual provisions. Only three provisions in Category I have negative signs. Of these, the only provision of major revenue consequence is the deduction of medical expenses which tends to aid the middle-income groups.[11] Other than that, exclusions for Social Security, retirement, and survivors benefits, workmen's compensation, unemployment benefits, and public assistance, all go to those in the lower-income ranges in much greater proportion than their share of income would dictate. Because of its built-in income restrictions, as intended, the earned-income credit is the most beneficial income tax provision for the poor.

A similar but asymmetrical situation explains the oppositely skewed distribution of general economic incentives. None of the nine provisions on which we have data have a positive sign. Further, capital gains, asset depreciation provisions, and research and development incentives, all of which are large, are distributed at the extreme upper ends of the income distribution – far more than proportionate to the income they receive. This category would undoubtedly be even more heavily weighted toward high-income earners if the incidence of corporate benefits of the investment credit were available, or data existed on the All Savers Certificates, which were designed to have a tax-free interest of 70 per cent of Treasury Bill rates and thus only makes them attractive to investors in higher income brackets. Curiously, the least skewed provision in this category is the exclusion of a portion of dividend income. This is because the provision only excludes what, for the well-off, may be a small amount of dividends, and thus it disproportionately benefits the small investor. However, there is no escaping the conclusion that broad investment stimulus through the tax system leads to substantial tax breaks that go almost exclusively to the rich.

Generalizations become more complex for the other groups. For example, the provisions that comprise Category III, special group benefits, are a widely diverse set of provisions. However, the most important provision in terms of revenue, the exclusion of military benefits, is heavily weighted toward low-income earners, and this has an overpowering effect on the total distribution in the category. The aggregate distribution would probably not be weighted as much toward the lower-income levels if data were available on the missing provisions, all of which probably benefit primarily upper-income groups. However, in terms of revenue they do not account for very much.

The tax equity and specific economic incentive categories also display this diversity, although in each of these cases some of the large provisions affect primarily the middle- and upper-middle income ranges rather than heavily subsidizing the rich. For tax equity provisions this is true for the deduction of taxes (state, local and real estate), 48 per cent of which go to those with incomes between \$20 000 and \$50 000; however, it is not true for the other sizeable provision in that category, the tax exemption of state and local bond interest, which goes almost exclusively to high-income earners.[12] The long and important list of provisions designed to encourage specific forms of behavior varies as widely in terms of distribution as it does in terms of the behavior and functions it subsidizes. However, once again the largest of these provisions, currently accounting for over 60 per cent of the category, accrue not to the very rich but to the middle- and upper-middle income, home-owning, wage or salaried employee. Of the combined totals of the exclusion of employer contributions for pensions and health plans and the deduction for mortgage interest, which together account for over 25 per cent of all tax expenditures, 60 per cent fall within the range of \$15 000 to \$30 000, with only 14 per cent going to those reporting more than \$50 000.

Disaggregating the over-all distribution of tax expenditures creates a somewhat different impression than the analysis of aggregate coefficients. Although it becomes clear where those with higher incomes gain their relative advantage, one is struck by the diversity of income tax benefits. The poor, elderly, and disadvantaged, with consistently low incomes, benefit from a range of income exclusion provisions tailored to their specific condition; the rich benefit almost exclusively from provisions designed to provide general capital incentives for the economy; and the middle class benefit from deductions for taxes and interest and the exclusion of rapidly expanding employer contributions to benefit plans. Thus in a very tangible way everyone gets something; a fact that may be more important to politicians than the complicated arguments about relative equity that are the stock-in-trade of the academic.

SUMMARY AND IMPLICATIONS

Growth of tax expenditures

The general conclusions presented above were that tax expenditures have grown dramatically over the 70-year existence of the income tax. This growth has occurred both in the number of provisions and in the amount of absolute and relative revenues lost. There was also evidence that the tax expenditure system has grown at a faster rate in recent years due to inflated values of a number of provisions and due to increasing use of the tax code to affect non-revenue policy goals. Two implications of this expansion are often discussed.

The first implication is the increasing complexity of the tax code. This has been a long-standing complaint of tax experts, dating back at least to Yale economist T.S. Adam's sneering characterization of the 1921 Revenue Act which failed to reform and simplify the tax code as Congress had declared:

> They (Congressmen) proposed 'to narrow some of these holes at this session of Congress and close some more of them in the future.' I do not sneer at this position. It is one that an honest and intelligent man could conceivably take. But it overlooks and forgets one crucial fact. It assumes that, four or five years from now, when we get around to the task of patching up holes in the income tax, we shall have the kind of income tax that can be patched up. *The probability is strong that in four or five years the income tax will, as a matter of practical politics, be past patching.* (italics in the original) (quoted in Mellon, 1924).

Although we have continued to 'patch' the system, there is a growing consensus that the income tax has grown unmanageable for the ordinary citizen. That concern has recently produced another wave of reform discussions, this time under the banner of 'flat tax' proposals (which are not flat at all). Given the growth and breadth of the tax expenditure system, and the uncertainty attached to any comprehensive reform, it is likely that these proposals will be added to the large stack of grand reform designs that have been advanced with regularity since the Second World War. Although no one questions that complexity has become steadily worse, unless wholesale tax avoidance threatens, and the withholding system for wage income currently prevents that prospect, the probability of lasting tax reform remains low.

The other implication of tax expenditure growth is that it directly threatens the revenue raising capacity of the income tax. Again there are long-standing arguments that, as the tax base erodes, and the political limit in raising marginal rates is reached, the income tax will decline as the major source of federal revenue. A recent study of the income tax base by Steuerle and Hartzmark (1981) indicates that indeed the tax base is beginning to shrink as a percentage of personal income, but that the decline has only occurred since 1970. The major reason is that from 1948 (the beginning point in their study) to 1969, real or inflated income (mostly the former) expanded the potential base, and that since the standard deduction and exemption levels were not raised proportionately during that period, they sheltered smaller percentages of income. Thus for the middle-class wage earner, a higher percentage of income became taxable and the base expanded. However, by 1969, the expansion in taxable income became very small as deductions and exemptions were raised and taxpayers began to benefit more from the tax expenditure system. Since 1970 the base has begun to shrink. Combine this phenomenon with the recent higher marginal rates being paid by the middle class, which Steuerle and Hartzmark also demonstrate, and one must question whether or not the revenue system can sustain the needs of government without accepting the large deficits currently projected for the future. Thus the explosion of tax expenditures in recent years may accelerate the already declining revenue share for the income tax.

Distribution of tax expenditures

The simple question of who gets what from tax expenditures unfortunately does not have a simple answer. Indeed there is evidence to support all types of positions, including some that are diametrically opposed – which in itself is a relevant conclusion for understanding tax politics. It was shown that if one assumes that the appropriate norm is equal division of the benefits, aggregate tax expenditures are heavily weighted toward high-income taxpayers. However, it was argued that, given that tax expenditures are not wholly, and perhaps not even significantly designed to affect income redistribution, other standards of comparison may be more appropriate. The distribution of pre-tax income and taxes paid are two such standards. It was shown that the distribution of tax expenditures is much closer to the distribution of adjusted gross income than to the distribution of returns, and very close to being proportional to the amount of taxes people actually pay.

Shifting the focus from aggregate coefficients that measure the distribution across the total income range, to shares for different income levels, the conclusions are somewhat different and also tend to vary considerably depending on the standard selected. By any standard, the very well-off get more than their share, and, conversely, the middle-income groups always get less. However, there is a significant range in these effects depending on the standard used. For the poor the range is especially dramatic. If the standard is based on returns, they do very badly, but if the standard is taxes paid, they get much more than they 'deserve'. Finally, the purposes behind different tax expenditures are reflected in clearly distinct distributional patterns. The most important conclusion was to reinforce the widely-accepted proposition that creating general economic incentives to save and invest requires conferring substantial tax benefits on the wealthy.

Several implications can be drawn from the distributional patterns of tax expenditures. First, they suggest that the popular image that the tax system is a welfare program for the rich is greatly oversimplified. The rich disproportionately benefit because they pay a disproportionate share of taxes and because they control capital, which government induces them to invest. Secondly, and perhaps more important politically, the immense tax expenditure system benefits very large blocks in society, usually in a selective manner. This broad conference of benefits, which is consistent with electoral incentives for legislators, makes tax reform or even pruning the tax expenditure system an enormous task. Although it is conceivable that, since many tax expenditures benefit selective minorities, congressional majorities could be generated to eliminate some provisions, such actions set precedents and imply political retaliation. Thus the breadth of the tax expenditure system enhances its self-defense. Indeed, if tax expenditures were the exclusive privilege of the wealthy, containing the system would be much easier. The prospect of large deficits may produce some trimming, but the historical pattern has been one of relentless growth in tax expenditures regardless of deficits. Based on the distributional effects described in this paper it is difficult to predict that the future holds anything different.

Notes

1. I thank Tom Vasquez of the Tax Analysis Division of the Department of Treasury for making available the estimates by income groupings. For all subsequent analyses I alone am responsible.
2. It was initially assumed that the original percentage standard deduction was the norm and the minimum standard deduction an added benefit for those for which it was an advantage. Similarly, since the original rate structure was 70 per cent in the top bracket, when an alternative 50 per cent rate for earned income was enacted, it was considered a tax benefit. In each case the differences were counted as tax expenditures. For both, the expenditures disappeared when the differential was eliminated by repealing the original provisions (the percentage standard deduction and the 70 per cent rate). In both cases this actually increased revenue losses.
3. The cases in note 2 are examples of broadening an initial provision to the point where the tax expenditure is eliminated. An example of a parallel benefit is the repeal of the tax exempt status of building and loans and co-operative banks in 1951. While their net income became taxable, they were given and still enjoy significant preferential deductions relative to other banks in terms of the percentage of loans they can deduct as ostensible loan defaults.
4. These data differ significantly from congressional testimony given by Alice Rivlin, the Director of the Congressional Budget Office, in which she cites a growth in tax expenditures from 1967 to 1981 as going from 50 to 104. Since no tax expenditure lists were presented in her testimony, it is impossible to evaluate her figures, although they appear to be exaggerated at both points in time (see Rivlin, 1981, p. 25).
5. Comprehensive estimates were first available for fiscal year 1975. Prior to that estimates were available for what today is considered a very small sample of tax expenditures. Summing tax expenditures yields an inaccurate estimate if the goal is to determine how much revenue would be gained by repealing any set of provisions. The reasons for this involve people shifting to the standard deduction if itemized deductions were eliminated, and the fact that repealing combinations of provisions would force people into higher marginal tax brackets, a fact not taken into consideration in the estimates of revenue loss associated with individual provisions. However, our goal is not to make such calculations but rather to estimate the relative size of the tax expenditure system and different types of tax expenditures, and to note changes over time. For these comparative purposes there is no reason to believe that the estimates are statistically biased.
6. Data presented in congressional testimony by Alice Rivlin, are even more dramatic in that they extend back to 1967. Her data indicated that the tax expenditure system had grown from 38 per cent of total income

tax receipts in 1967 to 73.5 per cent in 1982. However, the exact list of provisions on which such calculations are based were not presented and the comprehensiveness of the early data sets were questionable (see Rivlin, 1981).

7. The standard Lorenz curve depicts the cumulative per cent of the population on the vertical axis and the cumulative per cent of income on the horizontal axis. Since the population is ordered in terms of increasing income, any given cumulative population percentile must be less than or equal to the same income percentile.
8. In those few cases where the distribution crosses the 45-degree line, such as the deferral of capital gains in home sales depicted in Figure 9.1, the index is computed by subtracting the smaller area (L_{h2}) from the larger (L_{h1}), then computing the ratio and attaching the sign of the larger area. Such a distribution reflects a provision that disproportionately benefits middle-income groups in the range where the switch occurs. Although developed independently by the author, the general concept of this index was first reported by Daniel Suits for measuring the distribution of tax burdens. A detailed description of the calculations appear in Suits, 1977.
9. The 'preference' list for computing a minimum tax is an *ad hoc* list that includes many provisions which benefit high-income groups and are used to avoid or defer paying taxes. The major provisions on the list include half the excluded portion of capital gains, the excess of percentage over cost depletion for mineral extraction, accelerated depreciation on property, and income realized by exercising stock options. The effect of this income concept is to 'spread out' adjusted gross income by adding income which accrues to upper-income groups, while not adding in excluded income (such as Social Security) which primarily benefits lower-income levels.
10. Annual lists of tax expenditures vary in how they label the growing number of tax provisions that produce incentives in the energy field. My set, listed in Table 9.1, Category V, is a consolidation of the current method which depicts 9 separate provisions, some of which have subcategories (US Government, 1982).
11. The breakdown of medical deductions is 20 per cent going to those under \$15 000; 46.1 per cent, \$15 000 to \$30 000; 18.3 per cent, \$30 000 to \$50 000; and 15.6 per cent to those above \$50 000.
12. The reason for this is that the rate of return on tax-free bonds is only appealing for those in high marginal brackets. For others after-tax yields are higher on taxable bonds.

References

FREEMAN, R. A. (1973) *Tax Loopholes: The Legend and the Reality* (Washington, D.C.: American Enterprises Institute).

MELLON, A. (1924) *Taxation: The People's Business* (New York: Macmillan).

PECHMAN, J. A. and OKNER, B. A. (1974) *Who Bears the Tax Burden?* (Washington, D.C.: Brookings Institution).

RIVLIN, A. (1981) Testimony before the Budget Committee of the U.S. Senate, Hearings on 'Tax Expenditure Limitation and Control Act of 1981' (November 24): 24–5.
STERN, P. M. (1964) *The Great Treasury Raid* (New York: Random House).
STEUERLE, E. and HARTZMARK, M. (1981) 'Individual Income Taxation, 1947–1979', *National Tax Journal*, 34: 145–66.
SUITS, D. B. (1977) 'Measurement of Tax Progressivity', *The American Economic Review*, 67: 747–52.
SURREY, S. (1970) 'Tax Incentives as a Device for Implementing Government Policy: A Comparison with Direct Government Expenditures', *Harvard Law Review*, 83.
SURREY, S. (1972) 'Tax Subsidies as a Device for Implementing Government Policy: A Comparison with Direct Government Expenditures,' in *Joint Economic Committee, Federal Subsidy Program Papers*, 92nd Congress, 2nd Session (Washington, D.C.: U.S. Government Printing Office) 74–105.
SURREY, S. (1973) *Pathways to Tax Reform: The Concept of Tax Expenditures* (Cambridge, Mass.: Harvard University Press).
TURE, N. (1978) 'Taxation and the Redistribution of Income,' in Arleen A. Leibowitz (ed.), *Wealth Redistribution and the Income Tax* (Lexington, Mass.: D.C. Heath and Company) 3–42.
US GOVERNMENT (1974) The Congressional Budget and Impoundment Act, Section 3(a) (3).
US GOVERNMENT (1982) 'Tax Expenditures', in *Budget of the U.S. Government 1983*, Special Analysis G (Washington, D.C.: U.S. Government Printing Office).
WITTE, J. F. (1982) 'Incremental Theory and Income Tax Policy: The Problem of Too Much, Not Too Little Change', paper presented at the American Political Science Association Meetings, Denver.
WITTE, J. F. (1985) *The Politics and Development of the Federal Income Tax* (Madison: University of Wisconsin Press).

10 Microsimulation Models and State Tax Reform: The Case of Massachusetts

Andrew Reschovsky*

INTRODUCTION

The first half of the 1980s has been a particularly volatile period for state government finance. In 1980 and 1981, a large number of states reduced taxes in response to the 'tax revolt' movement initiated by California's Proposition 13. In 1982 and 1983 the trend towards lower taxes was reversed, as many states battled recession-induced fiscal crises by raising tax rates. In 1985 the trend was again reversed, as 14 states lowered their personal income taxes and one lowered its sales tax (Gold, 1986). The future direction of state tax policy is particularly uncertain given the possibility of federal tax reform, especially if it includes the elimination of state and local tax deductibility, and the likelihood of major cuts in funding of federal domestic spending programs and grants.

In order for state governments to be able to respond effectively to the changed fiscal environment, they must be able to rapidly design and evaluate state tax and spending policies. In recent years a great deal of attention has been focused on the impact of state fiscal policies on state economic growth and investment. Less attention has been paid to the distributional consequences of public policies. This paper describes a microsimulation model that has been developed to provide policy-makers with *ex ante* information about the distributional impacts of state income tax reforms. Although this paper concentrates on the state personal income tax, models of the type

* I would like to acknowledge the generous assistance of Heather Pritchard. Without her advice and guidance in building the simulation model this research could not have been carried out. The Massachusetts Income Tax Simulation Model is a direct outgrowth of models of the California state tax system which were developed with Howard Chernick. I relied heavily on his support and advice in developing the Massachusetts model. Daniel Pliskin provided able research assistance.

described here have been used to assess the distributional consequences of a wide range of tax policies.[1]

The model described in this paper has been developed for the state of Massachusetts. However, because the model uses US Census Bureau data, the same modelling strategy could be employed to analyze the income tax system in other states.[2] The next section describes the Massachusetts Income Tax Simulation model. Its operation is then illustrated by looking at the incidence of the income tax within Massachusetts. In the next section of the paper several examples are given to illustrate how these models can be used by policymakers to conduct *ex ante* policy analysis. The paper concludes with a brief concluding section.

MODELLING STATE INCOME TAXES

The personal income tax is used in 44 states and provided nearly $59 billion of revenue in fiscal year 1984. Following the assumption made by most previous studies of income tax incidence, the individual taxpayer is assumed to bear the full burden of the tax (see, for example, Musgrave, Case, and Leonard, 1974; Pechman and Okner, 1974; Phares, 1980). This assumption is based on the evidence that most taxpayers are unable to shift their tax liabilities to their employers by demanding higher wages to compensate for higher taxes. Modelling the income tax thus requires the calculation of the income tax liabilities of state residents. Because of the complexity of the relationship between the tax code and the economic and demographic characteristics of taxpayers, models based on summary data are generally inadequate for providing accurate predictions of tax liabilities. A more powerful tool for the analysis of tax policy involves the use of *microsimulation models* of tax systems to analyze large samples of individual household data. A microsimulation tax model is a complex computer model of a tax system which permits evaluation of both the current tax system and a wide range of possible reforms.

Over the past 15 years economists have begun to rely more heavily on microsimulation models to analyze a wide variety of complex policy issues, such as the feasibility of various guaranteed income plans, and of alternative means of financing the social security system (see Haveman and Hollenbeck, 1980, and Orcutt, Caldwell, and Wertheimer, 1976, for more information).

A microsimulation model uses data on individuals, families, or firms. The analyst incorporates this information into a series of algebraic expressions in order to represent economic behavior. For example, given information on a household's sources of income and demographic characteristics, the analyst can combine this information with knowledge of the tax code in order to accurately estimate the household's tax liability. The models are constructed so that it is easy to calculate the impact of changes in the environment (that is, the tax code) or in economic behavior. Because of the complexity of most economic systems, it is not possible to predict the outcome of any change in the system by analytic means alone. Simulation models of complex systems provide a means for achieving this goal.

The results presented in this chapter are based on data from the March 1984 Current Population Survey (CPS). The CPS is a large survey conducted by the US Census Bureau. It includes information on family structure and size, age, race, sex, ethnic background, and income. The income data are for the year 1983. The CPS income data, which are listed separately by source of income include income subject to taxation, such as wages and dividends, and income excluded from taxation, such as welfare payments, social security, and veterans' benefits. The only source of money income not included in the CPS are capital gains. These however, have been estimated based on detailed data provided by the Internal Revenue Service (IRS). The proportion of interest income that comes from tax-free government obligations has also been estimated based on IRS data on tax expenditures. The Massachusetts sample of the 1984 CPS includes data on 1475 families and 3645 persons. The sample is a weighted random sample, with the person weights summing to the population of the state. In order to provide policy simulations for calendar year 1986, the income data on the 1984 CPS have been inflated to 1986 values using data on per capita personal income growth in Massachusetts between 1983 and 1986.

The Massachusetts Income Tax Simulation model (MITS) is used to analyze these data. MITS consists of a set of new subroutines to the Transfer Income Model (TRIM) – a model developed during the early 1970s by the Urban Institute and the (then) US Department of Health, Education and Welfare. Since its development the TRIM model has been used to evaluate proposals for a large number of federal government programs. The MITS model is written in FORTRAN and operates on a large IBM mainframe computer. Adaptation of the model for use on microcomputers is being considered.

The model starts by defining as tax-filing units all single individuals or married couples who are not dependents of another taxpayer, regardless of whether they actually face positive tax liabilities. The MITS model determines tax dependency status by using data on the family relationships and income of each person within a household. The model next defines adjusted gross income (AGI) by combining income from the various sources subject to taxation. Finally, the model determines each filing unit's state income tax liability by first using the appropriate socioeconomic and demographic data from the CPS to calculate applicable deductions, exemptions, and credits.[3]

Because the CPS provides a weighted random sample of the Massachusetts population, the model generates a clear picture of the distribution of income tax burdens within the state. Moreover, a major strength of the MITS model is that it is relatively easy to calculate the impact – both on aggregate tax revenue and on the distribution of tax burdens – of any proposed change in the income tax. The model can also be easily adapted for use in other states by rewriting several subroutines to reflect state-specific tax code provisions.

Despite these strengths microsimulation modelling has not played an important role in public policy analysis at the state and local level. This paper will attempt to demonstrate how it can be used for the analysis of state and local tax policy.

Several states – for example, Wisconsin, Minnesota, and New York – employ models of their state income tax systems that are based on random samples of tax returns. These models have the advantage of relying on actual data on deductions, exemptions, and declared income. However, they also have important shortcomings. First, tax return data are only available for those who file returns. Many poor people, especially among the elderly, are not required to file tax returns. For example, for states that follow federal filing rules, couples with both spouses over 65 must only file returns if their income subject to taxation (thus excluding social security benefits), is in excess of $7400. In Massachusetts no return must be filed unless state adjusted gross income is greater than $6000. Using tax return data will generally result in overestimates of the tax burdens faced by the poor, because most people with zero tax liabilities will be excluded from the analysis.

The calculation of tax burdens requires a comprehensive measure of taxpayer 'ability to pay'. The best measure of ability to pay is a measure that includes income available to an individual or family from all sources, regardless of whether this income is subject to taxation or not. An important advantage of using data from the CPS is that it contains data on each family's total money income, whereas tax returns only include data on income subject to taxation. Using taxable income instead of money income to calculate tax burdens will seriously overstate the tax burdens of many taxpayers, but especially the poor and the elderly. A considerable portion of the income of the poor and elderly comes from income which is excluded from taxation, such as welfare benefits, unemployment and workers' compensation, and social security. The tax burdens of the rich will also be overstated if interest income from tax-free municipal bonds, and long-term capital gains are not counted as part of a taxpayer's ability to pay.

Many states have legal provisions against drawing a sample of individual tax returns, and thus these states must rely on aggregate data for analytic purposes. Data from tax returns are also not timely. In most cases a two- to three-year lag exists before these data become available. Although some precision is lost by updating the CPS income data, the richness of the underlying microdata set make it possible to conduct quite accurate tax simulations of current or even future tax years. This is obviously an important advantage in conducting *ex ante* policy analysis.

WHO PAYS THE MASSACHUSETTS PERSONAL INCOME TAX?

Massachusetts has a dual-rate state income tax. Earned income plus interest earned in Massachusetts banks is taxed at a uniform rate of 5 per cent, while most of unearned income, which includes all other interest income, dividends, and 50 per cent of long-term capital gains, is taxed at 10 per cent.[4] Taxable income is determined by subtracting a number of deductions and exemptions from the sum of earned and unearned income. In addition to a set of personal exemptions, limited deductions are allowed for a number of expenditures, for example, on payroll tax payments, rental payments, child care expenses, and medical and dental expenses.

Table 10.1 presents results of a simulation of the Massachusetts personal income tax for calendar year 1986. The data show that there are 3.1 million filing units in Massachusetts. Nearly 30 per cent of the total have money incomes below \$10 000, another 30 per cent have incomes between \$10 000 and \$25 000, 26 per cent have incomes

Table 10.1 Estimated number of filing units, adjusted gross income, and average tax liability, Massachusetts personal income tax, 1986

Total money income ($)	*Filing units* Number	*Filing units* Percentage	*Total AGI (billion $)*	*Average tax liability ($)*
Less than $5 000	446 316	14.2	0.6	0
5 000–9 999	476 212	15.2	1.4	37
10 000–14 999	342 443	10.9	3.1	250
15 000–19 999	322 289	10.3	4.5	469
20 000–24 999	284 982	9.1	5.4	679
25 000–29 999	225 689	7.2	5.2	847
30 000–34 999	195 345	6.2	5.7	1 185
35 000–39 999	163 861	5.2	5.6	1 377
40 000–44 999	125 296	4.0	5.1	1 736
45 000–49 999	110 690	3.5	5.1	1 993
50 000–74 999	301 946	9.6	16.9	2 596
75 000 and over	145 466	4.6	14.8	5 701
Average, all units				1 002
Total	3 140 535	100.0	73.4	

Source: Massachusetts Income Tax Simulation Model.

between $25 000 and $50 000, while 14 per cent have incomes over $50 000. Single individuals comprise 61 per cent of total filing units. Over four-fifth of all single filers have incomes below $25 000 compared to only a quarter of joint filers. Adjusted gross income (AGI) is quite unevenly distributed in Massachusetts, with only 3 per cent of total AGI going to filing units with money incomes less than $10 000, but over 43 per cent going to the 14 per cent of filing units with money incomes over $50 000.

The final column of Table 10.1 shows average tax liability by money income class. The average state income tax liability will be $1002. The average taxpayer with money income below $30 000 will pay less than this amount, while the average taxpayer with income above $30 000 will pay more. These average tax calculations include the one-third of all filing units who will owe no state income tax in 1986. The major reason why so many Massachusetts residents are exempt from state income taxation is that no taxpayer with adjusted gross income below $6000 ($10 000 for joint returns) is subject to taxation.

Although tax liabilities rise as income increases, tax burdens across income classes can only be assessed by comparing tax payments to

Figure 10.1 Tax burdens with and without federal offset, Massachusetts personal income tax, 1986.

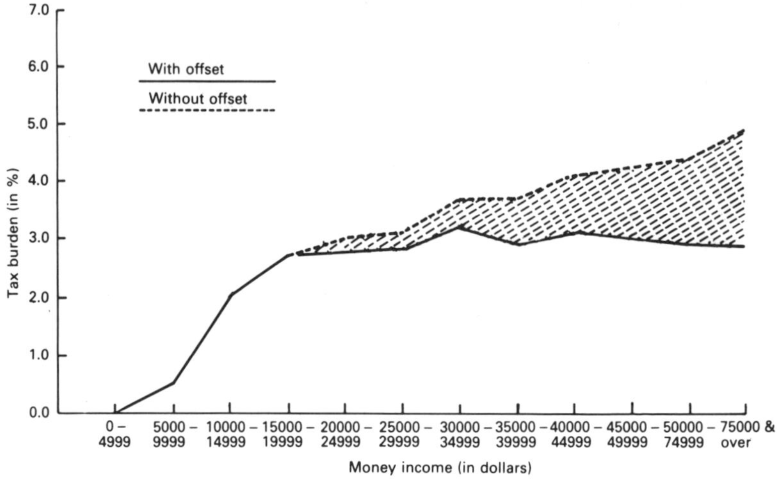

Source: Massachusetts Income Tax Simulation Model.

taxpayers' ability to pay, here measured by total money income. This measure of tax burden is often called an effective tax rate. The data represented by the 'without offset' line in Figure 10.1 show that the Massachusetts personal income tax is progressive. Most residents with incomes below $10 000 are not required to pay the income tax. Above $10 000 tax burdens rise rapidly to 3 per cent in the $15 000 to $25 000 income range. For taxpayers with income above $25 000, tax burdens rise reasonably steadily to an average rate of nearly 5 per cent for taxpayers with incomes over $75 000.

This pattern of effective tax rates overstates the degree of progressivity in the Massachusetts income tax. Although the average effective rate increases as income rises, 76 per cent of all those paying taxes face effective rates in the relatively narrow range between 3 and 5 per cent. The effective tax rate data discussed above also fails to account for the fact that taxpayers who itemize federal income tax deductions can, in effect, reduce their net state income tax payments by deducting their state tax liability from federal taxable income. Thus a family with a 30 per cent federal marginal tax rate and facing a $2000 state income tax liability can reduce its total tax liability by $600 (30 per cent of $2000). The reduction in state tax liability due to the deductibility of state taxes is called the *federal tax offset*. The average federal offset increases as income rises because both the proportion of itemizers, and the federal marginal tax rate rise as income rises.[5] The line marked 'with offset' in Figure 10.1 shows the impact of the federal offset. The state income tax is progressive only up to incomes of $25 000. Above that level of income tax burdens remain practically unchanged, with rich taxpayers facing the same effective rate (about 3 per cent) as taxpayers with $25 000 incomes.

An important attribute of microsimulation modelling is the ability it gives the analyst to explore the reasons for observed patterns of tax incidence. Microsimulation models allow one to disentangle the distributional impact of individual exemptions, deductions, and credits, and the impact of the differential tax treatment of income from various sources. For example, in Massachusetts the progressivity at the low end of the income distribution is due primarily to the fact that income from sources excluded from AGI, and the sum of exemptions and deductions fall as a proportion of money income as income rises. Income from sources excluded from AGI, such as welfare benefits, workers' compensation and the untaxed portion of capital gains, accounts for 28 per cent of money income for those with incomes between $10 000 and $15 000, but only 5 per cent of income for those with incomes in the $50 000 to $75 000 range.[6] Likewise, exemptions and deductions total 26 per cent of money income for those in the $10 000 to $15 000 income range, and only 12 per cent of income for those with $50 000 to $75 000 of income. Thus, the sum of exclusions, deductions, and exemptions, substantially reduces the taxable income of low-income households, but provides a relatively minor reduction in taxable income for the average high-income household.

The data show that the pre-federal offset progressivity of the Massachusetts income tax at the high end of the income distribution is due almost entirely to the higher rate of taxation of unearned income. Below $75 000 of money income, unearned income comprises approximately 5 per cent of Massachusetts AGI. However, unearned income averages over 17 per cent of AGI for taxpayers with money incomes in excess of $75 000.

Microsimulation models of tax systems can also facilitate the calculation of foregone revenue attributed to various provisions of the tax code, such as exemptions and deductions. These foregone revenues are often referred to as tax expenditures when they provide an implicit subsidy to an activity not related to the earning of income. As an example consider the provision of the Massachusetts income tax which allows tenants to deduct half their annual rent payments up to a ceiling of $2500.

A simulation using the MITS model shows that in 1986 the value of gross rent deductions will be $730 million, and the rent deduction will reduce state income tax revenues by $26 million. It is important to note that this revenue loss is approximately 30 per cent less than an estimate made from aggregate data by simply multiplying the value of the rent deduction by the tax rate. The primary reason for the difference in the two estimates is that although renter households with incomes below $10 000 claim 23 per cent of the total rent deductions, they receive only 3.5 per cent of the tax savings. This difference occurs because most of the state's poorest families face zero tax libilities even in the absence of the rent deduction. In addition, for many poor taxpayers, the value of the rent deduction exceeds their taxable income after the subtraction of other exemptions and deductions. These taxpayers benefit from the rent deduction only to the extent that the rent deduction exceeds taxable income.

The major beneficiaries of the rent deduction are renters with money incomes between $10 000 and $25 000. In this income range approximately one-third of all filing units are renters. Although only 40 per cent of all renters have incomes in this range, they receive nearly 50 per cent of the tax savings attributable to the renter deduction. On the whole, the rent deduction adds slightly to the progressivity of the income tax.

REFORMING THE STATE INCOME TAX

Microsimulation models can be powerful tools for evaluating alternative tax reform proposals. Their potential contribution to *ex ante* policy analysis can be demonstrated by using the MITS model to evaluate a number of proposal for reducing the state income tax burden of elderly taxpayers in Massachusetts. The fact that in Massachusetts most unearned income is taxed at twice the rate of earned income has generated considerable opposition from elderly taxpayers. The dual-rate structure has a larger impact on the elderly because, relative to the non-elderly, a much larger share of their AGI comes from unearned income. Complaints by the elderly have spurred a number of proposals to reform the state income tax. Although a number of these proposals have been seriously considered, as of this date none of them have been enacted. Before evaluating any proposals, it will be useful to see how the elderly are treated by the current state income tax.

The average elderly tax filing unit in Massachusetts (defined as any filing unit where the head *or* spouse is over the age of 64), faces an income tax burden that is only one-third of the burden faced by the average non-elderly taxpayer. This lower average tax burden occurs for several reasons. First, on average, the elderly are poorer than the non-elderly, with average money income of $19 000, compared to an average of $28 000 for the non-elderly. Secondly, a large portion of the income of the elderly is excluded from taxation. On average only 31 per cent of total money income of the elderly is included in AGI, compared to 85 per cent for the non-elderly. For every income class at least 60 per cent of the income of the non-elderly is included in AGI. However, only for the relatively few elderly with incomes over $30 000 (16 per cent), does AGI make up as much as 60 per cent of total money income. The consequence of this differential composition of income is that the average elderly tax burden is lower than the average non-elderly tax burden for all income classes below $50 000.

At every income class, income taxed at 10 per cent makes up a larger proportion of AGI for the elderly than the non-elderly. The importance of unearned income for the elderly, clearly increases their tax burdens. However, with the exception of taxpayers with incomes over $50 000, this effect is outweighed by the fact that most elderly taxpayers can exclude a sizably larger proportion of their total income from taxation than the non-elderly.

Single-rate taxation

Despite the fact that most elderly taxpayers face lower income tax burdens than non-elderly taxpayers, many people feel that the taxation of unearned income at a higher rate than earned income discriminates against the elderly. One solution to this 'problem' is to replace the current dual-rate with a single rate. To evaluate the single-rate proposal, we have chosen a tax rate that will generate the same amount of revenue as the current dual-rate system. The results of this single-rate simulation are illustrated in Table 10.2.

The data show that although a single-rate tax will reduce the state income tax burden of many elderly taxpayers, its major impact will be to substantially reduce the over-all progressivity of the income tax. Average tax burdens will be reduced for elderly taxpayers with incomes over $15 000, and non-elderly taxpayers with incomes over $75 000. For all other taxpayers, the poor elderly, and the non-elderly with incomes below $75 000, the move to a revenue neutral single-rate tax system will result in increased tax burdens. Looking at

Table 10.2 The impact of taxing all income at a single rate, Massachusetts personal income tax, 1986

Total money income ($)	*Non-elderly* *$ change in tax liability*	*Non-elderly* *Tax change as a % of Money income*	*Elderly* *$ Change in Tax liability*	*Elderly* *Tax change as a % of Money income*
Less than $5 000	0	0.00	0	0.00
5 000– 9 999	11	0.17	0	0.01
10 000–14 999	21	0.17	2	0.01
15 000–19 999	39	0.22	–12	–0.07
20 000–24 999	39	0.17	–2	–0.01
25 000–29 999	53	0.19	–65	–0.24
30 000–34 999	46	0.14	–211	–0.64
35 000–39 999	68	0.18	–124	–0.33
40 000–44 999	103	0.24	–284	–0.67
45 000–49 999	90	0.19	–215	–0.44
50 000–74 999	96	0.16	–580	–0.92
75 000 and over	–401	–0.24	–1 816	–1.47
Average, all units	20	0.13	–95	–0.15

Note: The rate is set at 5.412 per cent. This rate has been calculated so that the total tax change is revenue neutral.
Source: Massachusetts Income Tax Simulation Model.

the pattern of tax reductions as a proportion of money income provides us with an indication of the impact of the reform of tax progressivity. Larger proportional tax reductions for high income taxpayers imply a reduction in tax progressivity. The data in Table 10.2 show that single-rate taxation provides the largest relative tax reductions to all taxpayers, but especially to elderly taxpayers, with incomes over $75 000. These tax reductions are in effect paid for by tax increases borne by low- and moderate-income taxpayers.

Elderly exclusion of unearned income

In July 1984 the Massachusetts Legislature passed legislation (subsequently vetoed by the governor), which allowed each person over the age of 64 filing a single return to deduct up to $6000 of unearned (10 per cent) income. Couples with at least one elderly spouse would be allowed to deduct $6600 of unearned income. Interest income from Massachusetts banks would continue to be taxed, along with earned

Table 10.3 Impact of excluding elderly's 10 per cent income. Exclusion of $6000 of 10 per cent income for elderly taxpayers ($6600 for joint returns), Massachusetts personal income tax, 1986

Total money income ($)	*Average tax reduction*	*Total tax reduction (million $)*	*Percentage of total*	*Tax change as a % of money income*
Less than $5 000	0	0.00	0.0	0.00
5 000– 9 999	0	0.00	0.0	0.00
10 000–14 999	–10	–0.89	1.9	–0.07
15 000–19 999	–47	–2.91	6.1	–0.27
20 000–24 999	–30	–1.26	2.6	–0.14
25 000–29 999	–176	–6.79	14.1	–0.66
30 000–34 999	–335	–8.88	18.5	–1.02
35 000–39 999	–239	–3.41	7.1	–0.63
40 000–44 999	–346	–3.04	6.3	–0.83
45 000–49 999	–468	–0.67	1.4	–0.96
50 000–74 999	–514	–11.64	24.2	–0.86
75 000 and over	–605	–8.49	17.7	–0.55
Average, all units	–88			–0.23
Total		–47.98	100.0	

Note: Ten per cent income is defined as dividends, 50 per cent of capital gains, and interest income from sources other than Massachusetts banks.
Source: Massachusetts Income Tax Simulation Model.

income, at a rate of 5 per cent. Table 10.3 illustrates the impact of the legislation.

The major beneficiaries of this legislation would be elderly taxpayers with incomes in excess of $25 000. Although over three-quarters of all elderly filing units have incomes below $25 000, they would receive relatively small tax reductions (generally under $30) from this legislation. Because unearned income is concentrated so heavily among the highest income elderly, it is not surprising that in aggregate elderly taxpayers with incomes under $25 000 would receive about 10 per cent of the total $48 million tax reduction, while elderly taxpayers with incomes over $50 000 (7 per cent of total elderly taxpayers) would receive over 40 per cent of the total tax reduction. The last column of Table 10.3 provides further evidence that the exclusion of 10 per cent income provides negligible tax reductions for the average elderly taxpayer with income below $25 000.

Table 10.4 Impact of expanding the elderly exemption. Extra exemption of $3000 for each elderly taxpayer, Massachusetts personal income tax, 1986

Total money income ($)	*Average tax reduction*	*Total tax reduction (million $)*	*Percentage of total*	*Tax change as a % of money income*
Less than $5 000	0	0.00	0.0	0.00
5 000– 9 999	0	–0.06	0.2	0.00
10 000–14 999	–21	–1.97	7.0	–0.16
15 000–19 999	–48	–2.97	10.6	–0.27
20 000–24 999	–50	–2.09	7.4	–0.22
25 000–29 999	–151	–5.85	20.8	–0.57
30 000–34 999	–170	–4.52	16.1	–0.52
35 000–39 999	–132	–1.89	6.7	–0.35
40 000–44 999	–161	–1.41	5.0	–0.39
45 000–49 999	–230	–0.33	1.2	–0.47
50 000–74 999	–190	–4.30	15.3	–0.31
75 000 and over	–194	–2.72	9.7	–0.17
Average, all units	–51			–0.18
Total		–28.11	100.0	

Source: Massachusetts Income Tax Simulation Model.

Expanding the elderly exemption

Is it possible to design a tax reform that will reduce the tax burden for elderly taxpayers, but target tax reductions so as to provide a larger portion of the total tax relief to the low and moderate income elderly? The data in Table 10.4 show that the answer is clearly 'yes'. Massachusetts currently provides each elderly person with an extra exemption of $700. Table 10.4 illustrates the impact of increasing this exemption to $3000. A couple with both spouses over the age of 64 would thus receive an elderly exemption of $6000.

Expanding the elderly exemption more than doubles the proportion of the total tax reduction which would benefit taxpayers with incomes under $25 000, and nearly halves the tax reduction which would go to taxpayers with incomes over $50 000. The fact that most low-income elderly filing units currently pay little or no state income tax means that they receive relatively small additional benefits from an expanded elderly exemption. Elderly taxpayers with incomes between $25 000 and $50 000 would receive the largest relative benefit from an expanded exemption.

CONCLUSIONS

This paper has demonstrated the power of microsimulation models as a tool for evaluating and formulating state tax policy. When combined with a comprehensive data set that provides detailed socio-economic information about a state's population, these models are particularly well suited for analyzing the distributional consequences of tax policies. They provide great flexibility in modelling a wide array of tax proposals, and allow the analyst to explore the impacts of alternative tax incidence assumptions. Drawing on the example of income tax policies to reduce the tax burdens of the elderly, the paper demonstrates how *ex ante* analysis of tax legislation can pinpoint unintended consequences of even the most well-intentioned public policies.

Although this paper focuses on a model of the state income tax, the methodology described here can also be used to model other state and local taxes. In fact, models of local property taxes and state sales and excise taxes exist for several states. Linking these models together, and combining them with models of the federal income and payroll taxes will provide us, for the first time, with a clear picture of the total tax burden faced by taxpayers of different incomes and demographic characteristics.

Notes

1. The author and Howard Chernick have used microsimulation models to evaluate the distributional impact of California's property tax limitation, Proposition 13, to assess the distributional consequences of the partial taxation of social security benefits, and to evaluate federal income tax proposals (see Chernick and Reschovsky, 1982, 1985, 1986).
2. The data come from the Current Population Survey. The sample includes households from each state. However, the samples from some states are too small to provide a statistical foundation for a state-specific model.
3. See chapter 3 in Reschovsky *et al.* (1983) for a more detailed description of the MITS model.
4. In December 1985 a major reform of the Massachusetts personal income tax was enacted. The major provisions of the new legislation include the elimination of a 7.5 per cent surtax, and the replacement of a system of uniform personal exemptions with a system of personal exemptions which decline as adjusted gross income rises. Although the provisions of the new law will not be fully implemented until 1987, the simulations reported here assume full implementation in 1986.
5. We estimate that in 1986 35 per cent of Massachusetts filing units will itemize deductions on their federal returns. As not all filing units actually

file returns, it is likely that close to 44 per cent of federal returns filed by Massachusetts residents will be filed by taxpayers who itemize deductions.

6. The impact of income exclusion on the pattern of effective tax rates may be substantially changed if data were available on non-cash sources of income, such as employer contributions to pension plans and health insurance. In a recent paper Daniel Weinberg (1985) presents data that show that in 1979 the poorest 40 per cent of the US population received only 5.1 per cent of the federal tax expenditures on fringe benefits, while the richest 20 per cent of the population received 54.6 per cent of total tax expenditures on fringe benefits. On the other hand, although the total dollar amounts are much smaller, the value of noncash transfers received from the food stamp, Medicaid, Medicare, and housing assistance programs are greater at the bottom end of the income distribution, than at the top.

References

CHERNICK, H. and RESCHOVSKY, A. (1982) 'The Distributional Impact of Proposition 13: A Microsimulation Approach', *National Tax Journal*, 35 (2): 149–70.

CHERNICK, H. and RESCHOVSKY, A. (1985) 'The Taxation of Social Security', *National Tax Journal*, 38 (2): 141–52.

CHERNICK, H. and RESCHOVSKY, A. (1986) 'Federal Tax Reform and the Financing of State and Local Governments', *Journal of Policy Analysis and Management* 5 (4): 683–706.

GOLD, S. D. (1986) 'State and Local Tax Systems in the Mid-1980s', Legislative Finance Paper, No. 52, National Conference of State Legislatures, Denver, Colorado.

HAVEMAN, R. H. and HOLLENBECK, K. (eds) (1980) *Microsimulation Models for Public Policy Analysis* 2 Volumes (New York: Academic Press).

MUSGRAVE, R. A., CASE, K. E. and LEONARD, H. (1974) 'The Distribution of Fiscal Burdens and Benefits', *Public Finance Quarterly*, 2: 259–311.

ORCUTT, G., CALDWELL, S. and WERTHEIMER, R. (1976) *Policy Exploration through Microanalytic Simulation* (Washington, D.C.: Urban Institute).

PECHMAN, J. and OKNER, B. A. (1974) *Who Bears the Tax Burden?* (Washington, D.C.: Brookings Institution).

PHARES, D. (1980) *Who Pays State and Local Taxes?* (Cambridge, Mass.: Oelgeschlager, Gunn and Hain).

RESCHOVSKY, A., TOPAKIAN, G., CARRÉ, F., CRANE, R., MILLER, P., and SMOKE, P. (1983) *State Tax Policy: Evaluating the Issues* (Cambridge, Mass.: Joint Center for Urban Studies of MIT and Harvard University).

WEINBERG, D. H. (1985) 'Who Doesn't Bear the Tax Burden? The Distribution of Tax Expenditures', Technical Analysis Paper, No. 31, Office of Income Security Policy, US Department of Health and Human Services, Washington, D.C..

Part IV
Distributional Impact Analysis and Public Policy-making

11 The 'Group-Benefit' Method: A New Methodology for Distributional Analyses of Fiscal Policies in Developing Nations

William H. H. Cranmer

ORIGINS

In the 1970s I began searching for a method that, in Lasswell's phrase, would better describe 'who gets what, when and how' from fiscal policies in less-developed nations (see Cranmer, 1977, 1978, and 1982). For a variety of reasons I had become dissatisfied with other researchers' method of sorting and analyzing fiscal data.

I was interested in finding a method that would best reflect my goals of measuring which groups in less-developed countries historically have benefited the most from fiscal policies. I had found that many descriptive schemes commonly used in fiscal analyses either had other aims and were therefore irrelevant, or were poorly adapted to such a group-oriented study. As Meehan (1967: 13) comments, I wanted my descriptive categories to fit my own conceptual purpose.

The following essay outlines the specific reasons for my creation of the 'group-benefit' method, defines the method itself, and finally displays a sample of the things that the method can be used to do, employing data from my doctoral dissertation on Sri Lanka.

I was looking for a method of describing fiscal policy that would satisfy a variety of objectives. My primary goal was to create a scheme that would measure relative interest group success in fiscal policy distributions. Much past research on fiscal policy has either not had this aim, or had it in such a general way that the assumptions about the articulations between interest groups and particular fiscal policies were unclear (Tax Foundation, 1967; Fry and Winters, 1970; Pechman and Okner, 1974, are landmark exceptions).

I was also interested in creating a scheme that was relatively complete (see Peters, 1977). I wanted to include all relevant taxes, borrowing (domestic and foreign), and expenditures, and examine their interactions over a prolonged period. The inclusion of both revenue and expenditures is especially important because of the 'symbolic' ability of governments to take from Peter with one hand, then to give back all that was taken (perhaps with interest!) to Peter himself with the other (see Edelman, 1964; and Chandler, Chandler and Vogler, 1974). Unfortunately most analyses of government fiscal policies concentrate on either revenue or expenditure policies, ignoring the great potential interaction between them (exceptions are Tax Foundation, 1967; Fry and Winters, 1970; and Peters, 1974). Serious political studies of borrowing are even more unusual (exceptions are Wilkie, 1970; Cowart, 1978).

Another important goal was to create a scheme that could be applied comparatively to a variety of less-developed countries in the midst of the modernizing experience. As Hancock (1982: 17) has recently pointed out, most fiscal research by political scientists has been tailored to relatively developed nations. Some good single-nation studies (such as Rosen, 1967; Wilkie, 1970; Hayes, 1972; Snodgrass, 1974) have been made of fiscal policies in developing nations, but very few comparative studies have been executed (with the notable exceptions of Brunner and Brewer, 1971; Ames and Goff, 1975; Ames, 1977, 1980; Hill, 1976; and the studies of military-civilian expenditures summarized in Zuk and Thompson, 1982).

Yet another objective was to employ a time-series approach which could detect whether policies changed over time, and if so, precisely when they changed. The creation of such a time series of fiscal policies would permit both a more complete description of data, and the possibility of testing a variety of hypotheses, as other analysts have shown (see Peters, 1972; Chandler, Chandler and Vogler, 1974; Gray, 1976; Marquette and Hinckley, 1981).

Such an approach would permit the attainment of a final objective: the creation of a data set that could be employed in aggregated or disaggregated form for attempts either (a) to explain fiscal policies as dependent variables, or (b) to employ fiscal policy variables as independent variables in attempts to evaluate the degree of success shown by fiscal policies in conferring benefits. The explanatory goal is an aim widely shared among comparative fiscal policy analysts (see

Cutright, 1965; Pryor, 1968; Brunner and Brewer, 1971; Wilensky, 1975; Bunce, 1976, 1980; and the large body of work by Peters). Attempts to evaluate comparative fiscal policy efficiency in conferring benefits on either the nation or particular interest groups are, however, still rare among political scientists (among the few such studies are Cutright, 1967; Sharkansky, 1970; Peters, 1974, 1976).

DEFINITION OF THE GROUP-BENEFIT METHOD

In my research I have become interested in six national-level, socio-economic interest groups based on occupation (Small Rural Enterprise, Private Enterprise, State Economic Enterprise, and Security Forces), and economic class (Upper Economic Class, and Lower Economic Class).

I chose these groups, and not others, for several reasons. First, the political influence of each of these groups has been of considerable interest to other social scientists for more than a century. Secondly, each of these groups has an obvious stake in fiscal allocations, either as a major tax-paying group, or as a potential beneficiary of government expenditures.

Thirdly, more theoretically, I wanted to test Lowi's hypothesis (Lowi, 1966) that policies may generate different kinds of politics, according to the size of groups that would benefit. I felt that my larger, class-based groups would fall into Lowi's 'redistributive' policy area, generating intense zero-sum conflict over policy-making. I felt that my occupational groups, on the other hand, might fall into Lowi's 'regulatory' policy area, which would generate more regularized conflict.

Lastly, I chose nationally important groups, rather than smaller, or regionally important groups, because I was more interested for comparative reasons in policies affecting entire societies. I wanted to find a descriptive scheme that could be employed to measure fiscal success of interest groups in a number of less-developed nations. Such a concern does, of course sacrifice some specific information about fiscal policy-making in a particular nation, but it may gain much in return by showing comparable contrasts and changes in fiscal policy-making among different nations over time.

One should remember to interpret the results of such comparative research cautiously, because there are many non-fiscal policies, and implementations of policies that affect interest group status in different nations. If regularities do appear, however, in such an actually and symbolically important area of politics as fiscal allocation, the theoretical and heuristic benefits may be great.

In creating the method I have made the following simplifying assumptions: I assume these are political groups with clear economic interests in government policy, as well as socioeconomic groups. To the extent that members of these groups are politically active, I assume that they are primarily 'economic men' motivated by selfish concerns. Group members will therefore want lower taxes on themselves, and higher government expenditures on their group (in this I am similar to both Downs, 1957, and Schlesinger, 1970). I assume group members will not be primarily patriotic (for the common good), nor primarily altruistic, nor strongly ideological. I further assume members of groups will want lower taxes and higher spending on their groups for symbolic reasons, even if opposite government policies arguably would benefit them more in the short or long run.

I assume these groups may or may not be organized, with conscious memberships. I also assume that members of groups may or may not bring observable political or other pressures on decision-makers. Therefore, each of these groups is assumed to exist, not proven to exist.

The point of all these assumptions is very simple: to test when which of these interest groups has been more successful than other groups in the fiscal allocation process in a particular less-developed nation. If a particular group appears to have been more successful from the patterns of fiscal outputs, one inference might be that this group has been more successful in influencing decision-makers in its favor. Having detected such a clear pattern of favoritism, one may then investigate empirically why decisions were made in favor of certain groups, employing both statistical and historical methods. Thus group-benefit analysis may be used as an exploratory technique, as well as a descriptive method.

Although the groups are assumed to exist, conceptual definitions of each should be stated.

> *Small Rural Enterprise* interest groups are composed of members believing in the promotion of agricultural and rural economic development over other interests, and whose occupations or major sources of income stem from agricultural or rural enterprise. This would include agricultural landlords, free-holders, and tenants, and hunters, fishermen, foresters, and resident suppliers of goods and services to these groups.

Private Enterprise interest groups are composed of members believing in the promotion of private enterprise over other interests, and whose occupations or major sources of income stem from private economic enterprise. This would include plantation, manufacturing or commercial businesses which do not have a controlling government, or government corporation, degree of ownership in the operation of business.

State Economic Enterprise interest groups are composed of members believing in the promotion of state economic enterprise over other interests, and whose occupations or major sources of income stem from the public sector of the economy. This would include agricultural, plantation, manufacturing or commercial businesses which have a controlling degree of government or government corporation ownership, or participation in the operation of business.

Security Force interest groups are composed of members believing in the promotion of security force interests over other interests, and whose occupations or major sources of income stem from government security forces. This would include the central government-controlled military, militia, police and border guard forces and their supporting services.

Upper Economic Class interest groups are composed of members believing in the promotion of upper economic class interests over other interests, and whose occupations have high income levels, or whose wealth is much above the national average. This would include landlords, 'rich peasants', doctors, lawyers, and owners and managers of medium-to-large plantation, manufacturing, and commercial enterprises in both public and private sectors, plus high government employees.

Lower Economic Class interest groups are composed of members believing in the promotion of lower economic class interests, and whose occupations have low income levels, or whose wealth is below the national average. This would include subsistence agricultural landowners, tenant farmers, agricultural workers, plantation workers, and lower-ranking government, commercial, and manufacturing employees.

As one can see, the first four groups are mutually exclusive, as are the class groups taken by themselves. The economic class groups, however, overlap with the occupational groups, cross-cutting occupational loyalties with economic class loyalties. One may ascertain empirically whether occupations or class loyalties are in fact stronger in policy determination using my group-benefit method.

In order to describe fiscal policy from this group-related standpoint, I have divided all taxes, charges, loans to the government, and all government expenditures, into the following categories specifically appropriate for less-developed countries in the midst of modernization.

The group-related set of category definitions below is meant to be only a general guide. In applying this scheme to governments at different times, or in different nations, each analyst must be careful to see that functions nominally part of ministries or departments are actually performed by those agencies, or mainly by those agencies. Likewise, the analyst should scrutinize all expenditures and taxes to see if an entry logically belongs within a different fiscal category than that listed by the government. The actual incidence of taxes on various groups, too, should be examined to see what taxes should be placed in which categories.

I Revenue from taxes and charges[1]

Individual Income Taxes include taxes and surtaxes on individual incomes from any source.

Corporate Taxes include taxes and surtaxes on corporation (public and private) incomes, excess profits, exports, and contributions by corporations for social security for workers.

Wealth, Large Capital Transaction and Luxury Consumption Taxes include taxes on inheritances, gifts, wealth, capital balances, real estate purchases, automobile purchases, building construction, livestock inventories, automobiles, foreign travel spending, and luxury spending (jewelry, air travel, large appliances, entertainment, hotels, and so on).

Agricultural Capital Taxes are taxes on agricultural land and buildings.

Foreign Exchange Purchase Taxes are taxes on purchases of foreign exchange by individuals, private corporations, and public corporations.

Import Duties are any type of taxes on imports from abroad.

Production, Consumption, and Service Taxes on Widely-consumed Items and Services include taxes on production, turnover, retail sales, mass consumption items (liquor, tobacco, matches, salt, sugar, coffee, chocolate, petroleum products, and so on), government services (postal service, telephone, telegraph, banks, transport, electricity, water, natural gas, and so on), betting, profits from government lotteries, and government royalties on mining and petroleum production.

Individual Social Security Contributions include social security pension and insurance contributions from individuals in the public and private sectors.

Government Shares of Profits from Public and Private Enterprises include profits and shares in profits from government monopolies, public corporations, private corporations, interest on loans from the government, fees for government directors, income for the Central Bank from currency and foreign exchange transactions, repayment of loans from government and private corporations, and profits from government commercial undertakings.

Other Revenues and Charges include revenue from licenses, tolls, court fines and forfeitures, government services, gifts, sales of government property, rents and lease income, school tuition, health service fees, and miscellaneous.

II **Revenue from loans and grants**

Domestic Loans to the Government include loans and advances to the government by domestic individuals, private corporations, public corporations, and the Central Bank.

Foreign Civil Loans and Grants include loans and grants of money and commodities from supranational organizations, national governments, and subnational foreign public and private sources, when the funds are not tied to military uses.

Foreign Military Loans and Grants include loans from foreign governments and agencies to buy or make military equipment, and grants of military equipment and services from foreign governments and agencies.

III Government expenditures

Security Expenditures include spending by ministries or departments of defense, security, army, navy, air force, national police, prisons, militia, border guards, and security support services.

Rural Expenditures include spending by ministries or departments of agriculture, forestry, fisheries, state farms, irrigation, rural water supply, land survey, rural development (small enterprises, cottage industries, rural amenities), rural co-operatives, land development, land settlement, weather information, and government capital transfers to agricultural or rural development banks.

Private Enterprise Expenditures include spending by ministries or departments of commerce, economy, tourism and information, foreign and internal trade, shipping, plantation industry and subsidies (where plantations mainly privately held), exports, and government capital transfers to industrial development banks.

State Economic Enterprise Expenditures include spending by ministries or departments of state-owned industry, monopolies, factories, plantations, mines, or petroleum companies, the geological survey, and government capital transfers or loans to state-owned enterprises.

Non-agricultural Infrastructure Expenditures include spending by ministries or departments of public works (subtracting irrigation expenditures), communications and broadcasting, highways, transport, airports, state railways, ports and state shipping, posts, telephone, and telegraph services, state electrical utilities, and urban water supply.

Education and Public Health Expenditures include spending by ministries or departments of education, higher education, cultural affairs, museums, technical education, physical education, public health, medical services, indigenous (traditional) medicine, and sanitation.

Social Welfare Services, Housing, Labor, and Social Transfers include spending by ministries or departments of social welfare services, pensions, social security transfers, housing, labor, refugee settlement, emergency assistance, price controls, food distribution and rationing, probation, and government transfers to the sick, disabled or poor, and to dependent children.

Administration and Other Expenditures include spending by ministries or departments of the presidency, prime minister, courts, legislature, audits, planning, statistics and census, registration, justice, interior, foreign affairs, finance, customs, revenue, religion or religious endowments (trusts), public debt, local government liaison, archives, archaeology, immigration and emigration, personnel, government supplies, elections, natural resources, and miscellaneous expenditures.

In using the fiscal categories, I will compensate for inflation, and changing government proportions of Gross National Product (GNP) over time by the conversion of (a) each annual tax category total into a percentage of all taxes and charges for that year, (b) each annual borrowing category total into a percentage of all spending for that year, and (c) each annual expenditure category total into a percentage of all spending for that year. In using proportions of revenues and expenditures, I follow Hayes (1972), Peters, Doughtie and McCulloch (1977), and Zuk and Thompson (1982).

These percentages for each year in each fiscal category may then be used for the description of data, and as dependent or independent variables in research. Alternatively, they may be aggregated in different ways, depending on an analyst's descriptive purposes. We will employ these percentages both by themselves and in aggregated form later in the paper.

Having created these fiscal categories, we will now explore their relationships to the six interest groups I discussed earlier. In Table 11.1 below I define the presumed benefits associated with particular types of fiscal policies in relation to each interest group, including all relevant tax, borrowing and spending policies. By following Table 11.1 I expect an analyst to be able to measure the degree of government favor (or lack of favor) toward each interest group during a given period, and so to come to an over all judgment, based on strong empirical evidence, about which groups were most and least successful.

The reader will notice that the interest group benefits defined in Table 11.1 are quite different for four of the groups – Rural Enterprise, Security Forces, and the Upper and Lower Classes. These groups therefore seem to have few common fiscal interests.

Private and State Enterprise group benefits are, however, quite similar to one another, excepting only a few items. This mutuality of interests is quite deliberately incorporated into the definitions,

Table 11.1 Interest group benefits from fiscal policy

I. **Occupational interest group benefits**

A. *Rural Enterprise* interest groups would benefit from the following policies:

1. Low, declining, or relatively stable agricultural capital taxes.
2. High or rising levels of rural expenditures.

B. *Private Enterprise* interest groups would benefit from the following fiscal policies:

1. Low, declining, or relatively stable corporate taxes.
2. Low, declining, or relatively stable foreign exchange purchase taxes
3. Low, declining, or relatively stable import duties.
4. High or rising levels of foreign civil loans and grants.
5. High or rising levels of expenditures on private enterprise.
6. High or rising levels of expenditures on non-agricultural infrastructure.
7. High or rising levels of expenditures on education and public health.

C. *State Economic Enterprise* interest groups would benefit from the following fiscal policies:

1. Low, declining, or relatively stable corporate taxes.
2. Low, declining, or relatively stable foreign exchange purchase taxes.
3. Low, declining, or relatively stable import duties.
4. Low, declining, or relatively stable government shares of profits from public and private enterprise.
5. High or rising levels of foreign civil loans and grants.
6. High or rising levels of expenditures on state economic enterprise.
7. High or rising levels of expenditures on non-agricultural infrastructure.
8. High or rising levels of expenditures on education and public health.

D. *Security Force* interest groups would benefit from the following fiscal policies:

1. High or rising levels of foreign military loans and grants.
2. High or rising levels of security expenditures.
3. High or rising levels of expenditures on non-agricultural infrastructure.

Table 11.1 *continued*

II. **Economic class interest group benefits**

A. *Upper Economic Class* interest groups would benefit from the following fiscal policies:

1. Low, declining, or relatively stable individual taxes.
2. Low, declining, or relatively stable corporate taxes.
3. Low, declining, or relatively stable wealth, large capital transaction, and luxury consumption taxes.
4. Low, declining, or relatively stable agricultural capital taxes.
5. Low, declining, or relatively stable foreign exchange purchase taxes.
6. Low, declining, or relatively stable import duties.
7. High or rising production, consumption and service taxes on widely-consumed items and services.
8. High or rising government shares of profits from public and private enterprises.
9. Low, declining, or relatively stable domestic loans to the government.
10. High or rising foreign civil loans and grants.
11. High or rising rural expenditures.
12. High or rising expenditures on private enterprise.
13. High or rising expenditures on non-agricultural infrastructure.

B. *Lower Economic Class* interest groups would benefit from the following fiscal policies:

1. High or rising individual taxes.
2. High or rising corporate taxes.
3. High or rising wealth, large capital transaction, and luxury consumption taxes.
4. Low, declining, or relatively stable foreign exchange purchase taxes.
5. Low, declining, or relatively stable import duties.
6. Low, declining, or relatively stable production, consumption and service taxes on widely-consumed items and services.
7. Low, declining, or relatively stable individual social security contributions.
8. Low, declining, or relatively stable government shares of profits from public and private enterprises.
9. High or rising domestic loans to the government.
10. High or rising foreign civil loans and grants.
11. High or rising rural expenditures.
12. High or rising expenditures on education and public health.
13. High or rising expenditures on social welfare services, housing, labor and social transfers.

because both Private and State Enterprise groups would obviously benefit from many of the same revenue policies (relief from corporation taxes for example), and material and human infrastructural expenditure policies (better transportation for instance, and more educated, healthier workers). Thus in mixed economies, the logic of the similar interests of capitalists and state capitalists discussed by Marx appears much more significant than the assumptions of dissimilarity of interests usually claimed by propagandists for and against state 'socialism'.

In operationalizing the rules stated in Table 11.1, I will adhere to the following procedure, (a) employing statistical means to establish the relative levels of taxation, borrowing and spending in different periods, and (b) using regression (beta) coefficients descriptively to measure trends (slopes) in fiscal outputs over time (not using them inferentially, as is the usual practice).

1. I will score a maximum of two points for each item defined in Table 11.1 as benefiting an interest group. I will score one point if the arithmetical mean satisfies the 'high' or 'low' condition specified in a definition in Table 11.1. Likewise, I will score one point if the regression coefficient of a fiscal variable regressed against 'time' meets the condition specified as 'rising' or 'declining' in a definition. In the case of taxes I will assume that maintaining a 'stable' level of taxes within a category is a partial victory for the groups directly affected; thus for taxes I will consider a regression coefficient near zero equivalent to the success shown by a declining regression coefficient.
2. I will then sum scores for each of the interest groups, and convert these raw scores into percentages of the total points possible for each interest group.
3. Finally, I will rank-order the interest groups by their percentages of the possible number of points.

In practice, I will define a 'high' level of taxes to be 10 per cent of total revenues or above, and 'low' levels for taxes to be 5 per cent of the total revenues or below. I will similarly define 'high' levels of loans and grants to be 10 per cent of total expenditures or above, and 'low' levels of loans and grants to be 5 per cent or below. I will define 'high' levels of expenditures to be 12.5 per cent of total expenditures or above, and 'low' expenditures to be 5 per cent of expenditures or below.[2]

I will define a regression coefficient of plus 0.20 or higher to be a 'rising' trend, a regression of minus 0.20 or lower to be a 'declining' trend, and a regression coefficient between +0.20 and −0.20 to be a 'stable' trend.

This summary 'point' system, like any descriptive or inferential statistic, loses much information about variation – variation here within and between particular fiscal categories. Such a system for classifying group benefits does, however, permit systematic and consistent judgments based on quantitative evidence about which groups benefit more from fiscal policy-making, and how much variance there may be from time to time, or country to country in the relative success of these groups. The results of such a cumulation of points (as in Tables 11.3 and 11.5), while crucially important, therefore always should be shown following a display and discussion of the results of the categorization of revenues and expenditures (as in Table 11.2), so that the reader may understand on what base the quantification of 'group-benefits' stands.

APPLICATION OF THE METHOD

In this section I will show several different ways the group-benefit method may be used to measure which groups have most benefited from government policies. As I mentioned earlier, the data I use illustratively here are taken from my PhD dissertation on fiscal policy-making in Sri Lanka.

In Table 11.2 the basic data measuring the mean and trend for each substantive Sri Lankan fiscal category are displayed over a relatively long annual time series (1946–73). This Table shows the relative levels and trends of change in each of these fiscal categories during Sri Lanka's history of independence, up to 1973.

Table 11.3 shows the corresponding group-benefit profile for Sri Lanka during the same 1946–73 span. The scores leading to the groups' ranking are based on the data in Table 11.2, using the definitions and rules of scoring explained in the previous section.

Table 11.4 shows another way data from annual fiscal categories may be used. Here some of the data are added together in order to gain a more aggregated view of taxes, borrowing and expenditures in Sri Lanka. In some cases the aggregated data show a more rapidly rising or falling trend than one might have expected from the data in

Table 11.2 Statistics summarizing the absolute levels and trends of fiscal policies in Sri Lanka, 1946–73, rank ordering fiscal categories by means

Category	*Mean*	*Regression coefficient*
A Categories of revenues as a percentage of total revenues		
Corporate taxes	34.9%	−0.623
Import duties	25.9	−0.717
Government share of profit	8.6	+0.113
Other revenues	8.6	−0.155
Production, etc. taxes	8.3	+0.730
Individual taxes	6.8	+0.035
Foreign exchange taxes	3.0	+0.518
Wealth, etc. taxes	2.1	0.000
Individual social security taxes	1.8	+0.091
Agricultural capital taxes	0.1	+0.004
B *Categories of loans as a percentage of total spending*		
Domestic loans	10.3%	+0.838
Foreign civil loans	4.7	+0.409
Foreign military loans	0.0	0.000
C *Categories of spending as a percentage of total spending*		
Administration and other expenditures	26.8%	−0.103
Education and health	25.3	−0.282
Social welfare, etc.	19.9	−0.002
Rural expenditures	10.4	+0.070
Non-agric. infrastructure	8.7	−0.035
Security expenditures	5.5	+0.039
State economic enterprise	3.0	+0.164
Private enterprise	0.7	+0.058

Table 11.2, and in one case ('Import and foreign exchange taxes') a trend all but disappears. Thus, after fiscal category data have been classified and converted into percentages of total revenues and expenditures, they may be easily manipulated to answer an analyst's questions about some broader trends.

Table 11.5, the final Table, shows a series of group-benefit profiles for nine consecutive periods in Sri Lankan history, beginning with the colonial period in 1932 (when universal suffrage was introduced), and

Table 11.3 Rank order of interest groups benefiting from fiscal policy in Sri Lanka, 1946–73

Rank	*Interest group*	*Percent of possible score*
1	Small Rural Enterprise	50
2	Lower Economic Class	42
3	Upper Economic Class	39
4	Private Enterprise	36
5	State Economic Enterprise	31
6	Security Forces	0

ending in 1973. The periods chosen are arbitrary, most of five-year length, but one at each end of the interval is of three-year length. The end-points of these particular periods were chosen to be approximately simultaneous with elections in Sri Lanka, and with the beginning and ending of the Second World War. Other analysts studying this or other nations could use any periods they found suitable in order best to serve their purposes.

The picture that emerges from the foregoing data is a mixed one, showing both stability and change. As one can see in Tables 11.3 and 11.5, the relative ranking of interest group benefits tended to remain roughly constant during both colonial and independent Sri Lankan governments. Small Rural Enterprise groups continued to be the most favored, followed by Upper Class and Lower Class groups, which stayed about equal in status until the late 1960s. 'Modernizing' Private Enterprise and State Economic Enterprise groups were treated moderately well during the period, but favored less than the first three sets of groups. Private Enterprise and State Economic Enterprise were also treated relatively equally by different governments, except during the early 1950s. Security Force groups remained by far the least successful in obtaining Lankan government aid, except during and immediately after the Second World War.

This stability, and the relative equality of these groups in terms of government benefits (except for the Security Forces), suggest that most governments in Sri Lanka attempted to balance interest groups against one another, rather than choose clear favorites. Such a balancing act may, of course, have been inspired by the intense political party competition under democratic institutions in Sri Lanka from 1946 to 1973.

Tables 11.2 and 11.4 show further evidence of government aims to

Table 11.4 Statistics summarizing levels and trends of fiscal policies in Sri Lanka, 1946–73, in various combined and divided categories

Category	*Mean*	*Regression coefficient*
A *Combined categories of revenues as a percentage of total revenues*		
'Upper Class Taxes' (Corporate taxes + individual taxes + wealth, etc. taxes + agric. capital taxes)	43.9	−0.580
'Lower Class Taxes' (Production, etc. taxes + social security taxes + government share of profit)	18.8	+0.934
'Import and Foreign Exchange Taxes' (Import duties + foreign exchange purchase taxes)	28.8	−0.199
B *Combined categories of loans and grants as a percentage of total expenditures*		
Domestic Loans and Foreign Civil Loans and Grants	15.0	+1.247
C *Combined categories of expenditures as a percentage of total expenditures*		
'Economic Development Expenditures' (Agricultural + state economic enterprise + private economic enterprise + non-agric. infrastructure expenditures)	22.9	+0.256
'Industrial Development Expenditures' (State economic enterprise + private economic enterprise + non-agric. infrastructure expenditures)	12.4	+0.186

balance interest groups, through the rapid increase of revenues obtained from loans rather than from taxes. In the short run, raising revenues from loans does not inflict pain on particular social groups in the same way that increasing taxes does. Particularly in the 1960s, governments may therefore have employed large Sri Lankan loans to

Table 11.5 Interest groups benefiting from fiscal policy in Sri Lanka in different periods after the introduction of the Donoughmore Constitution, expressed in percent of possible group-benefit scores

Years	*Small Rural Enterprise*	*Private Enterprise*	*State Economic Enterprise*	*Security Forces*	*Upper Economic Class*	*Lower Economic Class*
1932–35	50	36	31	0	31	46
1936–40	50	36	31	33	42	35
1941–45	75	29	25	17	50	42
1946–50	50	50	50	33	46	54
1951–55	75	43	31	17	54	50
1956–60	50	36	38	0	38	42
1961–65	50	43	38	0	42	46
1966–70	75	36	38	0	54	42
1971–73	50	21	19	17	46	27

maintain the existing equilibrium between interest groups, and to forestall anti-government campaigns.

Tables 11.2, 11.4 and 11.5, however, also show significant changes in government policies toward several groups. Lower Class groups succeeded the most in the early years of Sri Lankan independence, and the least from 1966 to 1973, despite a Left coalition government from 1971–3 which included both Communists and Trotskyists in the Cabinet. Upper Class groups, by comparison, continued to fare rather well in the 1960s and early 1970s. Table 11.4 reveals a major cause of this relative change by the sharp decline of Upper Class Taxes compared with the very dramatic rise of Lower Class Taxes, measured by the decline and rise of their respective regression coefficients. In 1971 Lower Class Taxes surpassed Upper Class Taxes as sources of government revenue, thus ending government redistribution of income, and creating Lower Class financing of its own benefits among government expenditures.

Tables 11.2, 11.4 and 11.5 also disclose other important changes in policies. Although Social Welfare Expenditures and Education and Health Expenditures remained the largest two group-related outlays in the government budget between 1946 and 1973, allocations to development activities in the 1960s increased substantially, while Welfare, and Education and Health allocations stood still or declined relative to total spending. This increased concentration on development-related activities has been seldom noted by writers outside Sri Lanka. On the other hand, in 1971–3 fiscal benefits to both Private

Enterprise and State Economic Enterprise groups dropped remarkably, reversing the previous growth of economic modernization outlays.

Quite obviously, then, major changes began to occur in Sri Lankan fiscal policies in the 1960s and 1970s, benefiting some groups over others. Small Rural Enterprise, and the Upper Class stayed in government favor, while benefits to Lower Class, Private Enterprise, and State Economic Enterprise groups dropped sharply.

Equipped with such a provocative description of policy, and such a depth of revenue and expenditure data from Sri Lanka (or another nation), it is apparent ,that one could investigate many explanatory hypotheses, employing a variety of time-series techniques, to discover why such changes occurred. Group-benefit analysis indeed invites such research into policy causation, because it provides a panoramic view of policy and policy change which provokes one to discover how the more prominent features came into being.

Notes

1. Because of space limitations in this paper, I cannot explain some controversial definitions here and in Table 11.1. Readers seeking further explanation may find it in Cranmer, 1982, or by contacting me directly.
2. My threshold of significance for a 'high' level of expenditures (12.5 per cent) is slightly above a similar threshold for taxes (10 per cent). This was assumed because of the smaller number of categories of expenditures (8) compared with taxes (10). In both cases, I divided the total number of tax or expenditure categories into 100 per cent, and took the result as my threshold of significance. The threshold figures for loans and grants, however, are purely arbitrary, as are the lower thresholds for both taxes and expenditures.

References

AMES, B. (1977) 'The Politics of Public Spending in Latin America', *American Journal of Political Science*, 21: 149–76.

AMES, B. (1980) 'A Note on the Political Expenditure Cycle in Latin America', *Policy Studies Journal*, 9: 40–47.

AMES, B. and GOFF, E. (1975) 'Education and Defense Expenditures in Latin America: 1948–1968', In CRAIG LISKE *et al.* (eds) *Comparative Public Policy* (New York: Halsted).

BRUNNER, R. D. and BREWER, G. D. (1971) *Organized Complexity* (New York: Free Press).

BUNCE, V. (1976) 'Elite Succession, Petrification, and Policy Innovation in Communist Systems: An Empirical Assessment', *Comparative Political Studies*, 9: 3–41.

BUNCE, V. (1980) 'Changing Leaders and Changing Policies: The Impact of Elite Succession on Budgetary Priorities in Democratic Countries', *American Journal of Political Science*, 24: 373–95.

CHANDLER, M., CHANDLER, W. and VOGLER, D. (1974) 'Policy Analysis and the Search for Theory', *American Politics Quarterly*, 2: 107–18.

COWART, A. T. (1978) 'The Economic Policies of European Governments, Part II: Fiscal Policy', *British Journal of Political Science*, 8: 425–39.

CRANMER, W. H. H. (1977) 'Fiscal Policy-Making in Sri Lanka, 1946–1973: A 'Group-Benefit' Analysis', Paper presented at American Political Science Association convention, Washington, D.C..

CRANMER, W. H. H. (1978) 'Fiscal Policy-Making in Sri Lanka, 1946–1973: A Description and Interpretation', Paper presented at Wisconsin Conference on South Asia, Madison, Wisconsin.

CRANMER, W. H. H. (1982) 'Fiscal Policy-Making in Sri Lanka, 1946–1973: A 'Group-Benefit' Analysis', Unpub. PhD diss., University of Wisconsin–Madison.

CUTRIGHT, P. (1965) 'Political Structure, Economic Development, and National Social Security Programs', *American Journal of Sociology*, 70: 537–50.

CUTRIGHT, P. (1967) 'Income Redistribution: A Cross-National Analysis', *Social Forces*, 46: 180–90.

DOWNS, A. (1957) *An Economic Theory of Democracy* (New York: Harper & Row).

EDELMAN, M. (1964) *The Symbolic Uses of Politics* (Urbana, Ill.: University of Illinois Press).

FRY, B. R. and WINTERS, R. F. (1970) 'The Politics of Redistribution', *American Political Science Review*, 64: 508–22.

GRAY, V. (1976) 'Models of Comparative State Politics: A Comparison of Cross-Sectional and Time Series Analyses', *American Journal of Political Science*, 20: 235–56.

HANCOCK, M. D. (1982) 'Comparative Public Policy: An Assessment', Paper presented at American Political Science Association convention, Denver, Colo.

HAYES, M. D. (1972) *Policy Outputs in the Brazilian States, 1940–1960* (Beverly Hills, Calif.: Sage).

HILL, K. Q. (1976) 'The Within-Nation Distribution of Public Expenditures and Services: A Two-Nation Analysis', *American Journal of Political Science*, 20: 303–18.

LASSWELL, H. D. (1958) *Politics: Who Gets What, When, How?* (New York: Meridian).

LOWI, T. (1966) 'Distribution, Regulation, Redistribution: The Functions of Government', in R. B. RIPLEY (ed.) *Public Policies and Their Politics*, (New York: Norton).

MARQUETTE, J. F. and HINCKLEY, K. A. (1981) 'Competition, Control, and Spurious Covariation: A Longitudinal Analysis of State Spending', *American Journal of Political Science*, 25: 362–75.

MEEHAN, E. V. (1967) *Contemporary Political Thought* (Homewood, Ill.: Dorsey Press).

PECHMAN, J. A. and OKNER, B. A. (1974) *Who Bears the Tax Burden?* (Washington, D.C.: Brookings Institution).
PETERS, B. G. (1972) 'Economic and Political Effects on the Development of Social Expenditures in France, Sweden and the United Kingdom', *Midwest Journal of Political Science*, 16: 225–38.
PETERS, B. G (1974) 'Income Redistribution: A Longitudinal Analysis of France, Sweden and the United Kingdom', *Political Studies*, 22: 311–23.
PETERS, B. G. (1976) 'The Relationship Between Public Expenditures and Services: A Longitudinal Analysis', *British Journal of Political Science*, 6: 510–17.
PETERS, B. G. (1977) 'Developments in Comparative Policy Studies: A Brief Review', *Policy Studies Journal*, 5: 616–28.
PETERS, B. G., DOUGHTIE, J. C. and McCULLOCH, M. K. (1977) 'Types of Democratic Systems and Types of Public Policy: An Empirical Examination', *Comparative Politics*, 9: 327–55.
PRYOR, F. L. (1968) *Public Expenditures in Communist and Capitalist Nations* (Homewood, Ill.: Irwin).
ROSEN, G. (1967) *Democracy and Economic Change in India* (Berkeley: University of California Press).
SCHLESINGER, J. R. (1970) 'Emerging Attitudes Toward Fiscal Policy', in J. E. ANDERSON (ed.) *Politics and Economic Policy-Making* (Reading, Mass.: Addison-Wesley).
SHARKANSKY, I. (ed.) (1970) *Policy Analysis in Political Science* (Chicago: Markham) chapters 4 and 6.
SNODGRASS, D. R. (1974) 'The Fiscal System as an Income Redistributor in West Malaysia', *Public Finance*, 29: 56–73.
TAX FOUNDATION (1967) *Tax Burdens and Benefits of Government Expenditure by Income Classes 1961 and 1965* (New York: Tax Foundation).
WILENSKY, H. (1975) *The Welfare State and Equality* (Berkeley: University of California Press).
WILKIE, W. (1970) *The Mexican Revolution: Federal Expenditures and Social Change Since 1910* (Berkeley: University of California Press).
ZUK, G. and THOMPSON, W. R. (1982) 'The Post-Coup Military Spending Question: A Pooled Cross-Sectional Time Series Analysis', *American Political Science Review*, 76: 60–74.

12 Politics and Distributional Impact Studies: The Dilemma of Economic Analysis in the Policy-Making Process

Kent E. Portney

Over the past decade or so social scientists have increasingly focused their attention on the economic analysis of the distributional impacts produced by various public policies. The preceding papers in this volume exemplify the kinds of analyses currently being conducted on a variety of public issues. They also extend distributional impact analysis to some areas which have been untouched until now, and sometimes present new methodologies for this type of examination. It is probably safe to say that never before have we paid such explicit attention to the distributional impacts produced by our governments.

At the same time, a growing body of literature suggests that policy analysis has little direct effect on our policy-makers (Dunn, 1981). In other words, public policy analysis does not seem to constitute a major influence on policy-makers' decisions. If this pattern applies to distributional impact analysis as well, then this seems to present us with something of a dilemma. On the one hand, we have fairly unambiguous studies which explain who will benefit and who will be burdened by particular courses of public action. Such studies may or may not turn out to be accurate in the long run, but are usually fairly authoritative when written. On the other hand, we have policy-makers who apparently pay little attention to these studies when actually deciding which courses of action to pursue. Although this is undoubtedly an overstatement of the case, it does present the dilemma which constitutes the focus of this paper.

In this paper I examine this dilemma by explaining what I see as some of its specific roots. To do this I will rely on some concepts and terminology from policy-making process research. Although many of the terms are similar to those found in economic analyses, they have somewhat different meanings and underlying concepts in policy-making process research. I hope to clarify the points of convergence between policy impact research and policy-making, and to begin specifying some of the conditions under which the political system, manifested as the policy-making process, is capable of using policy analysis.

THE RISE OF DISTRIBUTIONAL IMPACT STUDIES

One of the more quickly-developing types of policy research describes and predicts who actually will benefit and be burdened by various public policies. Such research may also address the nature of the tradeoffs which might be involved with any policy decision. Thinking of public policies in these terms is certainly not new, as differential benefits and burdens have long been of concern to economists and political scientists alike (Lasswell, 1936; Garvey, 1952: 27–47). What may be new is the level of rigor and explicitness now involved in such studies. We have been able to expand our understanding of the entire range of economic impacts that our governments have on people.

From its early roots in education (Hansen and Weisbrod, 1969a, 1969b), and taxation (Pechman and Okner, 1974), this type of analysis has become diffused into almost every area of public policy. In this volume alone we have presented studies of social security indexing and taxation, the welfare 'safety net', child support systems, federal income tax expenditures, and state taxation. Other distributional impact studies have addressed issues of inflation (Browne, 1975; Foster, 1981), affirmative action (Eisinger, 1980), mass transit (Hefner, 1972), energy and the environment (Peskin, 1978; Navarro, 1981), unemployment compensation (Feldstein, 1973), gasoline rationing (Dorfman, 1981), urban zoning (Proudfoot, 1979), national health insurance and Medicaid (Stuart, 1972; McGuire, 1981), and income transfers (Haveman and Hollenbeck, 1980), to name a few.

As researchers develop the methodologies of distributional impact studies, we are increasingly finding that public policies never thought to produce much in the way of distributional impacts do indeed have differential effects. To analysts examining distributional impacts, *all public policies* may be expected to have some differential effects. In other words, we are increasingly willing to entertain the hypothesis that any policy has differential impacts. In some cases, such as Witte's paper in this volume, we are finding that policies which we assumed to have major differential effects (in this case federal income tax expenditures) really do not have such effects.

At the same time, however, such studies are often confronted by a policy-making process which clearly does not deal with all policies as though they have such consequences. And this produces something of a dilemma for policy analysts. To understand this dilemma, we can turn to some concepts developed in policy-making process research.

POLICY ANALYSIS IN THE POLICY-MAKING PROCESS

To the professional policy analyst, perhaps one of the most formidable challenges is that policy-makers do not always respond to public policy analyses even when such analyses have been conducted with the most flawless and 'value neutral' methods. This tends to be frustrating to many analysts because they often initiate their research with the basic expectation that their conclusions will provide important information. In many instances analysts begin with the implicit assumption that if their methodologies and methods are impeccable, then policy-makers will almost automatically heed their results. Of course, all too often this does not occur, and it may be safe to say that it never happens automatically.

But analysts should remember that the policy-making process is unavoidably political. In some sense the scenario I have developed resembles what Wildavsky (1979) calls 'speaking truth to power'. From one perspective, 'power' is not always interested in the 'truth'. It may be more accurate to say that the policy-maker's 'truth', or political context, is much different from the policy analyst's 'truth', or analytic context. There are numerous examples of the political process 'manipulating' policy research for political ends (Portney, 1986: 67, 76–7, 130), a reflection of the very different contexts in which analysis is conducted.

The policy-making process context of policy analysis has some peculiar problems when policy analysis context focuses on distributional impacts. To better understand the differences between these two contexts in particular, we can contrast what I have suggested are some distributional impact assumptions with some policy-making process concepts.

'DISTRIBUTIVE AND REDISTRIBUTIVE' POLICIES IN THE POLICY-MAKING PROCESS

In the literature on the policy-making process, one predominant set of concepts is the distributive-regulatory-redistributive policy typology described by Lowi (1964, 1972) and developed by others, including Ripley and Franklin (1980). This policy typology helps us describe and understand the different kinds of policy-making processes which exist. While the terminology may appear comparable to that which is associated with distributional impact analysis, the underlying concepts are very different. Because we use these concepts we should be clear about what they are.

Often, in distributional impact research, the terms distribution and redistribution are used almost interchangeably. In policy-making process studies, these terms connote very different types of policies. Redistributive policies consist of courses of action where policy-makers (including legislators, agency officials, and so on) *perceive* that the *intent* is to take something from (create burdens for) one group of people in order to give something (distribute benefits) to another group of people. For example, social security became a redistributive issue when policy-makers began to see the clear trade-off between providing benefits to retirees and taxing workers.

But not all public policies are considered redistributive by policy-making process researchers. The typology usually recognizes 'regulatory' and 'distributive' policies. The distributive type of policy is of particular importance here. This term is used much differently by policy-making process researchers, who use it to classify policies where our policy-makers believe that the course of action intends to benefit numerous groups of people simultaneously (Ripley and Franklin, 1980: 21–2).

This typology has been the source of some confusion. Most of the confusion revolves around exactly what makes some policies distributive and others redistributive. Researchers have at times mistakenly tried to classify policies based on their actual distributional impacts (Wade, 1972: 9–10; Greenberg *et al.* 1977) But it is my contention that this is something of a misreading of what these policy typologies were meant to convey. As I have implied above, the policies are different because distributional impacts refer to actual distributions, while redistributive policies refer to distributions as *perceived* by policy-makers. My support for this contention comes from Lowi's statement that 'the nature of a redistributive issue is not determined by the *outcome* of a battle over how redistributive a policy is going to be. *Expectations* about what it *can* be, what it threatens to be, are determinative', (Lowi, 1964: 691) (emphasis mine).

This point has not been totally lost in the policy typology literature (Steinberger, 1980), although the argument has been less than fully convincing. Ostrom, for example, argues that the Lowian and Steinberger approaches suffer from similar problems; the categories or policy types are neither mutually exclusive nor exhaustive (Ostrom, 1980). My point here is that the reason why these typological approaches are thought to be non-mutually exclusive and non-exhaustive is that researchers who use them lose sight of the fact that perceptions are the key.

It would be difficult to argue that the Lowian typologies, keeping in mind that perceptions are the referrent, are impossible to measure. Research in psychology provides us with numerous ways of measuring perceptions. This is not to say that it would be easy to measure the perceptions of policy-makers. I am merely arguing that it is theoretically possible to do so. Thus, it seems plausible that if we were to measure policy-makers' perceptions on policy issues, we might in fact find that they can be classified into mutually exclusive and exhaustive categories. In energy policy, for example, it does not seem likely that a legislator would perceive the oil depletion allowance to distribute benefits and burdens in more than one way. Some legislators may perceive that the oil depletion allowance is designed to provide benefits to the oil industry and burdens to no one. Other legislators may perceive that it is designed to provide such benefits at the expense of consumers. But the same legislator is not likely to perceive it both ways. As for the other policy categories (competitive and protective regulatory policies in particular), there may well be some overlap. But this is beyond the scope of my argument here.

The idea here, then, is that many policy-makers actually do believe and often act as though some policies are positive sum games where no one in particular has to pay for the multiple benefits accrued by various groups. Ripley and Franklin suggest that much of our domestic federal policy is of this nature (Ripley and Franklin, 1980). For example, decisions about various federal grants-in-aid to states and local governments are perceived as policies which benefit all states and local governments simultaneously (although the concept allows some states to benefit a little more or less than others). Many public policies in the states can also be said to be distributive (Morehouse, 1982).[1]

The principle political consequence of policy-makers' beliefs that such distributive policies exist is that the policy-making process is quite different than it would otherwise be. Not all policies are perceived of as distributive. Those federal policies which are distributive have political processes which tend to be very stable and predictable, characterized by a high degree of co-operation among members of Congress, and between Congress and executive agencies. This helps create an environment conducive to successful logrolling. Perhaps the most important implication of the political consequences of public policy types is that policies are difficult to change because the policy-making process has become entrenched.

Clearly, in the dynamics of the policy-making process, specific policies may become transformed over time from distributive to redistributive and vice versa. To some degree, policy-makers would probably like to convert all policies into distributive policies, since to do so in essence almost ensures that legislators never have to say 'no'. For example, US energy policy before the 1973 'crisis' provided benefits to practically every type of energy producer and consumer without much consideration of specific costs and tradeoffs (Ingram and McCain, 1978; Jones, 1979a, 1979b).

Often, because of external constraints, such as the function of the economy or the development of crises, policy-makers are increasingly being forced to think of policies which were once distributive as redistributive. Conversion of distributive policies into redistributive ones also seems to be one major strategy employed by the Reagan administration to achieve budget reductions.

One might expect that distributional impact analysis would constitute primary vehicles by which such conversions take place. Yet this seems not to be the case. And so we might wonder why. If we compare the message being sent by distributional impact analysts to policy-makers in the existing political context of distributive policies, we can readily see a major point of incompatibility. For the purposes of my argument it matters not whether the conversion is motivated by politics or other events.

THE PROBLEM WITH DISTRIBUTIONAL IMPACT STUDIES

Now that we are clear about some major aspects of the distributive policy-making process, we can begin to state the problems that distributional impact studies must confront.

The initial message sent to policy-makers by distributional impact analysts is that policies which have multiple benefits and no burdens probably do not exist. When an analyst demonstrates that one region of the country gets more benefit than another region from some policy, this implies that one region benefits at the expense of others. When an analyst shows that wealthier people benefit more than lower-income people from tax expenditures, the message is that wealthier people benefit at the expense of poorer people. In fact, most distributional impact analyses identify explicitly who benefits and who is burdened, or at least what tradeoffs might have to be made in providing benefits to any group of people.

Often the message sent by distributional impact studies asks policy-makers to redefine the policies on which they have been acting. The message tells the policy-maker that he or she can no longer hold the belief that many people benefit without creating specific burdens. In some sense it suggests that policy-makers have been deluding themselves. But policy-makers are not particularly receptive to this message. Perhaps most important, my contention is *not* that policy-makers are likely to disagree with the *conclusions* of distributional impact studies. It is that policy-makers face political constraints which often do not even permit them to entertain the possibility that a particular distributive policy might indeed have some differential impact on people.

For the individual policy-maker, redefining a distributive policy as a redistributive one would require a major reassessment of constituent benefits, and would threaten existing relationships with other policy-makers. In other words, the policy-maker would have to become convinced that constituents and other policy-makers really desired a distribution of benefits and burdens different from that produced by existing distributive policies. For the policy-makers taken in the aggregate, such a redefinition would require changes in the policy-making process, perhaps ultimately making the process more turbulent, less predictable, and more conflictive. Needless to say, this is asking quite a lot. For most policy-makers it is probably easier to ignore the distributional impact studies.

Nevertheless, there are some policy areas in which our policy-makers seem to pay substantially more attention to distributional impact analyses. Social security, employment training, and energy policy may be good cases in point. Policies in each of these areas were once thought of as benefiting large groups of people at the specific expense of no one. Clearly, our policy-makers' perceptions about how a particular policy distributes its benefits and burdens are subject to change over time. If distributional impact studies have been at all influential in the policy-making processes associated with these policies (and I'm not suggesting that they have been), then we might wonder what, if anything, such policy analysts can do to maximize the chances that policy-makers will not simply ignore their results. It is to this question that we will now turn our attention.

DISTRIBUTIONAL IMPACT STUDIES AND POLICY RESEARCH UTILIZATION

The question of what, if anything, can be done to maximize the chances that policy-makers will pay attention to distributional impact studies may gain some insight from analyses of research utilization. Numerous attempts have been made to study the conditions under which social science research becomes a useful input into the political process of making public policy. By examining some of these studies we can get a sense for what potential distributional impact studies possess, and prescribe how the utility of such studies might be maximized.

Policy-makers' use of social research seems to depend partly on the nature of the research itself, and partly on the political policy-making context in which the research is conducted. Perhaps the most influential research characteristic is the nature of the methodology. Studies which rely on methodologies which are considered to be 'standard' are more likely to be influential than those which develop new or obscure 'non-standard' methodologies. By and large, policy-makers seem to consider research using experimental designs with random sampling and quantitative measurement to be standard (Bernstein and Freeman, 1975). Therein lies something of another dilemma. Currently, most distributional impact analysis requires what is very likely to be perceived of as innovative or 'non-standard' methodologies. This is especially true of several of the papers in this volume. This fact, by itself, may limit the potential utilization of these studies. As such techniques as policy simulation become used more widely, this problem will likely diminish.

Policy research utilization is also partly reliant on the political context in which the research is interpreted. There is some evidence that there must be a close match between the structure of the policy question as perceived by policy-makers and the structure of the policy research as defined by the policy analyst (Ackoff, 1974).

Moreover, if policy studies are conducted in the absence of a process to permit interaction between researchers and policy-makers, research utilization is likely to be quite low (Weiss, 1977; Rich, 1981). This suggests a clear need to integrate policy analysis with policy-making processes.

INTEGRATING DISTRIBUTIONAL IMPACT ANALYSIS WITH THE POLICY-MAKING PROCESS

Prescriptions concerning how distributional impact studies can be made more 'useful' to policy-makers require substantial conjecture since we really have no good direct data with which to make an assessment. Nevertheless, given the apparent dilemma discussed earlier and what we know about research utilization in general, we can make some basic suggestions for distributional impact analysts.

First, and perhaps most obvious, distributional impact analysts must be clear about who their audiences are. If the primary audience consists of policy-makers, then analysts must begin to understand the political context in which those policy-makers operate.

Secondly, as part of understanding the political context, analysts must develop an idea of how policy-makers perceive the issues being analyzed. Specifically, it is important for them to be clear about whether policy-makers perceive the issue to be distributive or redistributive. The clear implication of the preceding discussion is that if policy-makers perceive the issue to be redistributive, then they will be somewhat more receptive to distributional impact research than otherwise. Conversely, if policy-makers perceive the issue as distributive rather than redistributive or regulatory, then they are likely to be much less receptive to the researchers' basic framework of analysis.

But not all policy-makers will be supportive of the existing policy in a given area. Many policy-makers will probably desire to alter existing policies. Such people may recognize that changing perceptions concerning the distribution of benefits or burdens of the policy in question probably constitute necessary (although not sufficient) conditions for policy change. Thus, such policy-makers may well be the most receptive to distributional impact analyses which question existing wisdom. For example, a policy-maker advocating de-control of natural gas might be expected to be fairly receptive to a distributional impact study showing that regulation of natural gas produces undesirable distributions of burden or benefit.

Thirdly, it seems likely that policy-makers will be more receptive to distributional impact studies when social and economic events begin forcing them to confront the redistributive implications of their actions. For example, once policy-makers were convinced that there were indeed energy shortages they became somewhat more interested in knowing more about the tradeoffs involved with alternative policy responses. Thus, the time is most ripe for distributional impact studies when social and economic events create something of a 'need to know'. Just as crises open 'windows of opportunity' to get new policy proposals on to the public agenda, so too do crises permit the redefinition of problems once thought to be distributive. During such periods, policy-makers are much more likely to pay attention to research which questions common 'distributional impact' wisdom.

Fourthly, distributional impact analysts should come to recognize that innovative methodologies may work against the chances of analysis being used. Reliance on understood methodologies, where possible, seems to be desirable if distributional impact research is to be influential. Of course, one of the dilemmas is that distributional impact research often requires innovative methodologies. In a sense, this type of analysis is likely to be less influential than other types of research until their methodologies are well established and well understood. Indeed, one of the purposes underlying this entire book is to broaden understanding of the methodologies on which distributional impact research will increasingly rely.

Finally, the distributional impact analyst confronting a distributive issue must recognize that the framework of analysis itself may in fact challenge basic beliefs of policy-makers. The underlying hypothesis that the policy could be redistributive may be as great a challenge to policy-makers as any conclusions might be. This would suggest that in these circumstances, distributional impact analysts must first and foremost be prepared to help policy-makers entertain the possibility that a policy they consider to be distributive might indeed have distributional impacts. This must be considered an important component of distributional impact studies conducted on distributive policies. Yet it is a component which is often underdeveloped or conspicuously absent in such analyses.

Note

1. I was made aware of this point by my colleague Andrew Reschovsky in discussing the potential for influence of distributional impact analysis in Massachusetts.

References

ACKOFF, R. (1974) *Redesigning the Future: A Systems Approach to Societal Problems* (New York: John Wiley).

BERNSTEIN, I. N. and FREEMAN, H. E. (1975) *Academic and Entrepreneurial Research* (New York: Russell Sage Foundation).

BROWNE, R. S. (1975) 'Some Redistributive Aspects of U.S. Inflation', *Journal of Black Political Economy*, 5 (2): 134–42.

DORFMAN, N. S. (1981) 'Gasoline Distribution Policies in a Shortage: Welfare Impacts on Rich and Poor', *Public Policy*, 29 (4): 473–505.

DUNN, W. N. (1981) *Public Policy Analysis* (Englewood Cliffs, N.J.: (Prentice-Hall) 28–9.

EISINGER, P. (1980) *Affirmative Action in Municipal Employment: The Impact of Black Political Power*. (Madison, Wisconsin: Institute for Research on Poverty) Discussion Paper, No. 621–80.

FELDSTEIN, M. (1973) *Unemployment Compensation: Adverse Incentives and Distributional Anomalies* (Cambridge, Mass.: Harvard Institute for Economic Research) Discussion Paper, No. 317.

FOSTER, E. (1981) 'Who Loses from Inflation?' *Annals of the American Academy of Political and Social Sciences*, 456: 32–45.

GARVEY, G. (1952) 'Inequality of Income: Causes and Measurements', *Studies in Income and Wealth*, vol. 15 (New York: National Bureau of Economic Research).

GREENBERG, G. D., MILLER, J. A., MOHR, L. B. and VLADECK, B. C. (1977) 'Developing Public Policy Theory', *American Political Science Review*, 71 (4): 1534–43.

HANSEN, W. L. and WEISBROD, B. A. (1969a) 'The Distribution of Costs and Direct Benefits of Public Higher Education: The Case of California', *Journal of Human Resources*, 4: 176–91.

HANSEN, W. L. and WEISBROD, B. A. (1969b) *'Benefits, Costs, and Finance of Public Higher Education* (Chicago: Markham).

HAVEMAN, R. H. and HOLLENBECK, K. (eds). (1980) *Microeconomic Simulation Models for Public Policy Analysis, Vol. I: Distributional Impacts* (New York: Academic Press).

HEFNER, J. (1972) ' Efficiency, Equity, and Pricing in Mass Transit Systems', *Review of Black Political Economy*, 2 (3): 38–44.

INGRAM, H. and McCAIN, J. R. (1978) 'Distributive Politics Reconsidered – The Wisdom of the Western Water Ethic in the Contemporary Energy Context', *Policy Studies Journal*, 7 (1): 49–58.

JONES, C. O. (1979a) 'Congress and the Making of Energy Policy', in LAWRENCE (ed.) (1979) *New Dimensions to Energy Policy* (Lexington, Mass.: D.C. Heath).

JONES, C. O. (1979b)'American Politics and the Organization of Energy Decision Making', in *Annual Review of Energy*, vol. 4.

LASSWELL, H. D. (1936) *Politics: Who Gets What, When, How* (New York: McGraw-Hill).

LOWI, T. (1964) 'American Business, Public Policy, Case Studies, and Political Theory', *World Politics*, 16 (4): 677–715.

LOWI, T. (1972) 'Four Systems of Politics, Policy, and Choice', *Public Administration Review*, 32: 298–310.
McGUIRE, T. G. (1981) 'National Health Insurance for Private Psychiatric Care: A Study in the Distribution of Income', *Public Finance Quarterly*, 9 (2): 183–96.
MOREHOUSE, S. M. (1982) *State Politics, Parties, and Policy* (New York: Holt, Rinehart & Winston).
NAVARRO, P. (1981) 'The 1977 Clean Air Act Amendments: Energy, Environmental, Economic, and Distributional Impacts', *Public Policy*, 29 (2): 121–46.
OSTROM, E. (1980) 'Is It B or Not -B? That Is the Question', *Social Science Quarterly*, 61 (2): 198–202.
PECHMAN, J. A. and OKNER, B. A. (1974) *Who Bears The Tax Burden?* (Washington, D.C.: Brookings Institution).
PESKIN, H. M. (1978) 'Environmental Policy and the Distribution of Benefits and Costs', in P. R. PORTNEY (ed.) (1978) *Current Issues in U.S. Environmental Policy*. (Baltimore: Johns Hopkins Press) pp. 144–63.
PORTNEY, K. E. (1986) *Approaching Public Policy Analysis* (Englewood Cliffs, N.J.: Prentice-Hall).
PROUDFOOT, S. B. (1979) 'Private Gains and Public Losses: The Distributive Impact of Urban Zoning', *Policy Sciences*, 11 (2): 203–26.
RICH, R. F. (1981) *The Power of Social Science Information and Public Policymaking: The Case of the Continuous National Survey* (San Francisco: Jossey-Bass).
RIPLEY, R. B. and FRANKLIN, G. A. (1980) *Congress, the Bureaucracy, and Public Policy* (Homewood, Ill.: Dorsey).
STEINBERGER, P. J. (1980) 'Typologies of Public Policy: Meaning Construction and the Policy Process', *Social Science Quarterly* 61 (2): 185–97.
STUART, B. (1972) 'Equity and Medicaid', *Journal of Human Resources*, 7 (2): 162–78.
WADE, L. L. (1972) *The Elements of Public Policy* (Columbus, Oh.: Charles Merrill Publishing).
WEISS, C. H. (1977) *Using Social Research in Public Policy Making* (Lexington, Mass.: D. C. Heath).
WILDAVSKY, A. (1979) *Speaking Truth to Power: The Art and Craft of Policy Analysis* (New York: John Wiley).

Index